By

Paul McNeil

paulmcneil@tactica.org.uk
www.tactica.org.uk

Published in March 2009 by emp3books,
Kiln Workshops, Pilcot Road, Crookham Village,
Fleet, Hampshire, GU51 5RY, England

ISBN-13: 978-1-907140-01-3

www.emp3books.com

For Bobbie, Ross, and David for bearing the distracted presence of a husband and father with a long Career in Sales and Management. To the salespeople who taught me how to make a living, the competitors who made me stronger, and Proxima Technology for letting me put all this into practice.

To Chris,
An inspirational
Leader.

P.S. McNeil

Table of Contents

Introduction

Starting at the end of the story, you are reading this book in order to achieve a happy ending, quite rightly, that's what we all want. *Tactica* provides a philosophy of excellence, a method to follow in order to achieve it, and a set of rules to act as a guide to implementing the Method, distilled from the accumulated knowledge of men who had more at stake than making a sales target.

Experienced Sales People, Sales Managers, and Sales aware frontline Technical Staff, will benefit by using the *Tactica* techniques it imparts allowing them to maximise chances and impact of success, and minimise the likelihood and impact of failure. Less experienced and new staff will have a model to aspire to and instructions on how to achieve it.

Tactica will allow everyone from Sales Team and Technical Support Engineer, to Sales Manager, and Sales Director to understand the Objective of the Campaign, what the correct Strategy is to achieve the Objective, and which Tactics to employ to enable the Strategy.

Tactica is organised in three parts:

Firstly the main Chapters on Strategy and Tactics, each is arranged in the following sections; Introduction to the author of the original military writings, an explanation of his theories, an explanation of why these are important to you as a salesperson, how to apply the lessons to sales situations, a sales example, a military example, a summary of what to do in order to use the lessons in practice, a Mnemonic summarising the lessons in a visual way, where applicable a section for the field manual, and lastly a bibliography.

Secondly There are three chapters with "Ripping Yarns", that is stories of three individual Military Leaders who show examples of how to "think out of the box" and how lessons can be drawn from their actions that can be applied in sales situations.

Thirdly some chapters have a field usable guide and these are pulled together in the last section of *Tactica* to provide the Plan of Campaign. Everybody directly involved in the Campaign should keep a copy of this to hand to ensure that a common Language, Philosophy, Methodology, and Practice can be employed. If this is done morale will be more easily maintained, the focus of the Campaign will not be lost, and all courses of action can be measured in terms of the desired Objective.

The chapter entitled **"The Principles"** based on the writings of General John Frederick Fuller explains the principles to apply to your chosen campaign, i.e. the way to correctly engage in it. By following his principles you are more likely to avoid mistakes and achieve results, minimising your failures and maximising your successes.

The chapter entitled **"The Pattern"** based on the writings of Lt General Sir Francis Tuker explains the generic types of sales situations you may find yourself in when you attempt to engage with an account. The types of engagement you start with will affect the type of campaign you will have to fight. Knowing the type of campaign you will have to fight will allow you to decide if this if favourable to your capabilities and timescales, and, if required, will allow you to plan to change the type of campaign.

The chapter entitled **"Tactics of Concentration"** based on the writings of F. W. Lanchester, is an extreme distillation of his work, the same work which has been used for decades by Japanese Industry to take on and defeat European and American competitors. It will explain how to mathematically concentrate your forces for maximum effect, and the way to fight on different fronts in order to beat a bigger opponent in detail, or how to stretch a smaller opponent to breaking point.

The chapter entitled **"The Indirect Approach"** based on the writings of Sir Basil Liddell Hart, explains how to penetrate and overrun an account once your campaign has taken you into contact with the prospect and or your competition. This section will show you how to get passed stubborn defences and collapse time frames to a decision.

The chapter entitled **"Leadership and The Effects of Ground"** is based on the story of Henry V and his climatic battle with the French at Agincourt. It illustrates the Principles outlined by Fuller in the **"The Principles of War"** section of the book. This will help you to bring the disparate Principles together, and allow the visualisation of a metaphor for their application by you in the sales world.

The chapter entitled **"Initiative"** based on the exploits of Nathan Bedford Forrest during the American Civil War, and illustrates what can be achieved by a mentality which does not recognise restrictions and rules, and believes only in maintaining advantage. It will show you how to "think outside of the box" in the most outrageous ways, in order to achieve results far outside of what will be expected from most individuals.

The chapter entitled **"Blitzkrieg"** is based on the writings of General Heinz Guderian, and illustrates how the various factors explained in the previous sections can come together in the real world to devastating effect. Following this example from the world of warfare and applying a similar philosophy to the sales market place will bring you similar results in the commercial world.

Follow the sections as they are presented, read them and consciously apply them, re-read them and reflect on whether you are actually applying them correctly. Don't worry about impressing others; hone your own skills for your own gratification, and cherish your skills as a badge of pride and honour.

The Principles

Based on
The Principles of War
Major-General John Frederick Fuller CB, CBE, DSO
1878-1966

Who was he?

John Frederick "Boney" Fuller was a WW1 British General who predicted the advent of mechanized warfare long before anyone else, and indeed became Chief of Staff to The Royal Tank Corps in 1916. He planned many of the WW1 tank offensives including the first at Cambrai. During this period he was at constant odds with the old school of the military hierarchy including Sir Douglas Haig remarking of the War; 'Though the Germans gave us a lot of trouble, Sir Douglas Haig and his phenomenally unimaginative General Staff gave us infinitely more.'

After WW1 he collaborated with Sir Basil Liddell Hart, on new and innovative plans for mechanized warfare, utilizing the works of F. W. Lanchester, the inventor, mathematician, and military strategist, to develop his theories. During his time he formulated his "Principles of War" which became refined into four principles and three accentuating factors.

Cantankerous, confrontational, and outspoken, he became disillusioned with the British Army and political establishment, which lead to him making the mistake of backing Sir Oswald Moseley, the leader of the British Union of Fascists, in the 1930s. This discredited him in Military circles due to his right wing anti-democratic political leanings.

Unfortunately the baby got thrown out with the bath water, and in Great Britain his teachings were discarded along with the man himself. Not so in Germany and Russia where they were studied avidly, in the former case at the expense of the allies in 1940.

Out of the mainstream military, he went on to have an illustrious career as a Military Historian. His legacy was that his teachings were later adopted by both the Americans and Israelis (ironically considering his early unpleasant anti-Semitic opinions). His work laid the foundation for a Scientific approach to Military thought.

What do the Principles teach?

Explanation of Theory

Fuller teaches Four Principles of Warfare and Three Accentuating Factors, these show you how to organise and engage in a campaign to its greatest effect. The Four Principles concern the fundamentals of setting yourself an objective and not loosing sight of it, making sure that your dispositions and movements are guarded from your enemy's actions, the importance of being able to move freely and if necessary change direction on your path to your objective, and the need to be able to unleash your striking power fully and effectively at the appropriate time. The Three Accentuating Factors show you how to make the most of the Four Principles by not wasting your resources, being able to concentrate them in the right place at the right time, and the effects of surprise. Fuller's teachings in their simplest form can be summarised in his "Boxing Analogy" to Warfare:

"...the primary elements of tactics are to be seen in their simplest form in a fight between two unarmed men. They are: to think, to guard, to move, to hit.

Before a bout opens each boxer will decide how to knock out his opponent; as the bout proceeds he may be forced to modify his tactics, but the aim remains the same. He must maintain an adequate defense, and advance under cover of this defence and manoeuvre his opponent into a position where his defence can be penetrated and an attack can be mounted to knock him out. In military terms objective, security, mobility, striking power.

If the two fighters are experienced they will understand the value of three accentuating factors. They will economise their physical force to ensure they can still function no matter how many rounds the fight goes to, they will concentrate their blows against decisive targets such as their opponent's chin, and solar plexus, and finally will attempt to take their opponent by surprise, by feints and jabs to get around his defence to land the killer punch. In military terms these factors are defined as: economy of force, concentration of force, and surprise."

So here are the four principles:

1. Maintenance of Objective (Think)
2. Security of Action (Guard)
3. Mobility of Action (Move)
4. Expenditure of offensive power (Hit)

And three accentuating factors:

1. Economy of force (Efficiency)
2. Concentration of force (Effectiveness)
3. Surprise (Control)

These principles are equally applicable to both Strategy and Tactics. But they are only "Principles" not "Laws", Fuller says that they can be discarded with impunity, but only after deep consideration.

Why are the Principles important to You?

Explanation of Benefits in Sales Situations

If you follow Fuller's teachings and apply them to sales situations you will find that;

1. You can fight Campaigns, not just a series of disjointed engagements.
2. You will gain much greater control of your campaign.
3. You will maximise your victories, and minimise your defeats.

Benefits associated with the Four Principles

Maintenance of Objective

Having an Objective that is worthwhile and provides the overriding measure of outcome makes you better able to take difficult decisions and weigh up the many choices that fate will throw you in a campaign.

Frederick the Great in his Military Instructions says:

"Your Strategy must pursue an important objective. Undertake only what is possible and reject whatever is chimerical."

The main reason for maintaining your objective is because it will prevent you from being distracted into less important areas thereby dissipating your energies which may ultimately lead to the failure of your campaign. Your objective will decide what you stand to gain, will allow you to calculate what resources you will need to achieve it, the likely timescales involved, and allow consideration from this of the risk vs the reward. Without a clear objective none of this is possible.

No plan is perfect, but again according to Frederick the Great;

"If you are not fortunate enough to follow a great plan through to its perfection, you will nevertheless go much further than the generals who, acting without a plan, make war from day to day".

Having a clear objective will not guarantee success, but **not** having a clear objective will often guarantee failure. Finally, as Frederick the Great says above, even if the ultimate objective isn't reached, it is likely that many gains will be made en route to it, maybe enough to justify the effort even without the ultimate goal being reached.

Security of Action

The essence of Security of Action is control of information. Ensuring Security of action will prevent your own miscalculations and enemy offensives derailing your campaign. Similarly identifying areas which prevent security of action will highlight areas that need to be avoided or where more ground work is required to ensure the success of your plan.

Security of action allows you to bring your forces together in a decisive way at the decisive point at the correct time. If your competition is unaware of your plans and movements it will not be possible for them to take steps effectively to stop them ahead of time. No matter how good your plan is, if your competition know abut it they may be in a position to counter it, or at least weaken it. Security of action prevents them from doing this.
Secrecy is defensive and provides security of action, which leads to the offensive accentuating factor of surprise. Conversely intelligence and experience can be thought of as offensive but will lead to the defensive accentuating factor of economy of force by ensuring that you don't waste your efforts in fruitless areas of endeavour.

Without security of action the likeliness of you being able to follow your objectives to a successful conclusion will be decided by chance and the actions of your enemies as much as by the actions you take. Without security of action you cannot maintain the initiative or be sure of reaching your objectives.

Mobility of Action

Because "You don't know what you don't know" you may have to change your plans due to unforeseen difficulties, or sudden opportunities. Either way you need to be able to amend your plans to avoid setbacks or exploit an advantage whilst still maintaining your Objective and benefiting from Security of Action.

Mobility of Action renders flexibility into your plan, and at the very least you must understand where the limits of your flexibility are and attempt to bypass these danger areas as quickly as possible during your campaign. Likewise you need to be able to identify and exploit potential advantages as they arise.

Being able to manoeuvre faster than your competition will allow you more time to gain objectives and advantages, and less time having to fight over them.

During WW2 German General Heinz Guderian was one of the war's greatest exponents of the teachings of Fuller, his view on mobility was summed up as:

"The engine of the Tank is a weapon just as its Gun is." ("Der motor des Panzers ist ebenso seine waffe wie die kanone").

Expenditure of Offensive Power
The ability to deliver a decisive blow in order to win the objective quickly, effectively and efficiently, must be the pinnacle of your. Unless your power is delivered in this manner your will not produce the optimum result.

Again General Heinz Guderian had a saying for it, and if he thought his men were applying less than decisive pressure in their attacks he would say;

"Bash them, don't splash them!" ("Klotzen, nicht Kleckern!")

Maximum force must be delivered in the most decisive areas, and at the most decisive times. Force must be controlled and directed, it must be reserved until required, and then unleashed to the optimum level required to ensure victory. There must be no holding back, no thoughts of humanity, no sympathy for your competition. The point of using your offensive power is to break your enemy's will to fight; they will only be defeated when they believe that they have lost and you believe that you have won. The expenditure of your offensive power must convince your competition that they cannot win; at that point they have lost.

Antoine-Henri de Jomini (one of Napoleon's Generals) summed up what is required in the expenditure of offensive power in his maxim:

"To throw by strategic movements the mass of an army, successively, upon the decisive points of a theatre of war, and also upon the communications of the enemy as much as possible without compromising one's own."

Benefits associated with the Three Accentuating Factors

Economy of Force
Assuming your resources are not unlimited, a profligate use of them will result in an inability to use them when and where they will be most effective. There are few things easier than making commitments in a customer situation, and few things harder than backing out of them when circumstances change and you need the people you have committed for a more important or urgent task elsewhere. So judging the worth of tasks and challenges before undertaking them will ultimately allow you to have resources on hand when they are needed.

If the resources used in a campaign can be kept to the minimum required to achieve the objective it will be found that planning and maintaining the objective is fast and simple with less dissention and extraneous opinions and actions, security of Action is greatly increased the fewer the people that are involved and aware of the objective, mobility of action is always faster with fewer people to control and direct to new areas, and even in expenditure of offensive power having just enough resources will allow a much faster, effective, and concentrated blow to be delivered without dissipating the force of the blow, if you have managed to save your forces till the decisive blow can fall then they are much more likely to be fresh with high morale, and therefore more effective in the engagement when it is required.

Conversely profligate salespeople will waste resources by soaking up all those which are available, if these resources are required, then that is excusable. If they are not required to achieve the objectives, having too many people involved in a campaign will make it less likely that an objective will be maintained due to too many opinions and agendas. Security of action becomes much more difficult to maintain as the more people who are aware of the plans and objectives, the more likely it is that there will be a leak that will reach your enemies. Mobility of action will be more difficult to achieve as it is much easier to react quickly and efficiently to changes in approach and plan with a small force than a large one, and you will find that it will become quite difficult to disengage and keep a low profile if heavy resistance forces the need for such change of approach

Concentration of Force
Concentration of force in space and time is the single most effective act that you can take during a campaign. Bringing your forces together to act in unison greatly magnifies their individual effects, and has a far greater impact on the psychology of a customer, and on your competition. Concentrating your forces in space and time will maximise their effect at the

decisive moment. If you concentrate your forces when or where they are not required renders them useless. You want them at the right place and at the right time in order to deliver the decisive blow to maximum effect. Once the time and place are right bring all necessary forces together to ensure a decisively positive outcome.

Surprise

Surprise allows you to psychologically disorient your competition, which allows you take gain the initiative and act before they have a chance to react. It allows a smaller force to beat a larger force, and multiplies the effect of numbers and speed, so manoeuvre is easier, and actions and results happen faster.

Surprise can produce a strategic and/or tactical dislocation in the enemy's mind, and should also produce a dislocation for the enemy at an operational level. The degree of the psychological dislocation will depend on your enemy's morale, the degree of dislocation at an operational level will depend on your enemy's ability to react quickly and calmly.

A surprise attack or move to your advantage will have three effects: The first being Tactical where you have the initiative and can therefore take advantage of time and space to gain an immediate win, the second is psychological, if the enemy feel they have lost the initiative and cannot effectively counter you, the enemy's morale will be lowered, thereby reducing their will to fight; thirdly it can destroy your enemy's plans as they will have to take actions to counter your move thereby becoming distracted from their own plans. So a successful surprise move can give you a tactical, psychological and strategic advantage.

How to apply Fuller's teachings to sales situations

The Four Principles

Maintenance of Objective

Plan your objective based on three things:

1. The resources you have at your disposal.
2. The time available to complete it
3. The reward vs the risks involved.

The entire decision process must be based around the maximum that can be realistically achieved. Objectives should be bold but not foolhardy, and should offer the greatest possible reward but with the most manageable risks If you get any one of these seriously wrong, you will not be able to maintain your objective.

From your Objective comes your plan i.e. your strategy to achieve it, and from your strategy flows your tactics. So your Objective is what you want to end up with, your strategy is your plan to achieve it, your tactics are the actions you will take to achieve your strategy. The converse is also true, if you have only one set of tactics at your disposal, then your strategy will be decided by these, and your objective will need to be tailored to this strategy.

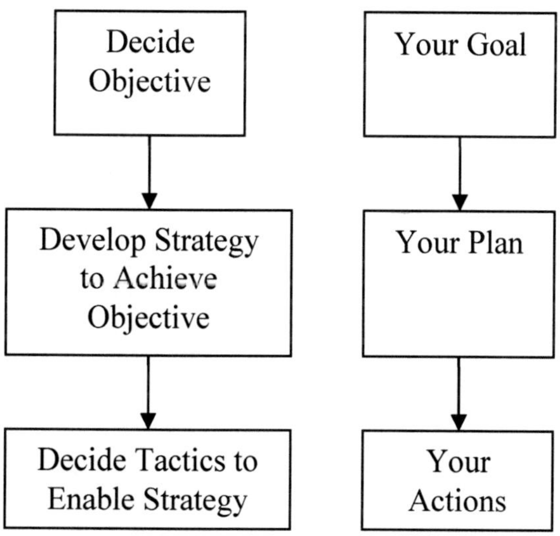

The problem you will face will be diversions from your objective, whether caused by your competition, the customer, or your own internal management. These must be avoided unless it is obvious that you have the wrong objective, and these diversions offer a better alternative. But generally they should be avoided as you will risk never reaching any grand objective if minor distractions continually pull you away from it.

Again Frederic The Great says:
"Give battle only when you have reason to hope that your success will be decisive, and fight not only to defeat the enemy but to execute the course of your strategy that would fail but for this decision."

If you do need to engage with your enemy, do not believe anything your competition says about their strength, unless you've seen the proof. Assume that they arc guilty and lieing until proven innocent. Do not let their propaganda dictate your actions. I cannot remember the number of times that inexperienced sales and technical people have come to me in a panic because of some new statement from a competitor, without any proof that it is true, acting as a fifth column on the competition's behalf spreading doubt within our own ranks, only to find, when fully tested, that their claims are pure fantasy with no empirical evidence or customer examples to support them. I have won scores of deals by rubbing my competition's noses in their false claims, but have never lost a deal because I forced them to prove their claims; nine times out of ten they will not be able to prove their claims, and the one time they do you will have discovered a highly valuable truth, and will know what to avoid in future. At the very least this course of action will bog them down in defensive work just to hold their ground. The main thing to avoid is distraction from your objective, into ambush by your competition. They will do this to break your momentum, to prevent you reaching a decisive position in space and time, and to destroy your strategy. Only spend time challenging them if it directly helps your objective.

Security of Action

In order for your actions to be secure, you must keep them as secret as possible; do not broadcast them internally other than to those who must know them, your colleagues may leave and join the competition and give away your plans, they may talk about them to other partners and customers which will alert your competition of your likely actions. Do not explain to your partners or resellers what your plans are other than what you must tell them in order to make them support your actions. Above all do not tell the customer what your plans are as they may use this against you and may actually tell your competition what you are doing thereby allowing them to take counter measures.

So, enforce your code of secrecy to your colleagues, your partners, and the customer, adjust what you tell them to how well you believe they will be able to be quiet about your plans.

Probe and scout for the best and easiest areas of engagement in the target customer account, do not spend time fighting in areas that are too difficult as this will show your enemies what your plans are and give them time to adjust their own plans to thwart you.

It is not possible to avoid risks altogether, and few worthy objectives exist that do not contain an element of risk; it is a matter of weighing up the risk vs. the reward available to you in taking any particular line of action in the pursuit of your overall objective. You must make judgments as to when to push hard and when to withdraw, pushing too hard at the wrong time or in the wrong place will show your hand to your enemies, conversely withdrawing too soon will rob you of the chance to achieve your objective. Follow the advice of The Duke of Wellington; "All the business of war, and indeed all the business of life, is to endeavour to find out what you don't know from what you do."

The greater your experience of similar campaigns, the greater your likelihood of understanding the risks you face in this one. However a word of warning from Frederick The Great: " A mule who has carried a pack for ten campaigns under Prince Eugene will not be a better tactician for it." the value of any previous experience will be multiplied or divided by the intelligence and aptitude of the commander. No matter how good the teacher or the lessons, an Ass can never learn them.

Mobility of Action

The key to this section is the conjunction of the two adjectives "Mobility" and "Action" moving on its own is not enough your movement must be to deliver an action, and your action should either move your campaign forward to its objective, or help secure your position for future moves. You must look for the Line of Least Resistance and when in doubt be prepared to strike out and take the initiative.

The key is to look at a number of different potential outcomes and choose to follow a route which will lead to the optimum benefit whilst either allowing lesser objectives to be reached en route, or that would allow a switch of emphasis to an alternative profitable conclusion. In order to do this you must build in flexibility of timescales and personnel, and have your stockpiles of arguments, proposals and counter arguments arranged along your route for use as necessary depending on the changing circumstances.

One of the biggest mistakes made by less able salespeople is to fixedly and inflexibly try to batter their way via an impossible route which will never allow them to reach their Objective, in order to avoid having to do the complex work of thinking through the alternatives, and arguing for changes to the plan.

Potential obstacles to success may be caused by the competition, the customer, or by your own organisation. The competition may buy time by asking the customer to wait a few months until the have a new product available, the customer may have their budgets cut, or you may find that your offering does not work as well as you had been lead to believe by your Marketing and Development teams.

Conversely you may come across unforeseen opportunities, you may uncover a particular weakness in a competitor's solution, you may find a particular customer need in a new area which could offer an opportunity, or your R&D department may come out with a particularly beneficial feature which will accelerate the take up of your solution.

All of these factors and more, must be assessed as they occur and your plan must contain the flexibility to either deal with them or at the very least you must understand where the limits of your flexibility are and attempt to bypass these danger areas as quickly as possible during your campaign. But most importantly you must be prepared to take action in order to exploit potential advantages as they arise, quickly and decisively.

You must calculate what will happen and lay plans to deal with it. Think of the worst that the competition and the customer may throw at you, and draw up your plans in advance, for example, if your customer has budgetary constraints, what will you do; offer a cheaper solution, defer payment, offer a rental rather than a capital purchase, or perhaps sell to individual departments rather than a group-wide deal? Or give up and hand the account to your competitors.

Expenditure of Offensive Power

Only use as much offensive power as required to move towards your objective. Save your decisive blow until you are concentrated in the right place, and at the right time. Save your killer blow until in a good position to deliver it. You need to identify the centre of Gravity of your prospect, the "Schwerpunkt" and hit it hard and decisively leaving no room for your competition.

When you do deliver it do so with supreme force and confidence. It must be done as effectively and efficiently as possible. Make it "an event" do not hold back on your delivery, make it stick in your customer's mind.

If possible apply successive blows to a limited area, but always with the intention of breaking through any initial organized resistance in order to reach the real decision makers and budget holders thereby winning them over and effectively "decapitating" the customer's command and control structure, if you can do this, the rest of resistance will collapse much faster.

The Three Accentuating Factors

Economy of force
Choose your forces carefully and precisely. Give them specific tasks which will avoid overlaps in responsibility and shared responsibilities between groups and individuals, this will prevent different groups reinventing the wheel and tripping over each other in the customer account.

Delegate responsibility, accountability, and above all else power to carry out tasks. If your people aren't empowered then you cannot expect them to take either responsibility or accountability for actions and outcomes.

Do not waste time on unnecessary meetings, and when meetings are necessary make sure that you set them up with the objective in mind, do not invite anyone other than those absolutely required, do not take any minutes other than actions given to people with the timescales for their completion.

Plan ahead to ensure that you will have the necessary resources available when you require them, and get commitments from other groups if necessary to ensure that this happens. In most situations where salespeople complain of a lack of resources, what they generally are suffering from is a lack of planning.

Concentration of force
The key to any campaign is to be in the right place and at the right time, one without the other will lead to a failure or only a partial success.

You must bring your forces to bear on a limited front, so that your numbers have a greater effect, and in relatively greater numbers than your competition, or better still somewhere where you competition are absent. All else being equal, these circumstances on their own should be enough to guarantee the success of your offensive.
Once you have identified the customer's Schwerpunkt, concentrate on that one area (or as few as possible) at any given time, focus the customer's mind on that one area, and have all your arguments and resources ready to deliver a series of successive blows in the shortest possible time frame to that area. Ensure that each blow either weakens customer resistance or moves past resistance to further your progress to your objective; each blow should ideally get you

past a level of resistance to another level within the customer's decision making process. Make sure that when you deliver each blow success criteria and outcomes are agreed upfront with the customer, i.e. when I deliver x you will give me y.

Surprise

You will achieve surprise through security of action and mobility of action. Keep your plans on a need to know basis, internally with your colleagues, and externally with your partners and the customer. Focus your resources on each component of the plan, do not let them drift into other areas which may expose more of your plan than would be helpful to the customer or your competition.

Move quickly and quietly within the customer account until you find the schwerpunkt. Engage with unexpected areas and departments within the customer, socialize with the customer to find their personal needs and wants, what will give them a personal win and you a surprise advantage over your competition? Once found, hit these areas quickly and silently.

Sales Example

Maintenance of Objective (Think)

Our Overall Objective was to break into the Managed Services Arm of a major Hardware Supplier who had not spent any money with us for some time despite having an agreement in place, but did regular business with one of our competitors.

I needed to find an area that lent itself to our solution, at a time when they would need to make a fast decision, and likewise I needed to contact someone in a position powerful enough to make a decision and back it up with action, to do this I needed to provide a personal win for them.

I did my initial research and found that there were three reasons why we had not made headway with them before, these were; firstly that we had concentrated our efforts on the major geographies where they were being well serviced by our competition, secondly that their sales people in the major geographies were not bothering to sell new third party solutions because they had more than enough to do selling their own solutions to a huge market, and thirdly that we did not have a reference account for our product that they could judge us on internally. So our efforts had previously been concentrated in Geographies which were highly competitive, lacked incentives for the partner, and we were relatively mistrusted through lack of familiarity.

So my Strategy became to attack an area where our competition were weak or mistrusted, where the local teams would have an incentive to sell third party products, and where we could quickly produce a referenceable account at no risk to the partner.

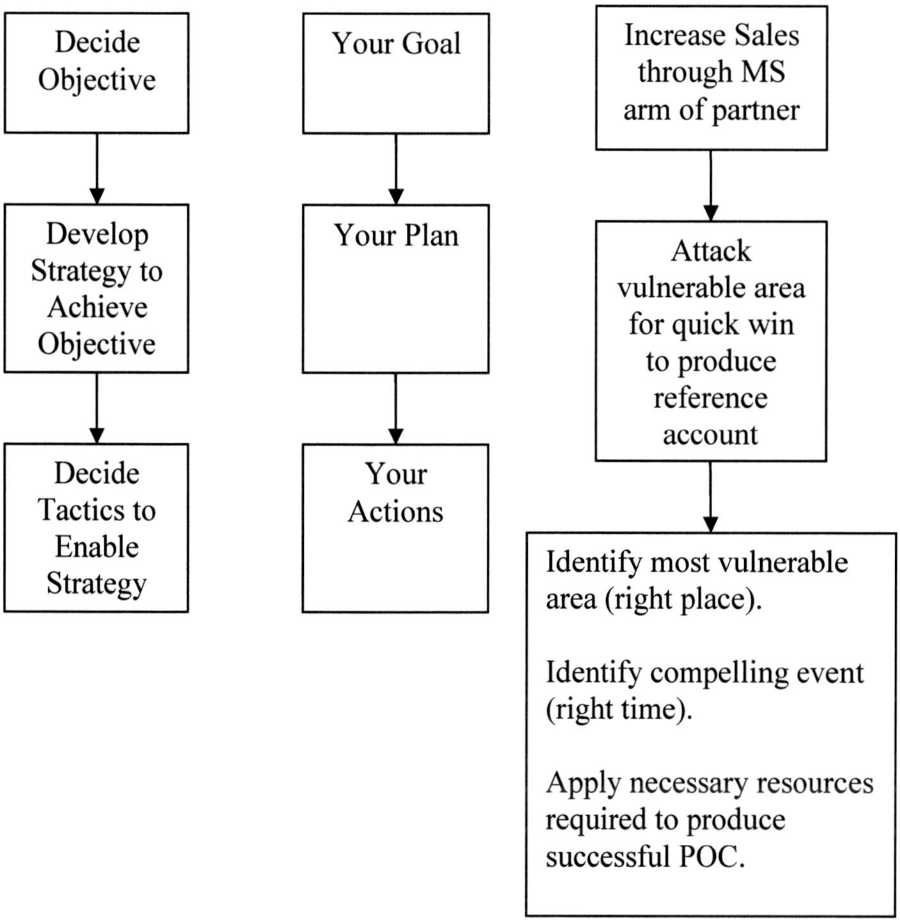

Having done some research with various high level contacts at the partner, probing for information that would lead me to the area I needed to attack, I found out that in some of the smaller geographies in Europe they owned a high proportion of the hardware install base which meant that it was very hard for them to drive new sales, and they made most of their business from upgrades, which was good business, but limited in revenue and a hard market to drive, because of this the salesmen in these areas had a much greater dependence on the Managed Services arm to engage to provide solutions in order to flatten out the dips in revenue that the account Managers would normally be subject to. I also found out that the preeminent position held by our main competitor meant that they had become arrogant and were starting to impose tougher conditions on deals in order to meet their needs rather than the needs of the Managed Services sales people at the partner, this was straining relationships, most especially at the management and sales level rather than at the technical level, where relationships were still strong. I now knew the general areas to attack in the company, i.e. smaller geography with high market share, and at a management/sales level rather than technical.

I researched my subject and came up with a number of possible targets mainly in the French speaking geographies including France, Belgium, and Luxembourg. France was my first try, they had a relatively large penetration of a large market, I managed to get in to see them but it was obvious that they did not wish to engage with an Englishman when our competitor had a local French presence, and a solution that they were used to and reasonably happy with, next I tried Belgium, a much smaller market, but with a good presence by our partner especially in the Government area, I could only reach the procurement people, and was told by them that they were happy with their current agreements and that I should try again in the following year when they were reviewing their budgets etc, I then tried The Netherlands, as although not French speaking was part of the "BeNeLux" (Belgium, Netherlands, Luxembourg) management region in our partner's setup; but drew a blank as I could not get a reply to calls, emails, or letters from them. This left little Luxembourg. I considered whether a market this small was worth the effort, and decided to do a bit more research to find out. It transpired that the partner had 70% of the install base, making it a virtual monopoly for them, which would mean that it would be incredibly difficult for the Account Managers to grow their market on hardware alone. The other advantage was that being a small country Managed Services were managed by a single man who new intimately the ins and outs of all the accounts in his territory and could therefore take decisions quickly and without having to involve a committee to discuss them. So after all the other knock backs I had finally discovered the right place; I just needed to be there at the right time. The key here was that I had walked away from any opportunities that looked too difficult as I needed to keep up the momentum driving us to the final objective and not be side tracked into attempted heroics to overcome a "No" from a country that didn't realise they had a need for us, I sacrificed the tactical for the strategic.

So, I engaged with the Managed Services Director for Luxembourg using introductions from friendly contacts in other geographies, and started to gently educate him about our solutions (I was wary given my failures with all the other countries in his region), the fact that I would fly out to Luxembourg to meet with him on a regular basis made a very good impression, as our competitor tried to run him as an account by phone from Paris. So again I put time into this phase which was out of proportion to the tactical short term gains, but utterly in keeping with the Strategic Objective.

Then we got a break, some people would call it luck, but personally I put it down to what Richard Branson says; "99% of selling is just being there." I was at lunch with the Director (he chose, I paid) when his mobile rang, he apologised and said that he had to take the call, fortunately I could understand enough French to know that he was having an argument with the person at the end of the phone, who it turned out was our competitor, and the argument concerned money and timing. Having finished the call he had gone from red in the face and very loud to very pale and silent. I asked him to tell me what had happened, he replied that he had put one of our competitor's products into an account in a proof of concept (POC) which was currently ongoing, this meant that there would be no payment from the customer (a major financial institution) until the end of the POC when they would decide whether the solution had achieved what was required. Despite this our competitor was now demanding payment from the partner prior to the partner receiving payment from the customer and were threatening to withdraw their product if it wasn't forthcoming, telling the Partner Managed Services Director that "…his company was big enough to go and find the budget."

This was a startlingly arrogant position for our competitor to take, born of false confidence in the strength of their position. Of course it put me in the right place, and now at exactly the right time. It was now up to me to seize the moment.

I poured us both another glass of wine and asked the Director to explain to me what was happening at the customer, i.e. the products being used, the timescales, etc etc, and that if he did this, I would do everything in my power to help him if I could. It turned out that they were engaged at a very tough client, one of the few fully managed installations in Europe, and to fail in this instance would mean the customer inviting the partner's competition in to prove what they could do instead, it also transpired that although in production use, the POC had only been happening for a short time, so our competitor's product was in a fairly raw form, with very little customisation to cement it into the customer's installation. So it was obvious that our competitor knew the importance of the account to the partner, had waited till their product had been put into production use, and had then attempted to spring the trap on early payment, their timing had been impeccable, but they hadn't planned on me being there when they sprang it. Getting the money and paying the competitor was possible but would but the Director under great personal exposure, and should the POC fail, and the customer refuse to

follow it up and pay for the competitor's product, the Director will have had to have written off a large sum of money and would face aboard of enquiry into his competence.
Timing indeed. I looked the Director in the eye and said;

"What if I can replace the competitor's product and allow you to carry on with the POC?"

He was distracted by the emotion of his phone call, and asked;

"But can you replace a product in production, and what are you going to charge me?"

I replied;

"I will charge you nothing for my product unless, and until, you get paid for it, and I will make a phone call now to my technical department to see if a production level swap out is feasible, if it is I will only ask that you cover the daily rate for my guys to come over and do it, if it can't be done I will not bring up the subject again."

This was a small commitment in my eyes for the chance to be placed within striking distance of the first part of the objective.

He agreed to my offer, I called the Manager of my technical group explained the situation, he agreed that we could do it, and as our competitor's product had not been heavily customised for the customer environment, he believed that it would take about a week of a consultant's time. I handed the phone to the director and let my technical manager explain what we could do, so that he could see that it wasn't just sales bullshit from me. The director's mood lightened somewhat, but he still had nagging doubts over the costs, I reiterated again that I would charge him nothing for the product unless and until he got paid by the customer, and told him the daily rates for my technical guys five days, then asked him what he thought he could afford without too much pain, and negotiated a fixed price within his budget by including travel and hotel costs (which we could control) in the daily rate. I had left him no reason to say no. We shook hands on the deal, but I insisted on one proviso; that he would not discuss what we were doing with either our competitor or any of his own staff who did not need to know.

My technical consultant was on a plane that evening to the account, and not only did he implement our solution in parallel to the competitive one, but he did it in three days instead of five, seeing this I took the opportunity to hit even harder into the director's good books by offering to either give him the money back for the two days we hadn't needed, despite the fixed charge agreed, or to allow him two extra days of training for his people in our solution, needless to say he jumped at the offer, and in fact used the days to get his people trained.

Our competitor was then cut out of the communications loop with the account and the partner technical people on site, so had no visibility as to what was happening, their temporary password on their product eventually expired, and they confidently sat back to await developments, and the expected call from the director agreeing to pay them what they had asked for.

So the POC continued, and proved to be a success, we nursed the installation through, trained the partner technicians, educated and advised them on the best approaches, and delivered a solution that their customer could only agree had delivered on what had been asked for. Once this point was reached I was invited to lunch with the director again, and had the pleasure of this time hearing him call our competitor and advise them that he wouldn't be doing business with them again. It was their turn to have their lunch ruined.

However the story didn't end there. The director now faced the problem of getting the customer to pay for the solution (remember this is the French speaking world, where negotiations don't finish just because you have an agreement, they finish when you have the money in the bank, and start again on the next phase the following day!). His issue was that the customer had decided that he wasn't happy to pay an upfront cost for a piece of software, as his agreement on services from the partner was on a quarterly basis. I discussed this with the Director, and it gave us a dilemma as we would normally expect the full costs upfront, but the overall objective of this deal was to break into this partner's portfolio of best loved products, not to maximise short term gain from one deal, so winning this deal was not the objective, the objective was to use this deal as a bridgehead to get us into the rest of the partner's geographies as a standard offering in preference to our competition. So I changed our rules. I agreed to let the partner charge the customer for our solution on a quarterly rental basis in line with his own charges for services, I adjusted the costs to add some interest payments within the charge, and then added more on top of each charge that the partner could either keep as a payment for themselves, or pass on as a discount to the customer. So once again I made it very easy for the Director to do business with us, and offered him an additional benefit on top.

The net result of all this, was that we made considerably more from the rental of the product than we would have done from a straight upfront purchase, and a few years later, the customer was so impressed with the product that they agreed to purchase it outright, which doubled the amount of money we made in total. If this had been all that happened then it would have been a good result, but the bigger objective was also met; the Director broadcast far and wide, at every opportunity his praise of us and our solution, first into Belgium, then into France, and eventually this message seeped out into Spain, Italy, UK, Germany, and the USA, giving us a seven figure revenue stream worldwide, all from one encounter in tiny Luxembourg. We had reached our Objective.

Security of Action (Guard)

My objective was never revealed to the Partner, nor to my own staff, they did not need to know, and as long as each part of the plan could be moved along successfully there was no need to explain further. As far as the Director was concerned I was fixing his short term problem, my long term plan was not his concern. So strategically there was no immediate possibility of our competition knowing what we were doing.

Tactically we needed to protect each stage of the approach. When we met with high resistance we immediately withdrew, researched, and took an alternative path, we did not spend our time making a noise in false heroics and drawing attention to our activities within the Partner company, and indeed to our competition.

When we did find the right place i.e. Luxembourg, it was considered a backwater, treated with contempt by our competition, which marked it out as an area which again would draw little attention to our activities from the competition or from their allies in the partner account.

When we found the right time, i.e. when the relationship between the Director and our competition reached crisis point, we still made security of action paramount; I insisted that if we were to help him he must not tell our competition what we were doing, and indeed he should not tell anyone of his own staff other than those who needed to know until the POC was complete.

Mobility of Action (Move)

Movement and indeed speed of movement was key to meeting our objective both strategically and tactically. Being in the right place at the right time is a matter of being in the perception and thoughts of your target, in the right place and at the right time, and this means being in many places all of the time psychologically speaking. You need not only a massively high work rate, but also the ability to inspire your targets to "join your ranks" and the judgement to know when this isn't going to work, at least at that time, in which case you must continue to move along the target front looking for other vulnerable spots to engage.

Strategically we wasted no time in probing the geographies that were openly hostile to change, we keep scouting until we found the one that was a fit for our strategic approach and our tactics. We did not spend a lot of time trying to change the minds of intransigent people, we moved on quickly and efficiently causing a s few ripples as possible which also helped our Security of Action. We probed all aspects of our strategic approach by geography looking for the right sized country, by Language group looking for cultural affinity to independent thought, and by market size and penetration comparing market opportunity with the partner's likely need to sell outside of the base products, and finally by constant communication in the geography (the sales equivalent of scouting movements) were managed to pin down the right person to engage with at a time that he needed us. This entailed continuous "movement" and manoeuvre at an intellectual and communications level, until a combination of the right elements were discovered in Luxembourg.

Expenditure of Offensive Power (Hit)

Finally we did not mount futile campaigns in unproductive areas. We maintained our movement to both keep our competition unaware of our plans and look for the optimum time and place and circumstances to give battle. Once we had found it we absolutely forced the issue to fight the battle there and then. If I had let that opportunity pass, we may never had had it again, decisions would have been made, and actions taken that would have forever taken away the opportunity to deliver a decisive blow to our enemy. The Director would have just paid them off and continued with their solution, or another competitor may have come in and swapped them out before we did, or someone elsewhere in the partner organisation may have decided to standardise on the competitor's product, any of which would have defeated us without a chance to put the matter to the test, and all our time and efforts up till that point will have been wasted.

The key to fighting the battle was not only being in the right place at the right time, but then having the perception to understand that a frown on a partner/customer's face, that wasn't put there by you, gives you a clue to a problem that needs solving, and if the frown has been produced by your enemy then this is the area in which to launch your attack, this is the right ground on which to fight. This window of opportunity must be grasped and exploited ferociously; there was no way that I was going to leave that lunch in Luxembourg without having agreement that we would have a chance to get our product into the customer site, that was in absolute harmony with my strategy, and the tactics I adopted were the ones required to ensure that the strategy would be carried forward, I hit the Director with the key solution to his immediate problem; I took away the need for him to pay any money in the short term, I called the my Technical Manager there and then from the restaurant to give assurances that what I was saying could be done without risk, and actually handed him the phone so that he could hear that for himself, I left him no reason to say "Non" (remember he was French) to us, and had a consultant on a plane and in the account the next day. That is how to Expend Offensive Power; in the right place, at the right time, focusing on maximum impact with the weapons and tactics at your disposal on the minimum area required to force the necessary victory, in this case our weapons were our confidence in our solution and people to be able to deliver, and our tactics were our speed of movement to give the director what he required for his immediate and overriding problem his immediate and overriding problem being the limited battle front that we had to engage the enemy in.

This battle ground was manufactured by our competitor. It was safe ground for them until we discovered it, and found that we were better able to fight on that ground than they were.

To summarise the Campaign from a business perspective using military analogies:

Our enemy had chosen a position that was not vulnerable to normal frontal assault. We were required to analyse the reasons for our lack of success in the past, and devise a strategy that would fit our weapons and abilities, and avoid repeating the same failures again. This was the thinking phase which gave us our objectives to be maintained.

Having arrived at our Objectives out of which would come our Strategy, we had to ensure that our enemies, not just our competitor, but also hostile elements within the partner account, were keep unaware of what our real Objective and plan was, when we hit a major obstruction we never spent a lot of time trying to subvert the defenders, we never discussed what our plans were with them, and we never threatened what we might do, or divulged what our next moves would be, and we never discussed what our approach had been up until then. Doing this gave us security of action, which meant that our enemies could not manoeuvre to counter our strategy or even forewarn other parts of their line as to what to expect from us.

Have our Objectives invisible to our enemies gave us freedom of movement, our moves were not being dictated in response to those of our competitor: We where able to move as we pleased; to take wrong moves and make mistakes without being punished for them; and to change direction when we became blocked. We could then look for the right place and be there at the right time, we went down many blind alleys or cul-de-sacs as the French might say, but did not let this slow our progress towards our objectives, the ability to move, react, and if necessary, move again, was paramount. You reach the right place by moving and probing many areas, you reach it at the right time by getting there quickly and persisting in your presence there.

Having found the right place, and ensuring that we were there at the right time without our enemies being aware of our presence, it was then crucial to unleash maximum effort in the most efficient and effective manner, ruthlessly and quickly to seize the moment of victory. We concentrated all of our required forces in time and space at the decisive point, during the most opportune time, on ground that suited us, and when our enemy was weakest, and kept up the momentum of our attack so that there was no time for doubt and reflection by our allies, and maintained the secrecy of our intentions even during the attack which prevented our enemies from changing their tactics to counter our attack.

The Three Accentuating Factors gave us the following:

Economy of force ensured that only those forces required were brought into action at any given time this helped us to move and react quickly without unnecessary delays, discussions, or breaches in security.

Concentration meant that we concentrated our forces only at the right time and in the right place, and in sufficient numbers to achieve immediate maximum effect over the shortest period of time.

Last but by no means least, all of these measures endowed us with the element of Surprise which robbed our competition of the ability to either prevent what we were doing or to react to our attack quickly enough to counter it, this meant that we could win with far fewer forces, more quickly, and decisively than would otherwise have been the case.

Military Example

Plan 1919

Fuller's initial crowning glory was his Plan 1919, which he formulated to end World War One Militarily on the Western Front. It was a synthesis of his principles applied to the tools at his disposal.

In brief the essence of Plan 1919 was:

1. Artillery barrage on target section of enemy line.
2. Breach the enemy line using Heavy Tanks.
3. Support Heavy Tanks with Ground Attack aircraft to pick off remaining targets.
4. Send fast moving Medium Tanks through the breach caused by the Heavy Tanks to attack Command and Control targets in the enemy rear.
5. Motorised Infantry follow through the breach in the enemy lines to mop up last enemy survivors, and hold the breach.

As it happened this plan was never put into place as the war ended in 1919 due to Germany's economic and civilian logistical collapse, but it formed the basic blueprint for theorists such as Sir Basil Liddell Hart and exponents such as Heinz Guderian, to formulate and exploit the Blitzkrieg tactics of the Second World War. Indeed it could be argued that it has formed the basic approach of direct armour tactics ever since.

The Four Principles applied to Plan 1919

Maintenance of Objective It contained a clearly articulated overall objective and each stage of the plan lead ultimately to the overall objective. The maintenance of the objective dictated the actions to be taken when choices presented themselves. The Objective was to break the stalemate of the trench warfare by breaching the German lines on a narrow front, surrounding the front line troops, wiping out the command structure in rear areas, before surrounding and overrunning the front line troops. To have performed this in multiple locations throughout France and Belgium would have brought about an irreparable breach in the German defences, and would have brought about a complete military collapse of all but the most fanatical units who could have been mopped up in detail.

Security of Action It relied on Security of Action, the enemy lines being denuded by artillery, before the Heavy Tanks reached them, when the Heavy Tanks arrived, they were supported by aircraft to ensure any threatening enemy artillery could be picked off, and the lighter armoured medium Tanks were only brought up after the breach was achieved, and the Infantry brought up last of all, being the softest target.

Mobility of Action was provided by motorising all the attacking troops, then exploiting the speed and manoeuvrability of the ground attack by aircraft which would engage with individual threats, and lastly utilising the fast moving medium tanks to surge into the enemy's rear areas and "decapitate" the enemy command structure.

Delivery of Offensive Power was provided in successively waves of first artillery, then Heavy Tanks and Aircraft, then Medium Tanks, and finally Infantry.

The Three Accentuating Factors applied to Plan 1919

Economy of Force was achieved by attacking a small front therefore less forces would be required, and also by matching the right offensive arm to the right offensive task, so the more vulnerable troops not being brought into play until the target was soft enough to allow them to engage with greatest economy.

Concentration was achieved again because of the limited front and by the waves of attack on such a limited front.

Surprise was achieved tactically by the speed of the attack, and the limited front, Strategic surprise was achieved by the quick exploitation of the breach and destruction of the enemy Command and Control centres.

Plan 1919 in practice

The nearest examples to his Plan 1919 before World War Two can be found in the Allied Tank attacks during the later part of World War One.

On 18th July 1918 the French Marshal Foch having been inspired by Fuller's teachings launched a counterattack against a successful German salient on the Western front and achieved complete surprise by unleashing masses of fast moving "Whippet" light tanks, and the German advance was turned into a retreat. However, reserves which had been intended to be used against the "neck" of the German salient were diverted to push back another German breakthrough. This meant that despite the successes of the tactical surprise achieved by the allied light tanks, the Germans were able to hold a defensive position which kept the neck of the salient open, allowing their retreating troops to pull back out of the salient without being cut off.

This use of armoured vehicles, especially Whippets and armoured cars, was once again highlighted on 8th August 1918, when Foch had Haig unleash Rawlinson's 4th army to recapture and extend his railway communications around Amiens. This attack included 450 tanks of various types, and was preceded by a period of secrecy and deception in order to double the size of Rawlinson's force just before the attack. This combination of two accentuating factors; surprise and concentration, allowed the attack to be made without pre-warning the Germans, Liddell Hart described this engagement as "...perhaps the most complete surprise of the war." .

The opening phase included a localised artillery barrage which was of very short duration compared to artillery engagements from earlier phases of the war, and was used to "creep" in front of the Heavy Tanks mainly to ensure that any local artillery (the Tanks main nemesis) was destroyed or driven away.

Stage 1
Sudden Attack, Limited Front

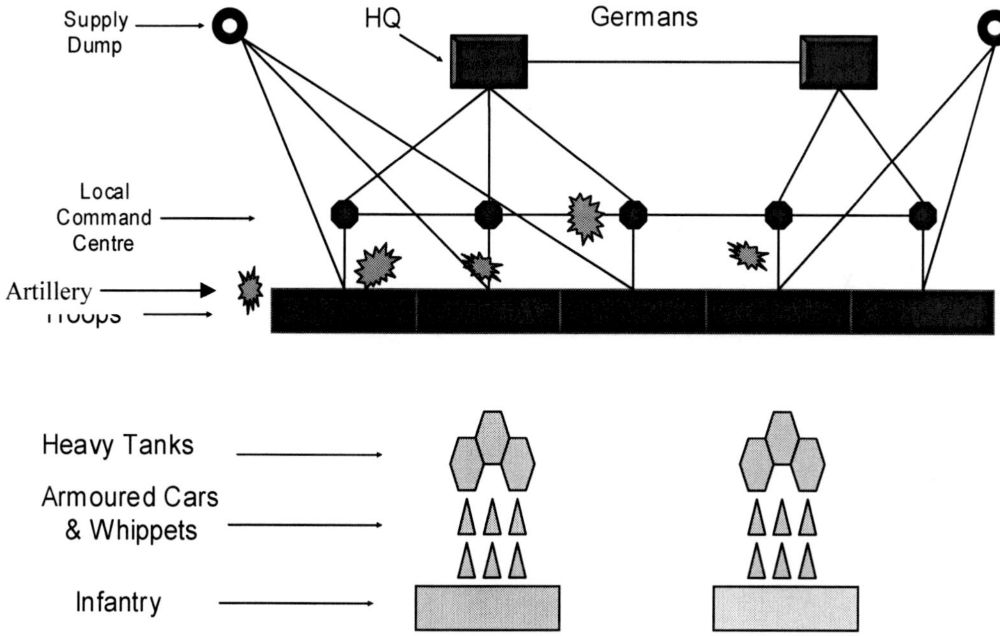

The Heavy Tanks were then used to blast the initial gaps in the enemy lines and to tow the armoured cars across the churned ground of no-mans-land, the gaps produced by the Heavy Tanks were then held by following infantry.

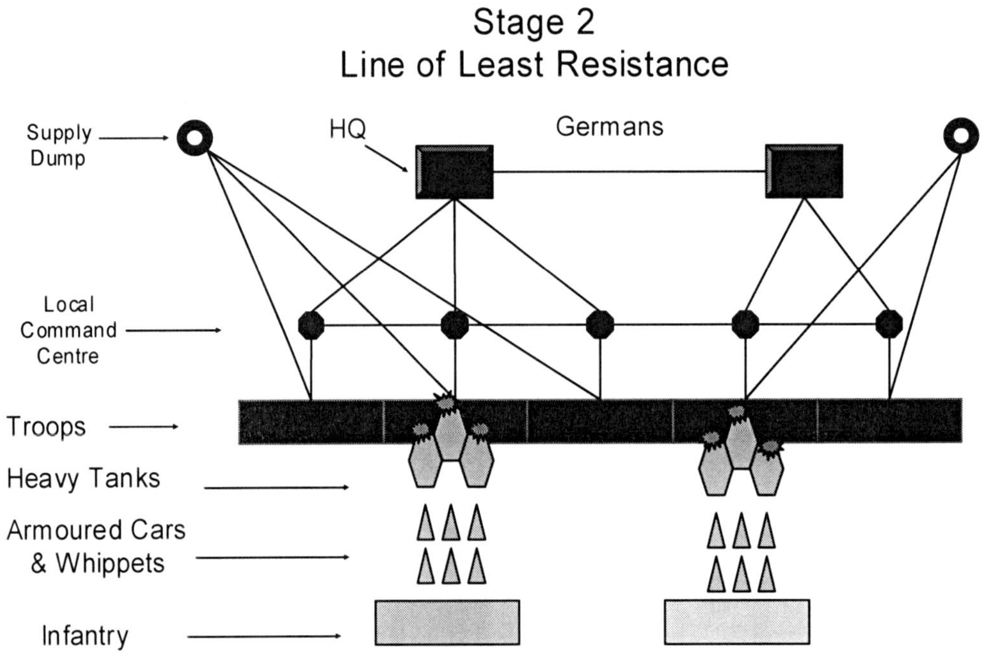

Stage 2
Heavy Tank Break-Through

Where the Germans managed to keep their artillery intact they exacted a heavy toll on the British Tanks, and also resorted to gas shells against Infantry making them resort to advancing in gas masks which slowed them down considerably. Where the allies had few tanks, as with the advancing French units, German machine gunners in defensive positions cut wide swaths through them, and were only overrun after heavy losses.

Stage 3
Exploit Gaps Hit Soft Targets

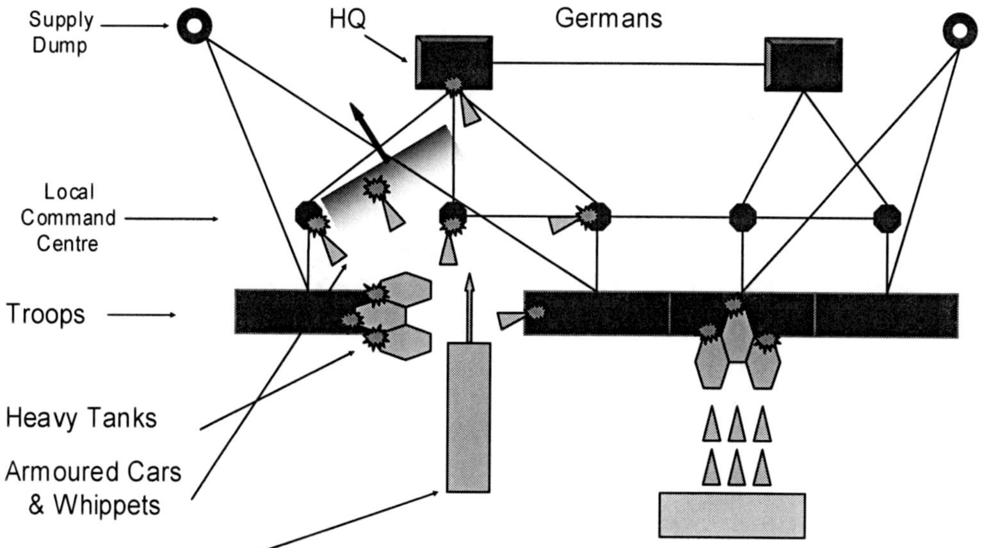

Stage 3
Whippets Exploit Gap

Where the Heavy Tanks had knocked holes in the German lines, the Whippets, armoured cars (now unhitched from the Heavy Tanks), and Cavalry units, then poured through these gaps, to spread chaos, terror, and confusion in their wake.

The cavalry suffered in this role, as one machine gun, or a platoon of infantry armed with small arms, or even a farmer's barbed wire fence could stop them in their tracks. To compound the problem the whippets were charged with supporting the cavalry. This had been warned against by the Tank Corps General Staff, and in practice it never worked. The problem was that the cavalry were forever charging off in advance of the Whippets, which would then motor past them as they came charging back in the opposite direction having been mauled by small arms fire. The whippets would then have to disperse the enemy, go back to gather up the cavalry, who would then charge off to punish their routed foes before being thrown back again by enemy action, and the whole situation would repeat itself. Eventually the cavalry would retire to water the horses and expect the Whippets to go with them. The one function the cavalry were able to carry out effectively was rounding up German prisoners.

The Whippets and armoured cars came into their own where they were either given free reign to roam behind enemy lines, whether this was through deliberate policy or where they managed to "loose" their accompanying cavalry units. Two striking examples of this come from accounts of an armoured car unit and a lone Whippet which were turned loose behind German lines.

The 17th Armoured Car Battalion consisting of 12 armoured cars managed to destroy a German transport column, knock out a train, and overran the local German HQ, running the Australian flag up over it. Next they attacked and destroyed a German Infantry unit as it sat down to lunch, and then routed a huge number of German Infantry units retreating from their trenches. They finished the day by shooting Lorries carrying German troops off the road, and joining a German transport column prior to opening fire on it at point blank range and destroying it.

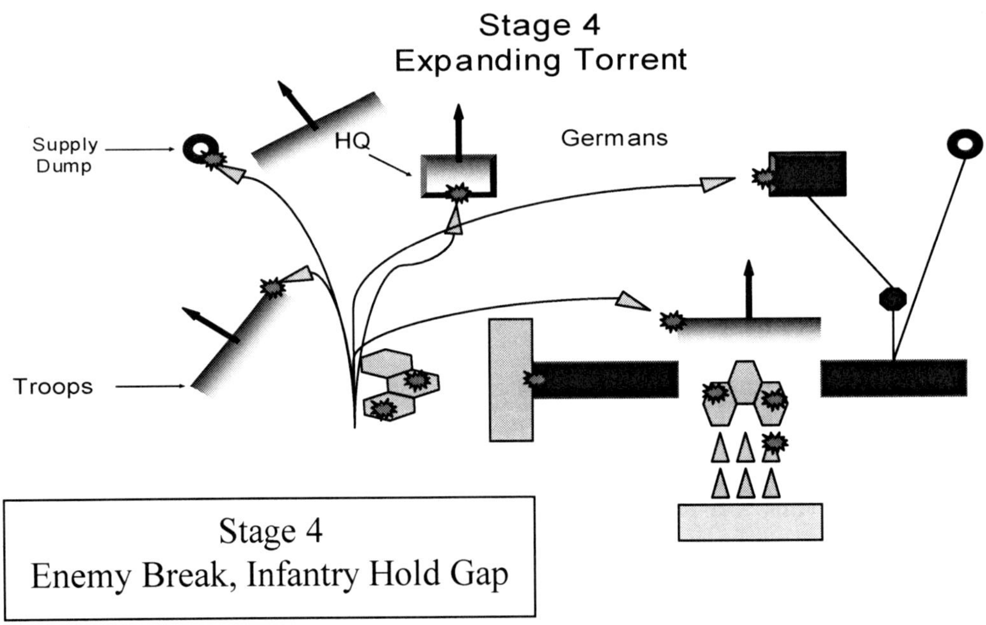

A lone Whippet, affectionately called "Musical Box" did, fortunately, manage to loose its Cavalry, and decided to act as an independent Guerrilla unit behind German lines. It overran an artillery battery, killed or wounded 60 Infantrymen packing kits ready for evacuation, attacked several retreating infantry columns, and finished its action by knocking out several transport columns.

Interestingly, although the German fighting troops managed to hold out without breaking, although with the loss of much ground, casualties, and prisoners, it was Ludendorff the German supreme Commander who threw in the towel. The line breaking tactics that the allies had developed and the intelligent use of tanks convinced him that the Germans would eventually loose the war, and he called for an armistice, which would eventually culminate in German surrender. The allies had won, strategically in line with Fuller's analogy of "decapitating" the enemy command structure, in this instance it was the German Commander's morale that had been decapitated, not just the command structure in the field.

Summary: What to Do

The Four Principles

Maintenance of Objective (Think)

a. Set overall objective that balances risk and reward.
b. Make sure that individual objectives are understood by personnel.
c. Periodically review strategy to ensure that it aligns with objectives.
d. Periodically review tactics to ensure that they support strategy.
e. Change Strategy if objective is becoming unreachable.
f. Only change objective if it will be impossible to achieve.

Security of Action (Guard)

g. Keep information on a "need to know" basis internally.
h. Do not advertise your strategy with partners or the customer.
i. Do not engage in unnecessary battles with the competition.

Mobility of Action (Move)

j. Probe as many areas as possible without loosing momentum.
k. Retreat from cul-de-sacs.
l. Pursue opportunities inline with maintaining your objective.
m. Continue to maintain momentum at all stages, do not stand still.

Expenditure of offensive power (Hit)

n. Find the customer's Schwerpunkt.
o. Attack Schwerpunkt with a succession on accelerating blows.
p. Deliver blows on as narrow a front as possible.
q. Deliver blows over as short a time frame as possible.
r. Agree criteria and outcomes with customer; "I do x you give y."
s. Do not hold back on forward assertive acts until objective is gained.

Apply the Three Accentuating Factors to the Four Principles

Economy of force (Efficiency)

a. Keep resources to the optimum required.
b. Avoid overlapping and shared responsibilities in your resources.
c. Plan and communicate resourcing requirements in advance.

Concentration of force (Effectiveness)

d. Make sure forces are concentrated at the right place at the right time.
e. Ensure a relative local superiority of resources over your competition.
f. Coordinate forces to maintain momentum of attack.

Surprise (Control)

g. Find unexpected routes to your objective.
h. Act quickly and decisively when surprise is achieved.
i. Exploit enemy operational dislocation to reinforce your success.

Mnemonics

The Four Principles

Think, Guard, Move, Hit

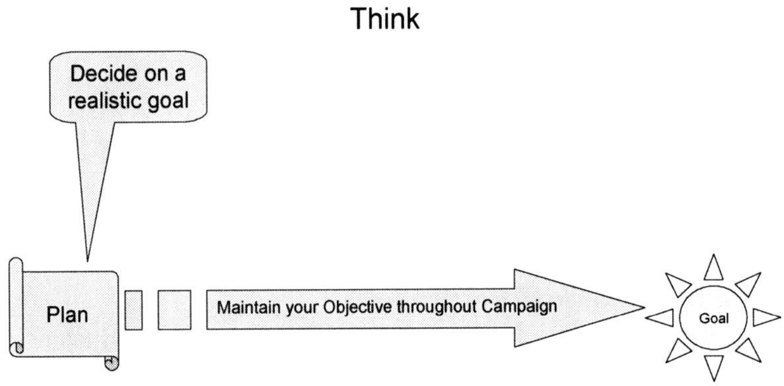

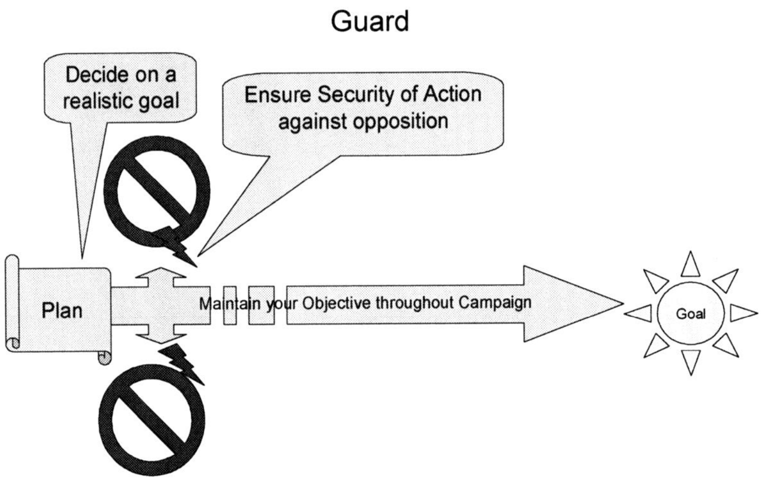

Move

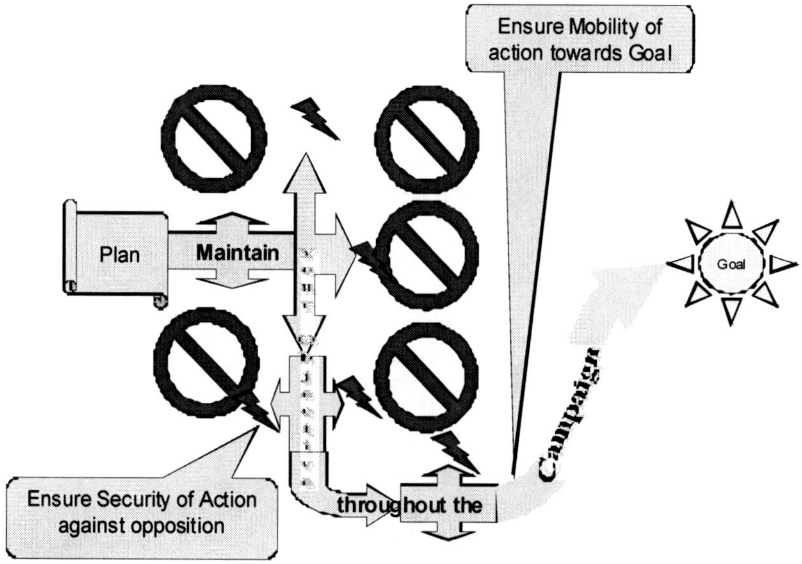

Ensure Mobility of action towards Goal
Plan
Maintain
throughout the
Campaign
Goal
Ensure Security of Action against opposition

Hit

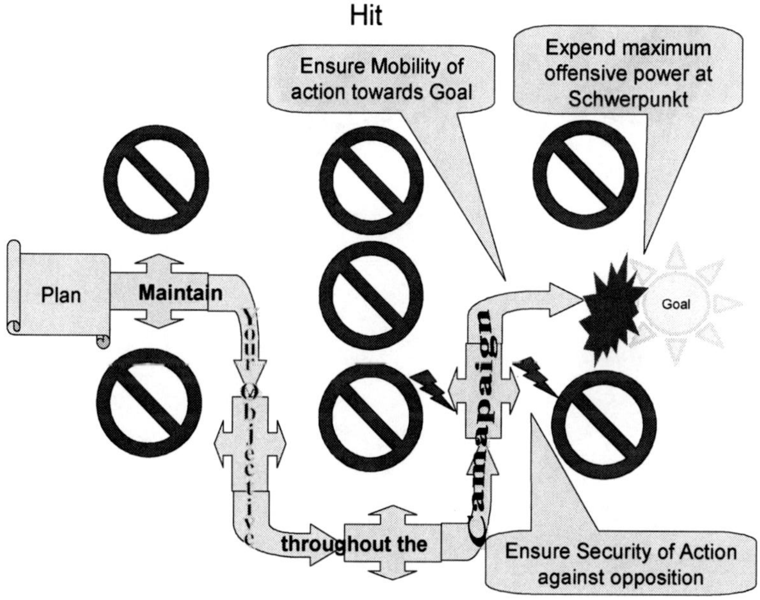

Ensure Mobility of action towards Goal
Expend maximum offensive power at Schwerpunkt
Plan
Maintain
Your
Objective
throughout the
Camapaign
Goal
Ensure Security of Action against opposition

The Three Accentuating Factors

Economy of Force, Surprise, Concentration of Force

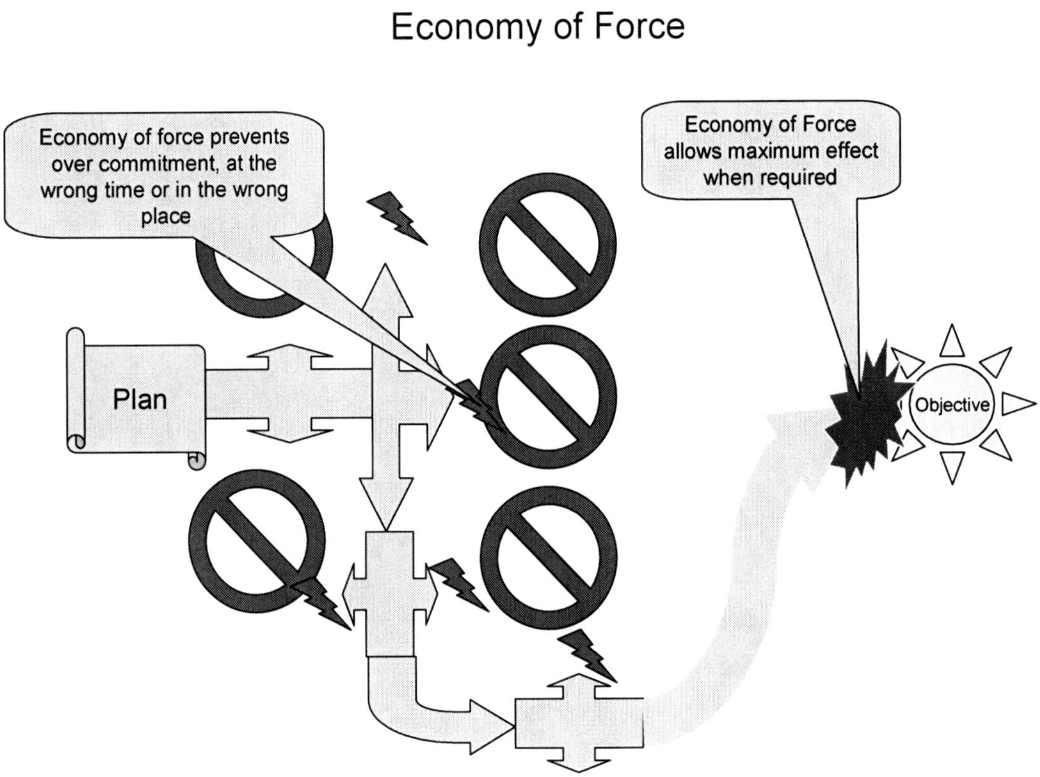

Surprise

Concentration

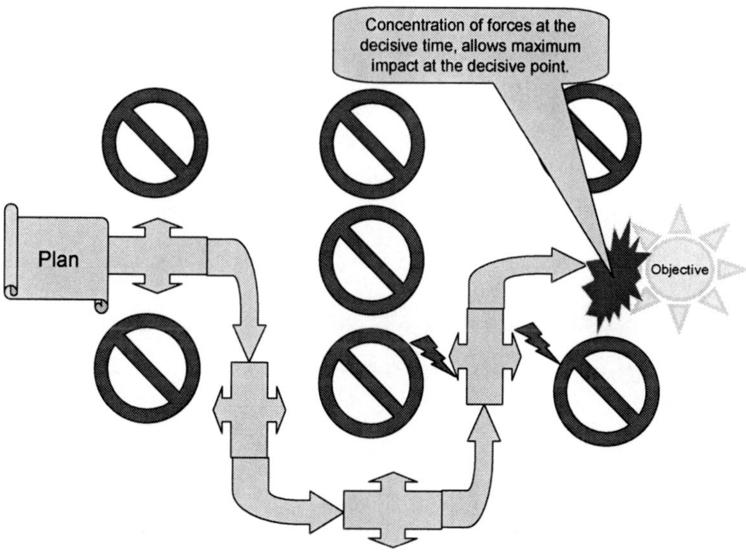

Principles Field Manual

Hear are two Templates to use in Planning and Executing your Campaign.

The First is the Plan of Campaign and should be filled by out by the Sales Leader and accepted and executed by all members of the Team. Having it agreed to by all members of the Team is the optimum result, but failing that acceptance and execution will suffice. This document should be reviewed by the Sales Leader periodically during the Campaign to ensure the Campaign is still on track, or amended if required, it will be the benchmark for all the actions of the Sales Team during the Campaign. A worked example of this plan is included earlier in this chapter.

The other document is the Campaign "Map" it can be used to document all relevant targets within the Campaign Customer Account. It will show points of strength and weakness, as well as areas of neglect and concentration. It should be continually updated to ensure accuracy. It represents the Topography or Hierarchy of the Account and should be filled in with the Name of the Individual, their directly responsible Budget spend, their Propensity to buy which represents both ability and willingness from -1 to +1, and Hostility which means would they rather support you or a competitor from -1 to +1, and this most important factor lets you shade each box so you can see at a glance red lights, green lights, and amber lights. This simple visual aid will prove of great value when making judgements about where to put your efforts in a Campaign. It can also be used at a rolled up level to represent whole departments, sections, and teams. Example below:

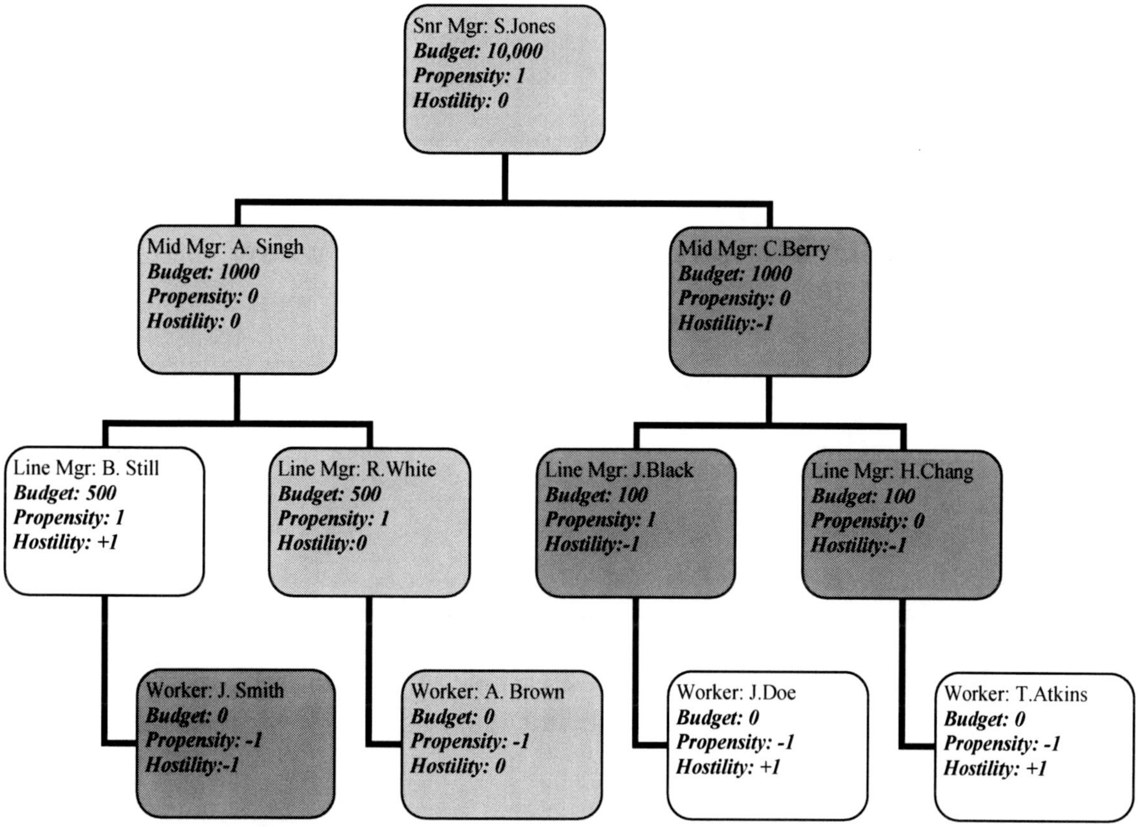
Snr Mgr: S.Jones
Budget: 10,000
Propensity: 1
Hostility: 0
Mid Mgr: A. Singh
Budget: 1000
Propensity: 0
Hostility: 0
Mid Mgr: C.Berry
Budget: 1000
Propensity: 0
Hostility:-1
Line Mgr: B. Still
Budget: 500
Propensity: 1
Hostility: +1
Line Mgr: R.White
Budget: 500
Propensity: 1
Hostility:0
Line Mgr: J.Black
Budget: 100
Propensity: 1
Hostility:-1
Line Mgr: H.Chang
Budget: 100
Propensity: 0
Hostility:-1
Worker: J. Smith
Budget: 0
Propensity: -1
Hostility:-1
Worker: A. Brown
Budget: 0
Propensity: -1
Hostility: 0
Worker: J.Doe
Budget: 0
Propensity: -1
Hostility: +1
Worker: T.Atkins
Budget: 0
Propensity: -1
Hostility: +1

Plan of Campaign for Account:

Time Period:

Define Objective (Precise Black and White Goals)

↓

Outline Strategy (Plan: What will you do in outline to reach Objective)

↓

Tactics (Actions: Who will do what and when? Issue tailored sheet to each person in Sales Team)

Account Campaign Map

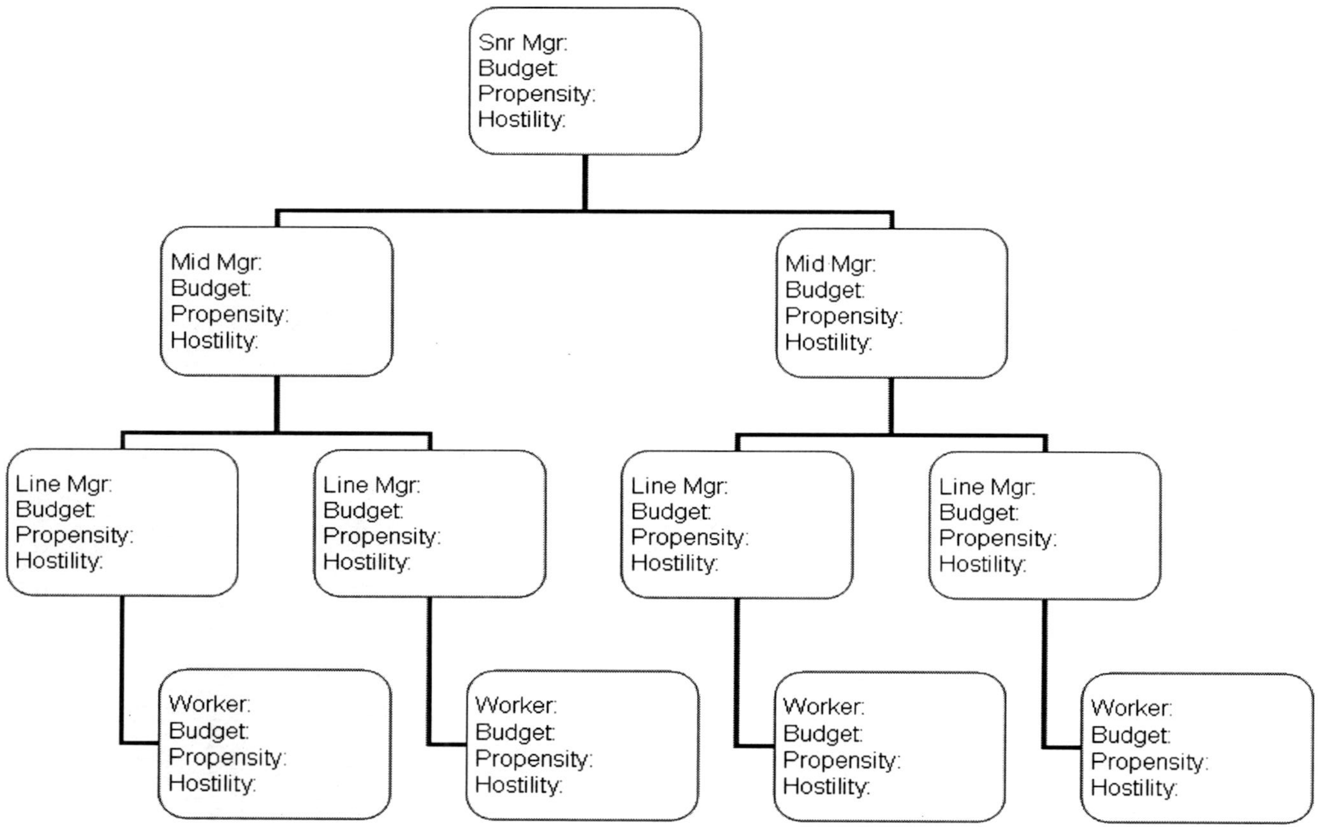

Where can I read more?

The Foundations of the Science of War

Colonel J.F.C. Fuller

Hutchinson & Co. Ltd
1926

ISBN

Summary:
In depth break down of philosophy and science of warfare. Very hard to get hold of.

The Conduct of War 1789-1961

Major-General J.F.C. Fuller C.B., C.B.E., D.S.O.

Eyre & Spottiswoode
1961

ISBN 978-0306804670

Summary:
Interesting description of warfare throughout the world and the way it has been influenced by the political background and ideas of the times.

Decisive Battles of the Western World

Major-General J.F.C. Fuller C.B., C.B.E., D.S.O.

Cassell & Co
2001 (first published, 1954, 1955, 1956)

ISBN 0-304-35867-3
ISBN 0-304-35868-1
ISBN 0-304-35869-X

Summary:
Everything you ever wanted to know about warfare from the earliest times to the Second World War.

The Generalship of Alexander The Great

Major-General J.F.C. Fuller C.B., C.B.E., D.S.O.

Wordsworth Military Library
1998 (first published 1958)

ISBN 1 85326 695 7

Summary:
Fuller breaks down the Campaigns of Alexander the Great, and expounds on his Principles and Accentuating Factors in the later chapters of the book, with reference to how these were used by Alexander.

The Pattern

Based on "The Pattern of War"

Lt General Sir Francis Tuker KCIE CB DSO OBE (1894-1967)

Who was he?

After Serving as a Captain in the Royal Gurkha Rifles in the First World War, Lieutenant General Sir Francis Tuker commanded the Fourth Indian Division of the Eighth Army during the victorious campaign in North Africa and Italy in The Second World War. He ended his career in 1948 as General Officer Commander in Chief Eastern Command India. He retired in 1948.

In his Book "The Pattern of War" Lt General Sir Francis Tuker sets out to show that warfare of all ages no matter what armaments are used follows a definite and unchanging pattern. Tucker illustrates this with discussions of campaigns from Alexander to Hitler, and makes, what turned out to be, highly intuitive predictions concerning potential nuclear engagements and the dominance of air superiority.

Tucker's "Pattern of War" can also be applied to sales situations, and you must understand the type of campaign in which they are involved; Linear, Area, and Siege.

In this chapter you will learn the relative virtues and drawbacks of these campaigns depending on whether you are attacking or defending, and how to change from one type to another in order to gain advantage.

In the process of describing the types of engagements you will also learn the definitions and roles of different forces. They are divided into; The Mobile Arm, The Arm of Defence, and The Siege Arm. These roles apply to the sales world in terms of what type of forces you need to use in order to gain new customers against opposition, defending against your competitors' moves against your customer base, and attacking your competitors' customer base.

What does Tuker's Pattern Teach?

Types of Engagements

Linear Engagements occur when an attack is launched against a static linear defensive position, prepared in advance and offered as a point of engagement by the defenders in order to force the attacker to expend his forces in the least favourable way, and with no room for manoeuvre.

Linear Engagements are an attempt by a defender to use a defensive position offensively. They differ from a siege in as much as they are used to actively force a conflict with the attacker in a specific area or fashion. It requires the Defender making his defensive deployment in the path of the attackers either actively or by placing them around a point that the defender believes the attacker will want to capture or engage. They represent the initiative lying with the defenders.

Area Engagements occur when an attacker is able to change position and direction of attack in order to seek advantageous circumstances that most favour the attacker's strengths, and refuse to engage where the attacker would be weakest, or the defender strongest.

These are campaigns of manoeuvre. They come about as a result of the attacker using varying degrees of speed of movement, and/or secrecy of movement, to gain a position of local advantage against an opponent and thereby force their opponent to fight at a disadvantage.

Area Engagements are far more fluid than linear engagements, and are initiated by a seizure of the initiative by an attacking protagonist, rather than by a defensive plan which is the defender's initiative.

Siege Engagements are actions by an attacker against heavily defended static positions, which are isolated points rather than part of an interconnected linear defence. They also differ from linear defences in that they are not generally offered up as deliberate points of engagement by the defenders, in the Linear Defence the defender actively seeks an engagement; but on the defender's terms. In a Siege the defense is passive, and is more concerned with denying engagement than promoting it, the idea being to hold the attacker long enough to force them to give up rather than to attempt to destroy the attacker through combat.

Identifying Current Engagement

Area vs Linear Campaigns

To know whether the Engagement before you is likely to be Area or Linear in its nature, Tuker gives the following three factors as determining the degree to which the engagement is likely to be an Area rather than a Linear Campaign:

First condition. Flanks shall be tactically open or it shall be possible to create a flank by a break-in and break-through.

Secondly, the mobile arm shall be predominant.

Thirdly, that it shall be possible to administer the mobile arm to the point at which it will decide the battle and gain decisive victory.

By weighing up the degree to which these three factors predominate the likely pattern of the engagement can be prepared for. So, if you are confident of finding an open flank or can break through the enemy line, with large proportion of your forces being made up of highly mobile troops, who can show initiative but follow orders to an ultimate winning objective, then an Area Engagement will be available for you to exploit and impose your terms on the defender. Conversely if you can find no weak flanks to the Linear defence, and are not able to break through decisively at a particular point in the defences, plus your troops are predominantly slow to move and take action, and your more mobile troops are difficult to control, then you will have little choice but to contend with a Linear Engagement on the defender's terms.

Tuker's basic premise is that mobile Area Engagements interspersed with sieges of isolated defensive strongpoints are the predominate pattern for warfare, and give greater scope for an attacker to win a quick and decisive victory compared to what can be achieved in Static Linear Engagements. Area Engagements also allow leaders to apply their tactical skills, and can allow superior tacticians to beat a more powerful enemy. He therefore advocates when on the offensive to attempt to convert Linear Engagements into Area Engagements.

He describes how to break a Linear Defence, how to turn it into an Area Engagement, and then how to win that Area Engagement.

Sieges

Sieges can be very long term affairs, maybe running for years, and therefore require dogged persistence, and, if they are to be successful, a very detailed understanding of the strengths and weaknesses of the account.

If sieges are so difficult, what is the point of attempting them? Well if strongpoints are left in enemy hands they provide them with a source of supply, a source of recruits, a place from which to mount attacks, and a rallying point for defeated units. For all of these reasons it pays to overcome enemy strongholds, and indeed to hold strongholds of your own.

The difference between a Siege and a Linear Defence Engagement is that in the later the customer actively invites an attack against prepared defences with a known prize behind them, he intends to buy, and therefore seeks an engagement, but on his terms. In a Siege the customer is not interested, maybe has no budget, or no intent to buy, or is occupied by your competition.

For these reasons they should only be entered into when either time permits or necessity demands.

Sales Definitions

Linear Engagements

The sales equivalent of a Linear Engagement involves the purchaser seeking engagement from vendors by initiating a Tender Process. This generally takes the form of some kind of a request for tender or proposal, which may be preceded by a scouting exercise, a request for information. It is important to understand what the customer's tactics are:

Requests for information are scouting exercises which allow the defender (customer) to assess the strengths of the likely attackers (vendors) before having to engage with them. They allow the defender to prepare their positions to ensure that any attacker (vendor) will need to jump through as many hoops as possible.

Requests for proposal or tender are the defences onto which the attackers are invited to launch themselves. They are designed to give an advantage to the defender (customer). They are generally simplistic but very detailed, have tight deadlines that generally slip in order to favour the least able bidder, take a long time to put together by the defenders and require an even more enormous effort on behalf the vendors to engage them.

Such Linear Engagements form a linear defence of the account inviting engagement, but removing the attacker's ability to manoeuvre.

They are also multi-vendor activities, requiring a race to be the first to breach the defences and overrun the critical point before the other attackers can, once the critical point is taken either the other attackers will be demoralised and withdraw, or they may mount an attack against the new defenders, which could turn into a siege.

Area Engagements
In a sales sense these represent seeking opportunity and maneuvering for advantage within an account hierarchy, in the normal prospecting/Account Management pattern, rather than simply waiting an initiative from the prospect or your competition. They are the campaign of choice for able sales teams.

Sieges
In the sales world these are represented by accounts or departments which actively attempt to avoid sales situations either through reticence on the behalf of the customer, or because your competition are already entrenched in the account.

The Strategy: Overcome the Linear Defence

Tucker advocates overcoming any linear defence with the intention of turning such a defence into an area combat. According to Tuker in "The Pattern of War" there are three conditions necessary to bring about an area engagement, as set out previously:

1. Flanks shall be tactically open or it shall be possible to create a flank by a break-in and break-through.

2. The mobile arm shall predominate.

3. It shall be possible to administer the mobile arm to the point at which it will decide the battle and gain decisive victory.

The Types of Forces and their Roles

Once you know what type of engagement you are in, you then must understand which side of the defences you are on. In a Linear Engagement are you helping man the defences or attacking the account? In a siege you will either be defending the position or attacking it. In an Area engagement both sides are likely to be maneuvering, although there may be local defensive engagements by either side where appropriate.

If you do not have the right type of forces at your disposal to match the type of engagement in which you find yourself, but your enemy has, then there is a good chance that you will loose the engagement. The reverse is also true.

Military forces throughout history have been comprised of between one and three of these components:

Arm of Manoeuvre

It is the responsibility of the arm of maneuver to probe for openings, exploit local successes to maximize their impact, lay false tails for the competition, engage and destroy the opposition's Arm of Manoeuvre, and relieve sieges of friendly strongholds (reference accounts) by attacking the besiegers. And as stated above maneuver the enemy into a position where they must fight on ground of your choosing.

You must avoid dissipating the force of maneuver, concentration is key, and the arm of maneuver must not be split to defend strongpoints.

Arm of Defence

The arm of defence must stand and fight, act as a rock against the enemy to blunt their resources and make them tire of the fight, blunt their morale, slow down their arm of maneuver, and defeat their arm of defence.

The arm of defence must man the defences of strongpoints, keep out enemy troops and sally out against the besiegers.

They must act as a strategic reserve to respond to enemy concentrations and thrusts, and mobile enough to cover a wide front without being tied to one location. Reference sites can be thought of as providing airfields to provide counter strikes.

Siege Train

The Siege Train represents a specialist group experienced in reducing well defended accounts, it must be prepared to be self sufficient and closely surround the account, it must specialise in the grinding work of wearing down defences and cutting off access to an account by any approaching enemy. It takes constant vigilance, patience and determination.

Why is the Pattern important to You?

Why Seek Area Engagements?

Area Engagements
As an active salesforce you should favour Area Engagements as they confer an advantage of time to an attacker, whether successful or not, and may also confer an advantage of position which may compensate for having to compete with a more powerful competitor.

These confer the initiative on you the attacker. They can gain you entry past the prospect's defences, help to overwhelm a more powerful or entrenched competitor, and quickly confirm whether you stand to gain a fast victory or that you can never win in the short term (and should therefore be prepared to withdraw and look for another target).

Linear Engagements
Customers like Linear Engagements for three reasons:

1. They flatten out the differences in the attackers, meaning that simple binary decisions can be made, generally on price, which will be driven down by the attackers inability to differentiate themselves, ensuring that whoever wins will gain much less than otherwise possible.
2. They are often decided on by committee, so that no blame can be apportioned directly to any individuals for the possible failure of the chosen solution.
3. They rob the attackers of any initiative, thereby allowing the customer to decide on what areas are open to attack, and thereby control, to a great extent, the actions of the vendors.

Unless you helped the customer to construct the tender requirements you must try to convert Linear Engagements into Area Engagements. The reasons for this are three fold:

1. If you didn't help construct the tender, one of your competitors probably did.
2. Linear Engagements are controlled by the customer; they therefore remove the initiative from you.
3. They tend to focus on price over value. With the result that the price is driven down, driving down the value of any potential deal to you.

How to apply the Pattern to Sales Situations:

Basic Rules

The Strategy: Overcome the Linear Defence

Once again according to Sir Francis Tuker in "The Pattern of War" there are three conditions necessary to bring about an area engagement, as set out previously:

1. Flanks shall be tactically open or it shall be possible to create a flank by a break-in and break-through.

2. The mobile arm shall predominate.

3. It shall be possible to administer the mobile arm to the point at which it will decide the battle and gain decisive victory.

Expanding on each of these:

1. You must be able to approach the enemy from an undefended position outside or at the edges of their main line of defence (a *flank*), or you must produce a flank by either overrunning a position in their defensive line (a *break-in*) and thereby be able to attack the defenders on either side of this break-in from a direction from which they were not expecting an attack (their now exposed flank), which leads to their line locally collapsing; opening up a way through for your maneuvering forces (this being a *break-through*).

2. You must launch your initiative with forces that are sales oriented; willing and able to engage and exploit the opportunities. Any group who may slow the initiative down must be in the minority and not the prime arm of engagement.

Your engagement team must see initiative and mobility of action as their prime driver. In business terms this means being willing and able to act to the limits of their capabilities, to grasp the initiative, and spread through an account rapidly looking for opportunities, and taking action to out maneuver the competition. They must be sales oriented and able to see opportunities before the customer or competition does, and then exploit that opportunity.

3. This means that the sales force must be able to be controlled or take decisions, either directly or through sales management without long delays whilst decisions are awaited from on high in the management structure. Management must be able to help guide and consult with the field force to ensure that the campaign goes to plan, and that all actions are coordinated.

It is important that the initiative is focussed and forced through, the initiative should have only one overall objective, and it is up to sales management to ensure that the sales team stays on plan. It must always be remembered that the plan is to further the sales opportunity at the expense of the competition and defenders, with the aim of closing the sale. No closure = no victory.

The Tactics to Use to Produce an Area Engagement

In the words of Sir Francis Tuker; "No army that is weaker in the mobile arm can hold a linear field defensive position which has an open flank or which can be penetrated"

1. Turn a Flank
In the words of Sir Francis Tuker; "**No army that is weaker in the mobile arm can hold a linear field defensive position which has an open flank** or which can be penetrated"

Look for an open flank. Assuming that you can find a flank to turn, if you can, then you can convert the Linear Defence into an Area Engagement.

The "Flank" itself is the side edge of the defenders' position, an *Open Flank* is a poorly or undefended area, allowing access to a wider area in the rear of the defenders' position. So you are looking for an area at the edge of the defenders' position which is either poorly defended or undefended. Flanks are usually located by reconnaissance and probing at the edges of the enemy position.

Gaining access to an open flank, called *turning a flank*, provides a route to further attacks from an unexpected quarter; this bestows the advantage of Surprise, the benefits of this being threefold:

1. The benefit of Morale. The defenders' morale, and therefore psychological ability to react, plan, and control, will be reduced due to the shock of your surprise appearance.
2. The benefit of Time. If the defenders' morale holds, the amount of time the defenders have to react and prepare to defend against your initiative will be minimised in direct proportion to your momentum.
3. The benefit of Position. When the defenders have used what little time they have to reposition against you they will have to do so by changing position to engage on a front of your choosing, which will put you at an advantage.

In summary turning a flank is a bold move, and must be unexpected in order to fully exploit the advantage of surprise, thereby maximising its chances of success. However, just turning the flank without exploiting surprise is not enough to win a victory. It will be the combination of your actions and the defenders' reactions that guarantee or deny victory. If your actions do succeed, the results will be rapid and spectacular, *rolling up* the defenders position by position, and leaving the competition reeling in its wake. The key is to exploit your advantages to the fullest.

Turning a flank in a Sales situation

Turning a flank in sales terms means finding a way to get behind the Linear Defence as represented by the tender process; you must therefore look for access at the edges of, or outside of the content of, the tender.

The flank is by definition likely to be an area not covered by the tender but one which may be related to the problem it is trying to solve. The key to finding where this flank area is, is to ask yourself the question "Which is the area of interest that is powerful enough to outflank the defender's concentration on the tender process?" It may require some "out of the box" thinking. This may mean finding a sponsor who owns a problem which you are fitted to solve, this will form the flank of the tender. Your ability to solve the customer problem will decide your momentum, and therefore your ability to turn the flank.

Having turned the flank the next stage is to exploit the advantage that surprise has brought you, in order to collapse the will to fight (morale) of the defence (and your competition) by using your new position to negate the continuance of the tender, or if this is not possible, to insist on new criteria set by you from your new position, and force the competition to fight on ground that you have chosen, before they have time to adequately prepare for the engagement.

Sales Example

Step by Step Explanation of Turning a Flank

Opening Positions

Customer sets out their Linear Defence for attackers to expend their energy against.

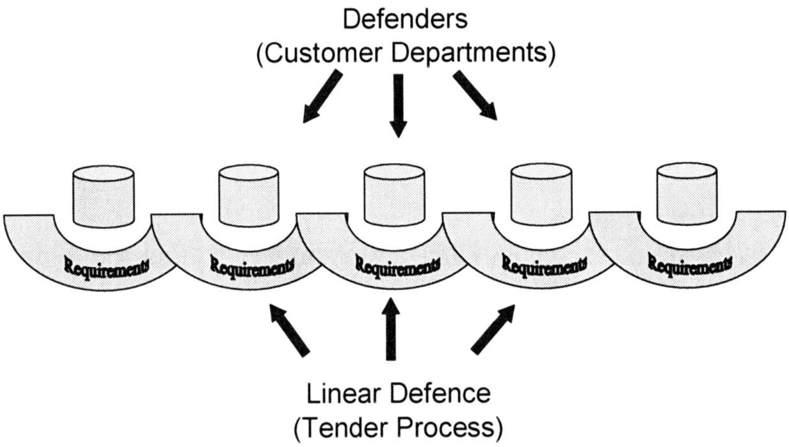

Vendors position to attack against the prepared defences.

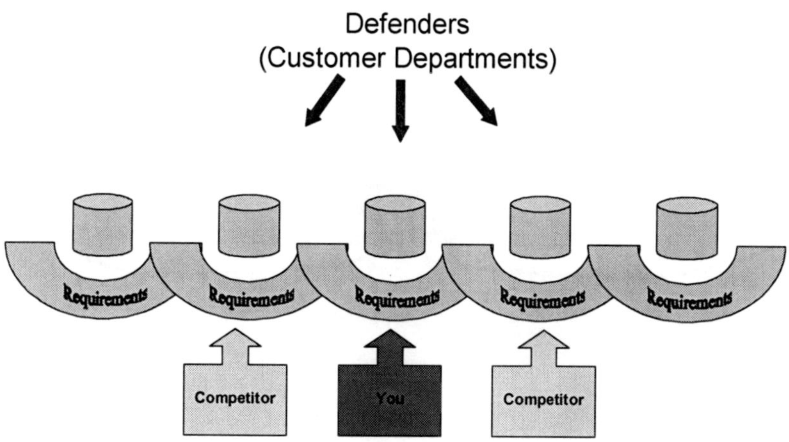

Scouting
Whilst continuing to engage the Linear Defence in order to hide your other plans, send scouting parties to look for a flank that can be turned.

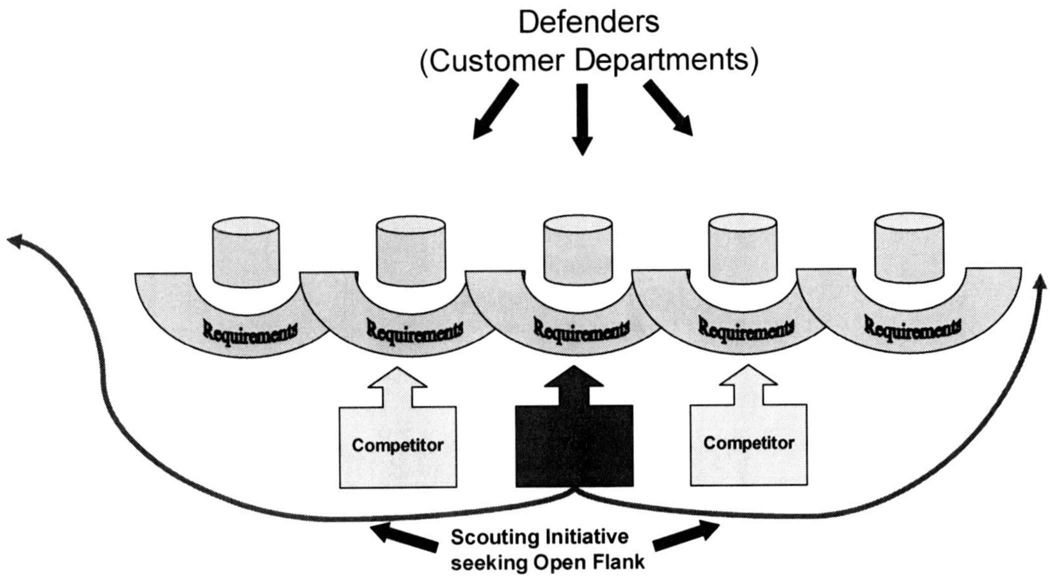

You may find that in some areas there is no open flank, whilst in others there are some opportunities, it is therefore important to spread far and wide to look for such opportunities but always as near to the main Linear Defence as possible.

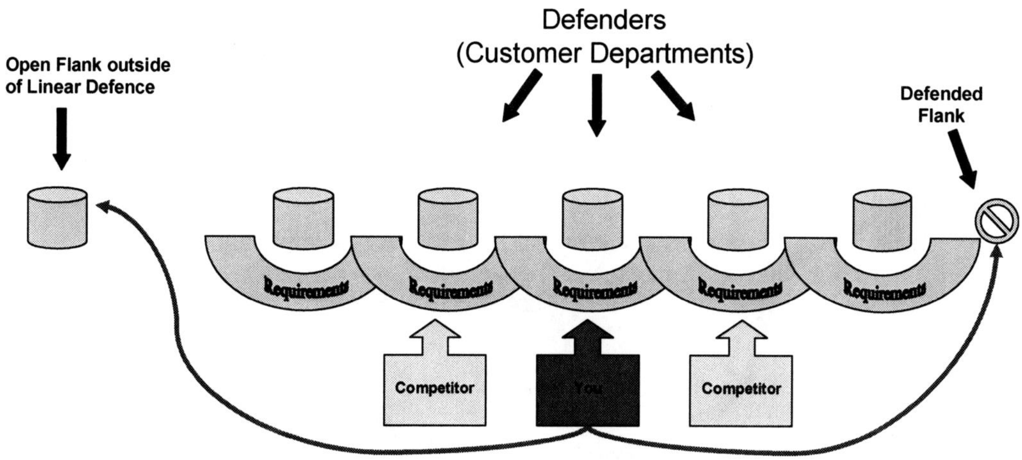

Turning the Flank

Once an open Flank is found concentrate your mobile forces against it in order to turn it as quickly as possible, whilst still engaging the Linear Defence with your less mobile arm. Speed is important as the faster you turn the flank, the less likely it is that your competition or the defenders will be aware of what your true intentions are.

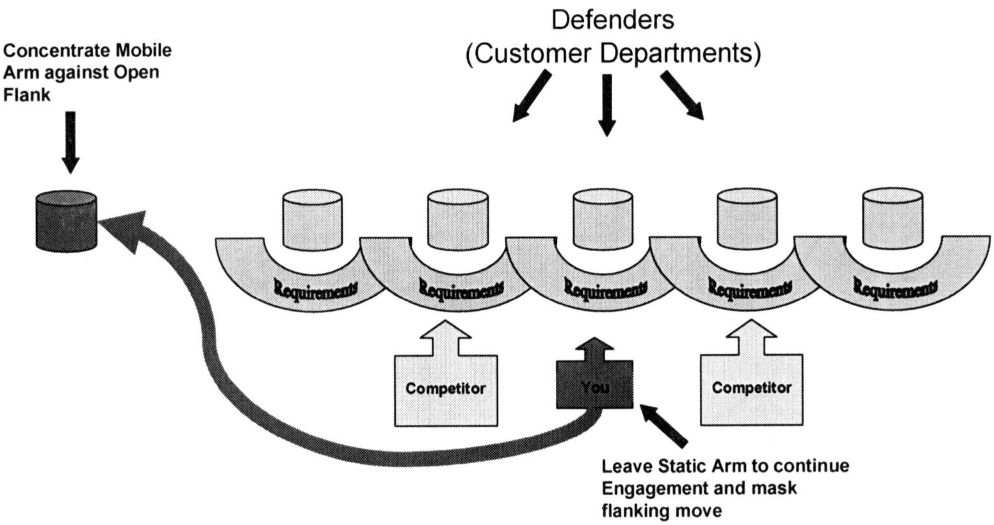

The momentum must be maintained, and the springboard provided by the collapsed flank must be utilised to allow a surprise attack from behind the Linear Defence, beyond the reach of your competitors. At the same time your more static troops should engage energetically with the Linear Defence, this will distract the defenders and your competitors from your flanking manoeuvre.

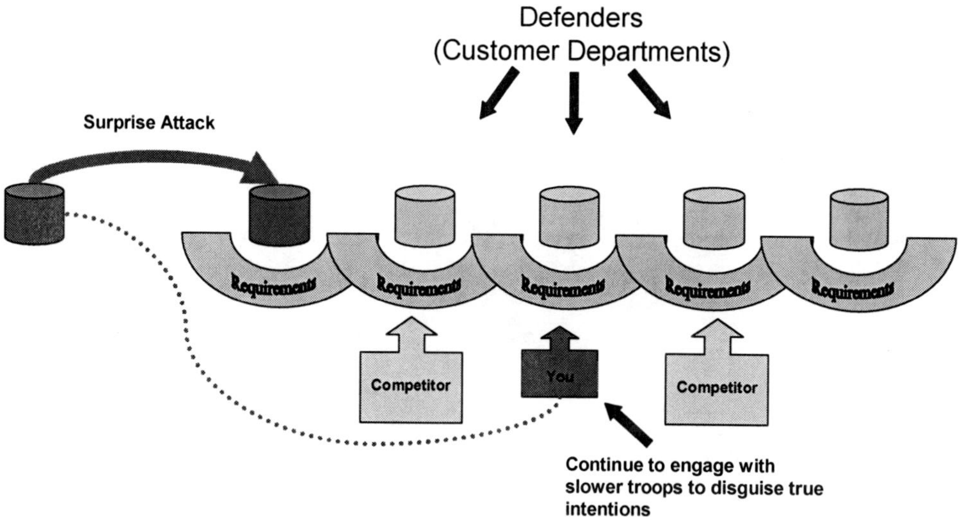

Roll up Defensive Positions from Unexpected direction

Once one part of the Linear Defence is overrun unexpectedly, it will lead to other parts of the Linear Defence becoming weakened, and as they fall will negate the efforts of your competitors.

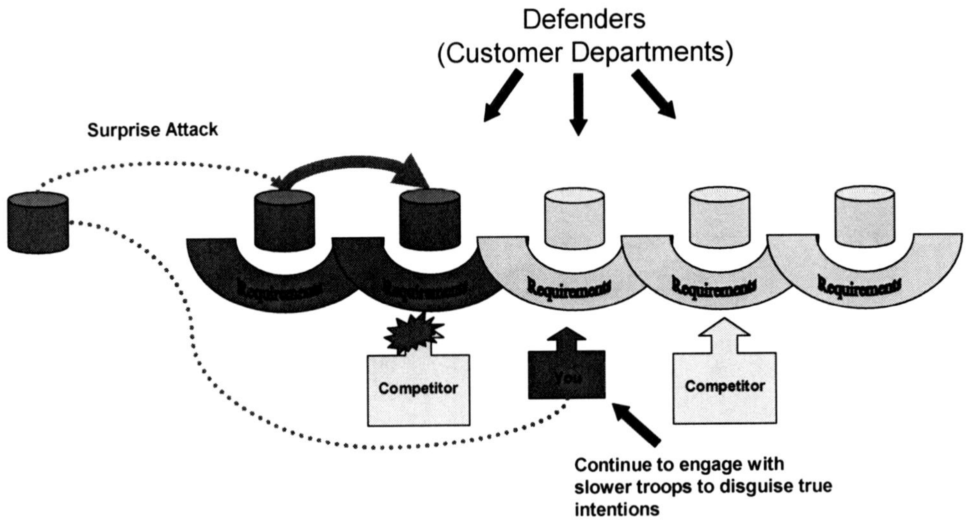

This will be multiplied as your success increase due to the collapse of the "will to fight" in the defenders.

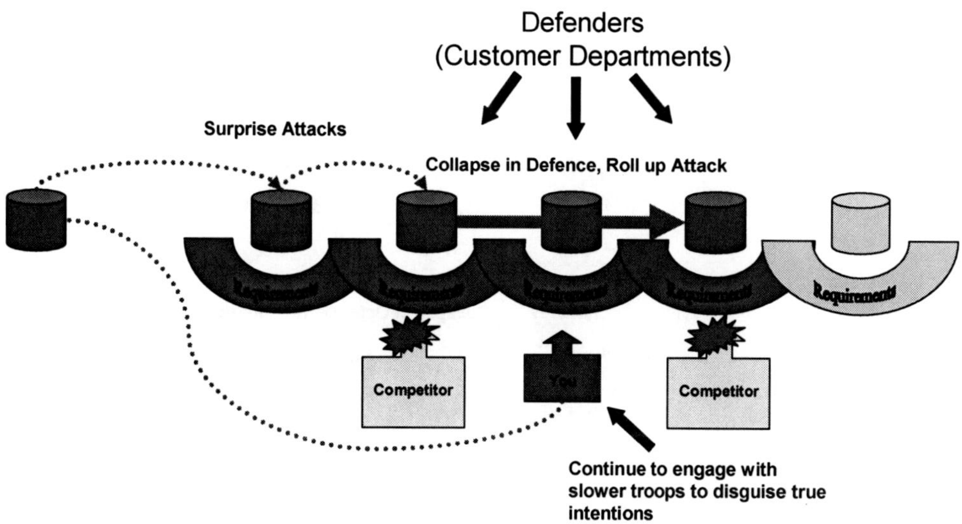
Defenders
(Customer Departments)
Surprise Attacks
Collapse in Defence, Roll up Attack
Requirements
Competitor
Competitor
Continue to engage with slower troops to disguise true intentions

Mopping up

Once the rollup is achieved, it is then a matter of mopping up any lingering hostile departments at leisure until all resistance is overrun.

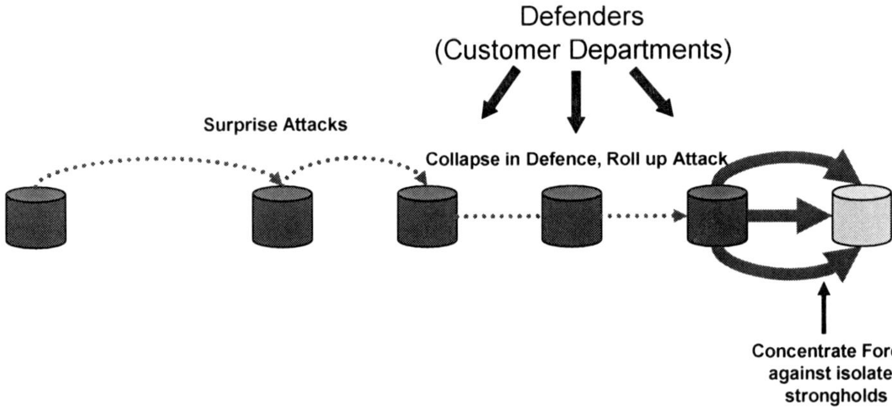

Break-in and Break-through in a Sales situation

In the words of Sir Francis Tuker; "**No army that is weaker in the mobile arm can hold a linear field defensive position** which has an open flank or **which can be penetrated"**

The second way to turn a flank is to *create* the flank *in* the Linear Defence rather than outside of it. Mounting a break-in attack at a point in the Linear Defence, followed by a break-through does this. The attacker needs an overwhelming advantage in a particular area compared to the other attackers, and it must be seen as so important to the customer that their defences crumble and allow the breakthrough, which then allows your attack to take on other areas from a position of strength "behind the lines of the defenders, i.e. from an unexpected direction; an internal flank. It is often the sponsorship of customer factions in the breakthrough area that gives strength to these attacks. In battle it is the equivalent of the defenders seeing the unit next to them break and run in the face of the enemy, forcing them to fall back or risk being surrounded. Or in business terms if the faction which "collapses" during the breakthrough is seen as significant enough, then other areas will "collapse" in the face of the flank attack caused by the breakthrough.

This is different from the "scouting" exercises mentioned previously, as the point here is to fully engage the defences, not to simply reconnoitre them. But of course good reconnoitring could lead to the commander identifying a good point to launch this breakthrough movement.

If the attacker has planned ahead then they have a chance to subvert a particular point in the defences, or perhaps all of them. Getting to this position may not be as hard as it sounds. Most Linear Defences are not homogenous, contain inconsistencies, gaps, and conflicting agendas, the important thing is for the attacker to have had the opportunity to get to see the defences before attacking them, preferably from behind their lines. If he can get forces into them or turn the loyalty of the defenders in a particular area before the attack then so much the better.

This is a matter of account penetration and influence prior to the tender, here you have the chance to set the agenda, and thereby subvert the defences in your favour.

To do this it is necessary to "help" write the tender. Any vendor who receives a tender without having been involved in writing it for the customer should ask themselves who did help write it, reading it should probably make this plain.

Getting to this position is not as hard as it sounds. Most tenders are written by committees, so often end up with inconsistencies, repetitions, and contrary agendas, the important thing is for the attacker to have had the opportunity to get to see the defences before attacking them, preferably from behind their lines. If he can get troops into them or turn the loyalty of the defenders in a particular area before the attack then so much the better. This is a matter of account penetration and influence prior to the tender, here you have the chance to set the agenda, and thereby subvert the defences in your favour.

Step by Step Explanation of Break-In and Break-Through

Opening Positions

As usual the customer sets out their defences to absorb the vendors' attack.

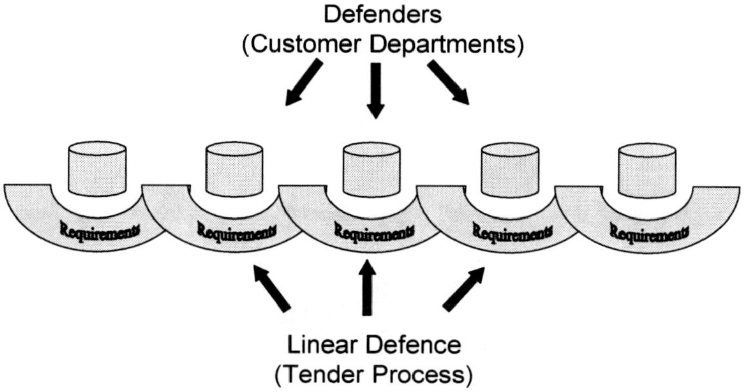

It is necessary to identify or create the weak point. Optimally it should be created by prior preparation, i.e. you should create it by involvement in the creation of the tender. Alternatively you may find a weak point as part of a scouting exercise.

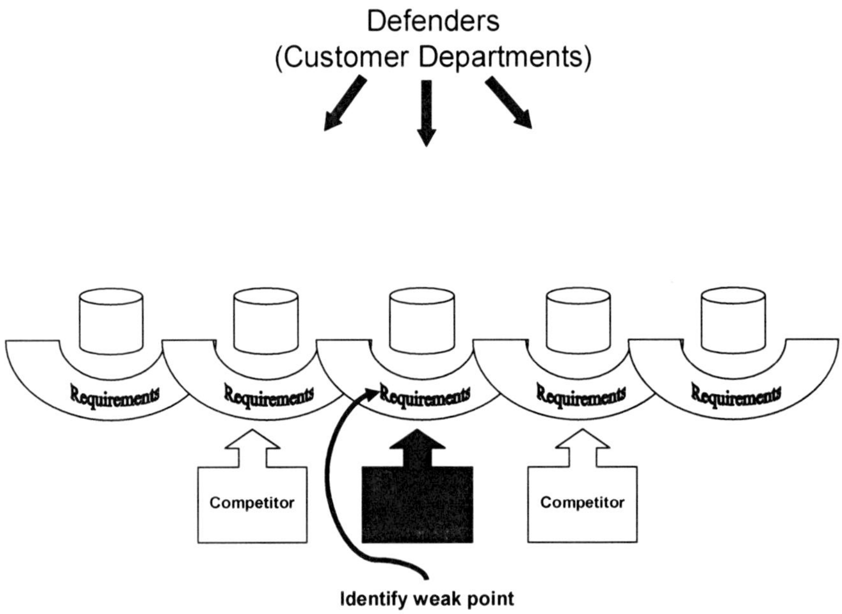
Defenders
(Customer Departments)
Requirements
Requirements
Requirements
Requirements
Requirements
Competitor
Competitor
Identify weak point

Break-In

Having identified the weak point you must concentrate all your force against it to ensure a rapid collapse of the weak defences, and create a Break-in in the defences.

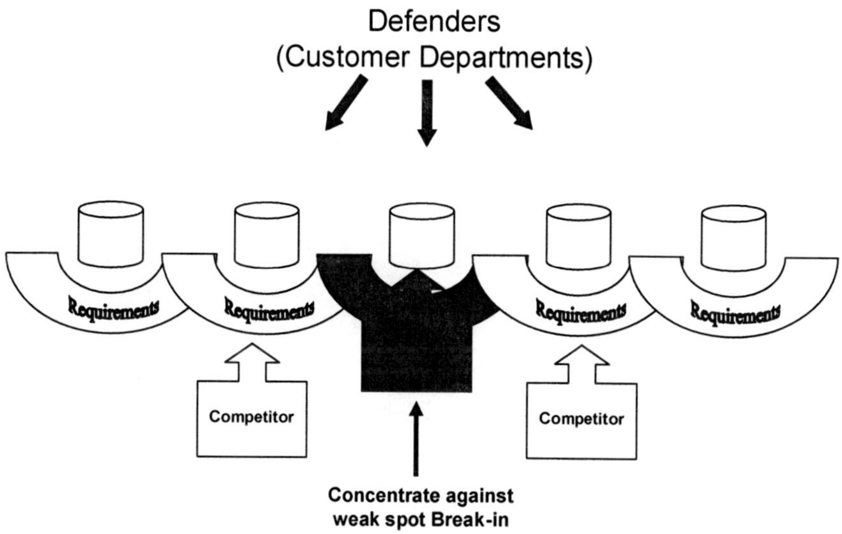

Break-through

Having broken in to the defensive lines only the less mobile Arm of Defence should be left to hold the gap, the Mobile Arm must immediately be used to turn the Break-In into a Break-Through.

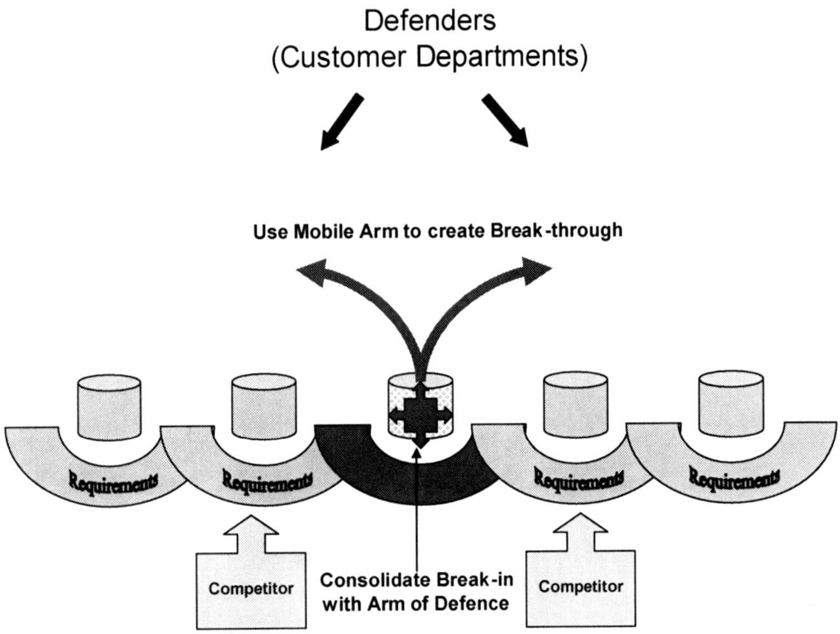

Produce Flank
Having broken through, it is now possible to use the space created to produce flanks from within the defences.

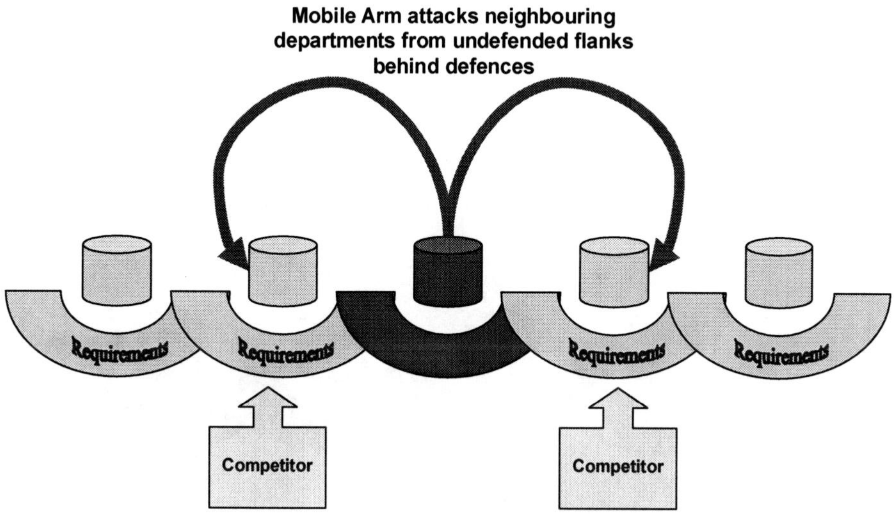

Roll up Defensive Positions from Unexpected direction

Once one part of the Linear Defence is overrun unexpectedly, it will lead to other parts of the Linear Defence becoming weakened, and as they fall will negate the efforts of your competitors. This will be multiplied as your success increases due to the collapse of the "will to fight" in the defenders.

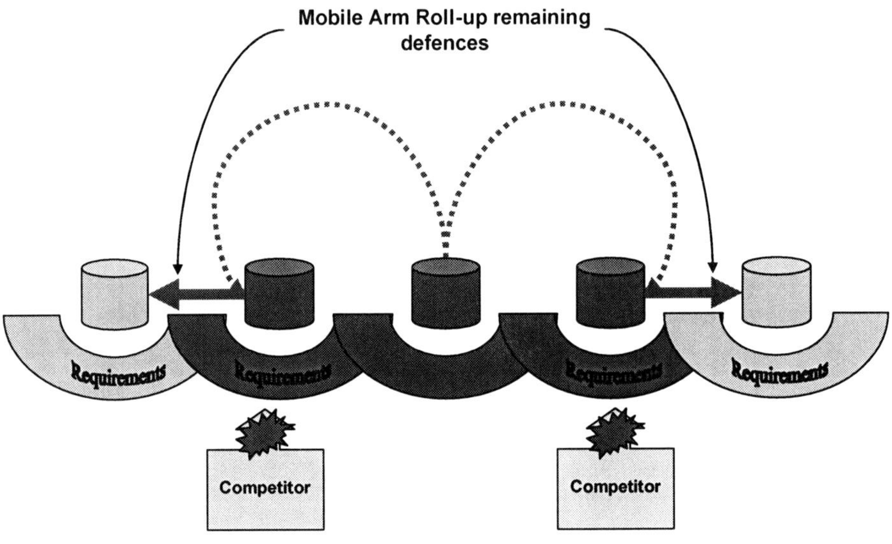

Once the rollup is achieved, it is then a matter of mopping up any lingering hostile departments at leisure until all resistance is overrun.

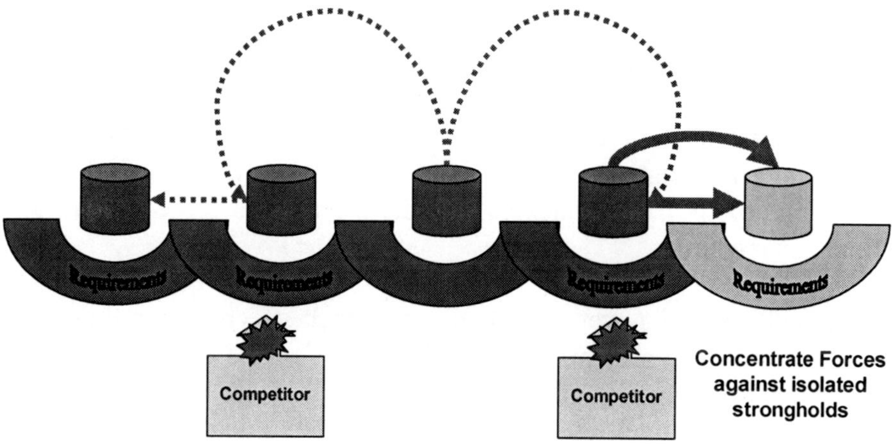

The Alternative: General Frontal Assault

This is the least favoured option to attack a Linear defence, but is the one the customer wishes to impose. A frontal attack can only be carried out at great cost in manpower and time. Although the defence is linear it is unlikely to be homogenous; some areas will be weaker or more tactically important than others. But if these areas aren't known then the attacker must be able to hit all points equally hard until the critical points are identified and then prove superior to the defenders in these areas as well as being stronger/faster than any other attacking forces in these areas.

Mounting the fight in these two areas will enhance the chances of an attack being successful, but will by no means guarantee it, especially if one of your rival attackers has more intelligence of the situation than you do.

In summary, the frontal assault strategy is the least efficient method of attack against a linear defence whether it works or not. It favours large organisations with the time and resource to soak up the punishment of a frontal assault, marching against the hail of lead from the defences until sheer persistence overruns the position, or the attack is defeated, or more likely outpaced by one of the rival attackers and the a retreat is forced with nothing to show but wasted time and resources.

A frontal assault should never be the the approach of choice; rather it is a position that unfortunate commanders may march into if they don't have the resources or inclination to do their scouting and intelligence gathering properly. Without knowing what the critical points are, it is necessary to attack the lowest common denominator which is always price, even when price "isn't an issue", it will be a differentiator, a cheaper price giving the customer more bangs for their bucks, and you as the vendor a more costly victory.

The Other Type of Engagement: How to win a Siege

The difference between a Siege and a Linear Defence Engagement is that in the later the customer actively invites an attack against prepared defences with a known prize behind them, he intends to buy, and therefore seeks an engagement, but on his terms. In a Siege the customer is not interested, maybe has no budget, and no intent to buy.

Sieges come about where the customer has no intent to buy, or there are no identified opportunities, the account may also be garrisoned by the competition. Sieges can be very long term affairs, maybe running for years, and therefore require dogged persistence, and, if they are to be successful, a very detailed understanding of the strengths and weaknesses of the account.

The attacker must look for small openings to exploit, must fight a war of attrition, blocking all routes for opposing forces to enter the account, and must try to wear down the defenders until an attack may be possible. It may require a small initial break-in by a minor force, but if this can hold its ground then there is a chance for a much bigger force to enter. Head on assaults are unlikely to gain any headway because of the inability to come to grips with the opposition, who is ensconced behind the walls of his lack of ability to buy. However there is ultimately no such thing as an impenetrable fortress.

If the account is garrisoned by the competition, they will move their forces to defend against the attacker's attempts to take the account by storm, they will counter mine the attacker's attempts to undermine the walls of the account with marketing activities, and continually look to open up access to their own supplies (marketing activities) to the account. In short the competition's account management activities will form the defence; it is this that must be broken down. The degree to which the defenders will actually defend will vary considerably, and they may take no aggressive action if they see no overt action from the besiegers, after all their sales force will be off looking for accounts with a willingness to buy, and will probably leave the defence of the existing accounts to garrison forces of technical staff, if any garrison is there at all. It is a fact that most companies give very few incentives to any of their staff to defend an account, incentives go to winning new business, whereas more predatory companies with competitive offerings often have the flexibility in their pay and discount structures to make an attempt on a hostile account worthwhile to their sales force.

Sieges succeed because of one of four reasons:

1. The besiegers starve the defenders out.
2. The besiegers storm the walls and overrun the defenders.
3. The besiegers use a technology that negates the defences.
4. Someone lets the besiegers in.

It must be remembered that an "impregnable fortress", in both military and business terms does not exist.

The besiegers starve the defenders out.
It's a long grinding process, camped out on site, banging away at the walls hoping to find a weakness, months of failure, every breach which is opened is repaired by the besieged again, a war of attrition, either the walls are eventually breached at a faster rate then the defenders can repair them and the attackers can gain entry, or one side or the other runs out of food and gives up.

This is the standard form of account management and may eventually work. Constant meetings, unsolicited proposals, fishing for an opening, the account looking for reasons not to spend money, the besiegers hurling ideas and products at the defences, the account taking the ideas and trying ways to achieve the same result using internal resources (repairing the walls).

Eventually either the sales management tire of paying a salesman to sit outside the city walls without reducing the defences, or the customer's will to resist is subdued by an original product idea. But this is only for vendors with a lot of time on their hands.

The besiegers storm the walls and overrun the defenders
In military terms this is very rare, usually either involving huge numbers of attackers and small, poorly defended, or weakly fortified fortifications, unlikely to provide glittering prizes in themselves, or come about because complete surprise is achieved by the attackers, a very difficult thing to achieve in practice.

Surprisingly this is what is usually asked of a salesforce. Not surprisingly it rarely goes to plan, and goes a long way to explaining why sales forecasts are usually completely in inaccurate, the gap between theory and practice being a large on in both battle and business.

The besiegers use a technology that negates the defences

Option 2 happened in three periods in history. Firstly in the classical period when the Egyptians started using battering rams, and scaling ladders, the Assyrians built on these ideas with more sophisticated siege towers and undermining techniques, the Greeks then added catapults and bolt throwers. Over time fortifications caught up and Engines rarely proved crucial against major fortifications built by the Romans and mediaeval states.

Fifteen hundred years later West Europeans adopted cannons for siege warfare which temporarily leveled all castles and city walls in their way, until again fortifications caught up via the French Military engineer Vauban and his contemporaries, with their Star Forts, sloping walls and counter batteries.

No further innovations of any great merit happened to change the balance until the coming of Airforce bombers, and ballistic missiles, five hundred years later. Even these now stand challenged by anti-ballistic missiles, fighters, and anti aircraft defences.

In other words, sudden innovations in products such as mainframe computers, PCs, and Office and accounting software products, may temporarily sweep the market, but having peaked, and with the adoption of innovations by the competition thereby breaking the initial technology monopoly, markets soon settle down to long sieges again.

Someone lets the besiegers in

In general in business when attacking a garrisoned stronghold account it is unlikely that you will have enough resources at your disposal to attack all points simultaneously and overrun the defenders, and the bigger the prize, the larger and more well defended the account is likely to be and therefore the harder it will be to use sheer numbers to overrun it.

It may be that you have a "killer" product that the customer cannot fail to need, want, and have the budget for, and therefore their defences will tumble before your "siege train" in which case you don't need this book.

You may find a small opening in the defences, which can be pounded until a bigger breach is made and a frontal assault can be attempted. But this is a long process may tie up resources for a long and grueling duel with the defenders.

By far the best option in terms of time, resources, and efficiency is get someone to open a gate and let you in. In military terms this often happened when the garrison ran out of food or water, but this could take weeks or months, in business terms it is the equivalent of the incumbent vendor deciding that it costs them more to support the account than it is worth, and they therefore remove or weaken their garrison, and this can take a long, long time. A much quicker way of being let in is through treachery.

Military Example

Turning a Linear Defence

As already mentioned Lieutenant General Tuker, was the supreme advocate of turning a linear defence, and in deference to him I shall describe the battle of Sidi Barani as outlined in his book The Pattern of War, as an example of how to overcome a linear defence.

Marshal Graziani of the Italian Army had mounted a successful invasion of British North Africa during World War 2, with a view to overrunning Egypt thereby cutting off the Suez Canal and preventing the passage of men and oil between the British Empire and the British forces in the Mediterranean. He was in control of part of North Africa in the West with a safe flank of the Mediterranean Sea protecting his left flank. He had temporarily given up the initiative and had his men dig in a linear defence near the town of Sidi Barani. His infantry, artillery, and anti-tank weapons covered the approaches to Sidi Barani to the East and South, the North was secured on the Sea, and there were only Italian troops to the West of these positions. Graziani had dispersed his tanks amongst his infantry positions to help bolster their defensive capabilities.

Against this the British had a mainly mobile force spear headed by the 4th Indian Division and 7th Armoured division. General Richard O'Connor the leader of the British Western Desert Force had decided on a reconnaissance in force to test out the Italian forces. In general, weaknesses can be found in the "join" between two forces, and O'Connor had identified a crucial 20 mile weakness in the Italian defences between two bodies of Italian troops called the Enba Gap near Nibeiwa. O'Connor was planning a five day raid behind the lines of the much stronger Italian force to create as much disruption as possible.

O'Connor had studied detailed RAF photos of Italian truck tracks to identify paths through the Italian minefields, and his force had stealthily penetrated to within striking distance of the

Italian lines moving by night and removing the windscreens of the trucks during the day to prevent reflection from the desert sun.

Whilst the extended Italian defences were being battered by the RAF and distracted by an infantry brigade and mechanised free French Marines, O'Connor used his mobile force to burst through the weak point at Nibeiwa, overrun the Italian positions there and perform a wide outflanking manoeuvre catching the Italians completely by surprise, taking their positions one after the other. The Italians had been attacked from the flank and rear, from directions that they believed to be occupied by other Italian troops, their guns and defensive emplacements were facing the wrong way. Some fought tenaciously and died at their guns, others threw down their arms and immediately surrendered. In this one manoeuvre the British captured 38,000 Italian troops, 60 tanks and 180 guns, for the loss of about 600 men.

O'Connor pushed on up the coast capturing all Italian held cities on the way, British tanks bursting through the gates of Beau Geste style desert fortresses, their commanders trading small arms fire with the defenders from their turrets. They eventually captured Tobruk, swept around the line of retreat of tens of thousands of fleeing Italians, captured them, and pushed the remaining Italians back 500 miles. 30,000 Allied troops including Australians, who had replaced the Indian units after their initial successes, had defeated 250,000 Italians, capturing 130,000 of them, plus 400 tanks, and 1290 guns, effectively knocking Italy out of the war in North Africa, and forcing Hitler to send in German forces under Irwin Rommel to try to win North Africa back, only to be beaten by Field Marshal Bernard Montgomery.

Summary

O'Connor had done his homework, studied the defences facing him in detail, found their weak point, used the tracks of the Italian trucks to show him the way through the Italian mine fields, concentrated his arm of manoeuvre secretly at the vulnerable spot and then committed the whole of this force to break through and form a flank and rear assault on the surprised Italian positions beating them in detail, so that despite his overall inferiority in numbers (about 8.5 to 1) he achieved local superiority in strength (if not always in numbers). Graziani had thrown away his opportunity to form a mobile reserve by dispersing his own armoured units amongst his defensive positions, which may have made sense if he had faced a frontal assault, but destroyed any chance of launching a counter attack once the line was breached.

O'Connor had managed to breakthrough a weak spot with his mobile arm, creating a flank, and allowing his arm of manoeuvre to be brought into play without having to attempt a frontal assault on prepared defensive positions. Doing this allowed him to command superiority of force (if not numbers) where ever he chose to attack. The difference between force and numbers is important. The Italians had far greater numbers, but at each individual decisive point, the British had a superior force, i.e. their numbers *even where smaller* were more effectively applied, because they took the Italians by surprise, so they were largely unprepared for an attack, and from a direction that bypassed their defences, and meant their heavier guns were pointing in the wrong direction, therefore their forces, even where smaller in number were applied more effectively.

This pattern was repeated in engagement after engagement. Eventually the net effect was a demoralisation of the Italian forces, which amplified even further the effectiveness of the British Troops, causing a mass retreat, which the British, using their arm of manoeuvre overtook and overpowered. Although outnumbered by nearly nine to one, O'Connor's raiding force destroyed the Italian army in North Africa. Although not well known, in terms of the scale of numbers overwhelmed, it is probably the most decisive battle in British military history.

Summary of Campaign

1. O'Connor approaches a gap in the line via an unexpected route through a mine field.

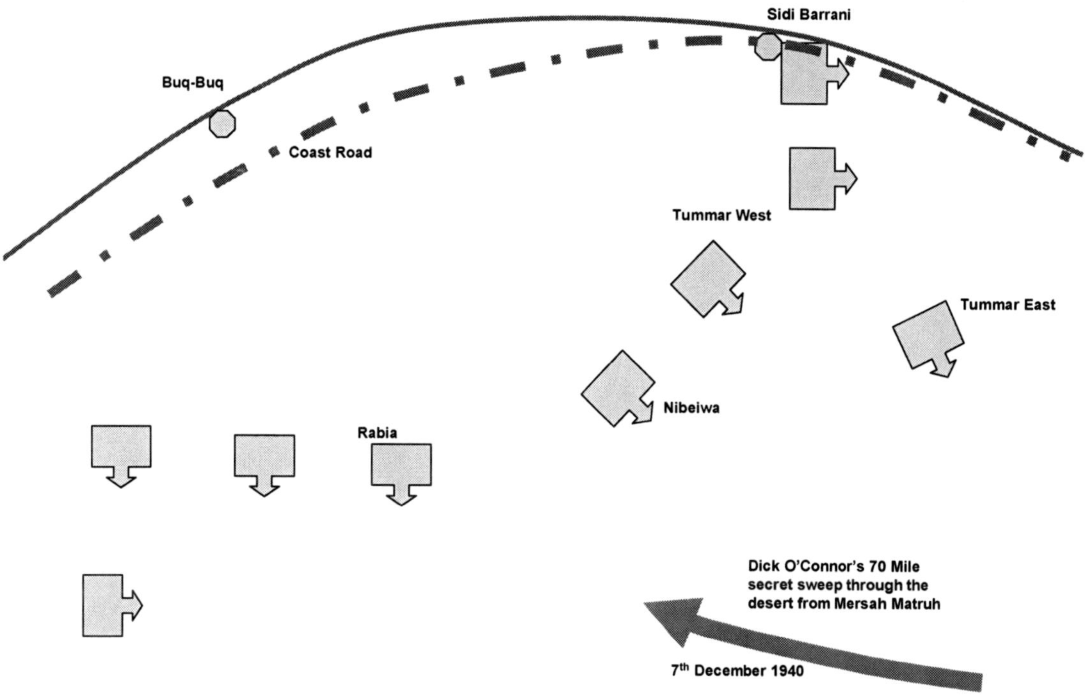

2. Element of surprise allows penetration of enemy Linear Defence.

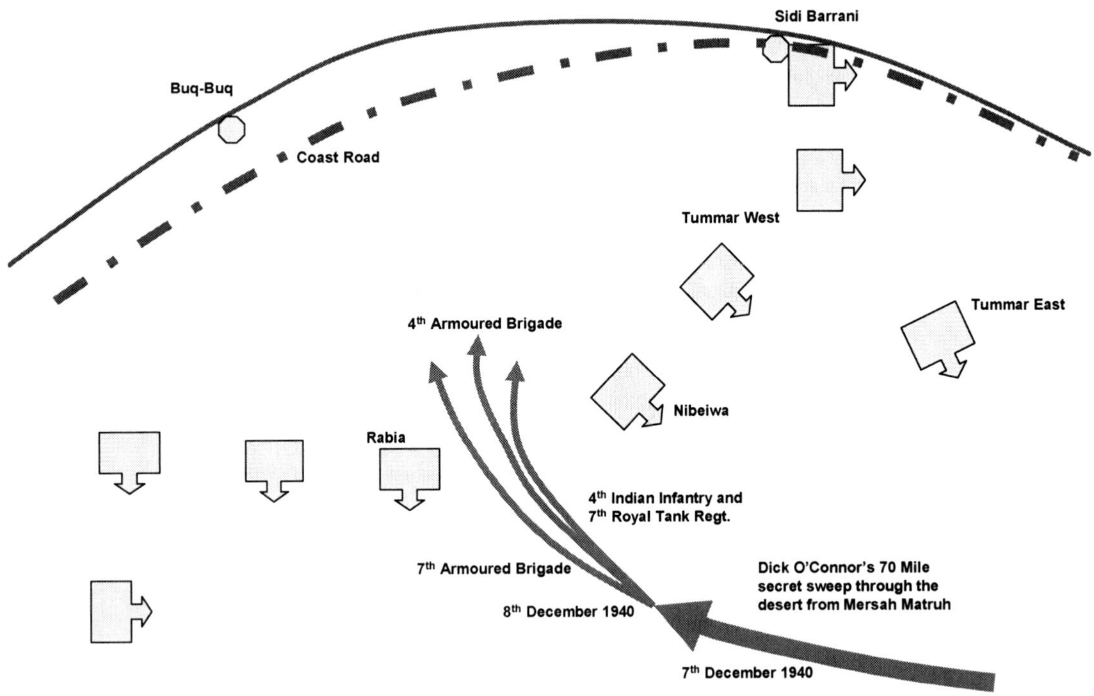

3. Main Mobile Arm approaches enemy strongpoints from unexpected dirction, and sends other mobile forces to secondary targets.

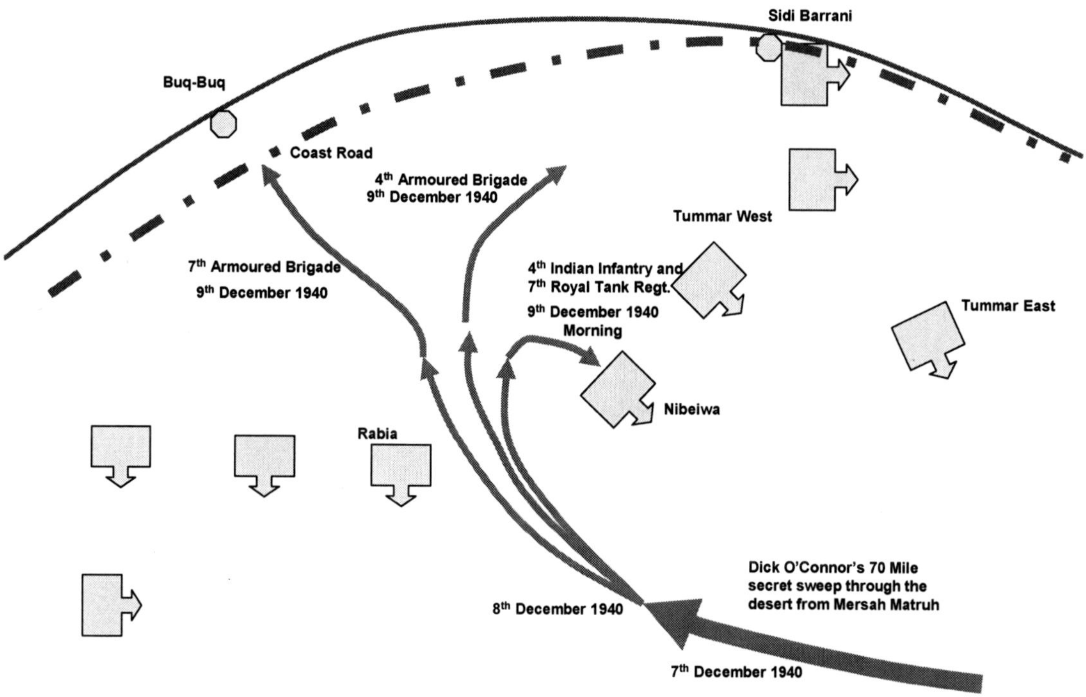

4. Surprise attack from rear allows relatively rapid overrunning of enemy position.

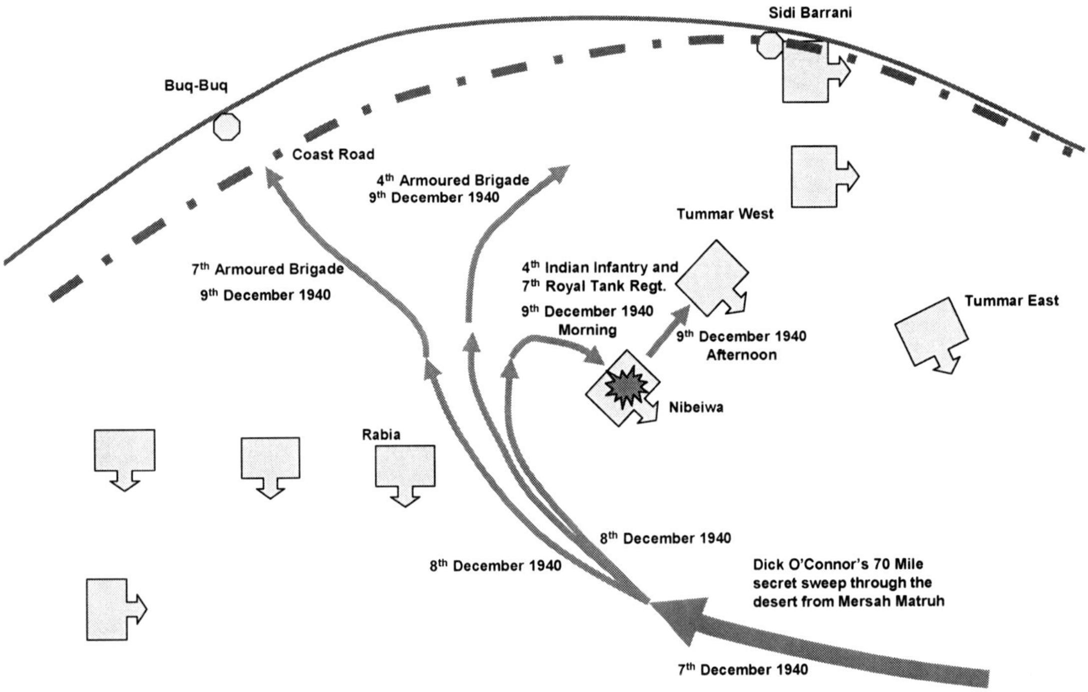

5. Once first position falls, adjacent positions can be attacked with relative impunity.

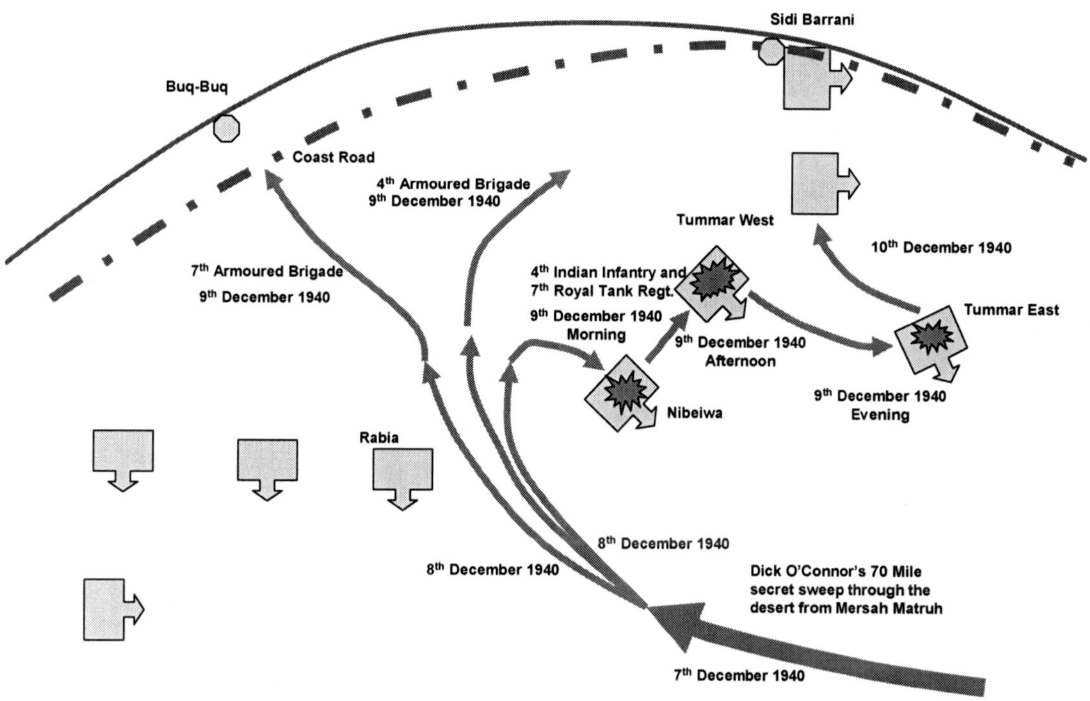

6. Once Linear positions begin to be rolled up mobile forces can join forces to attack major strong point.

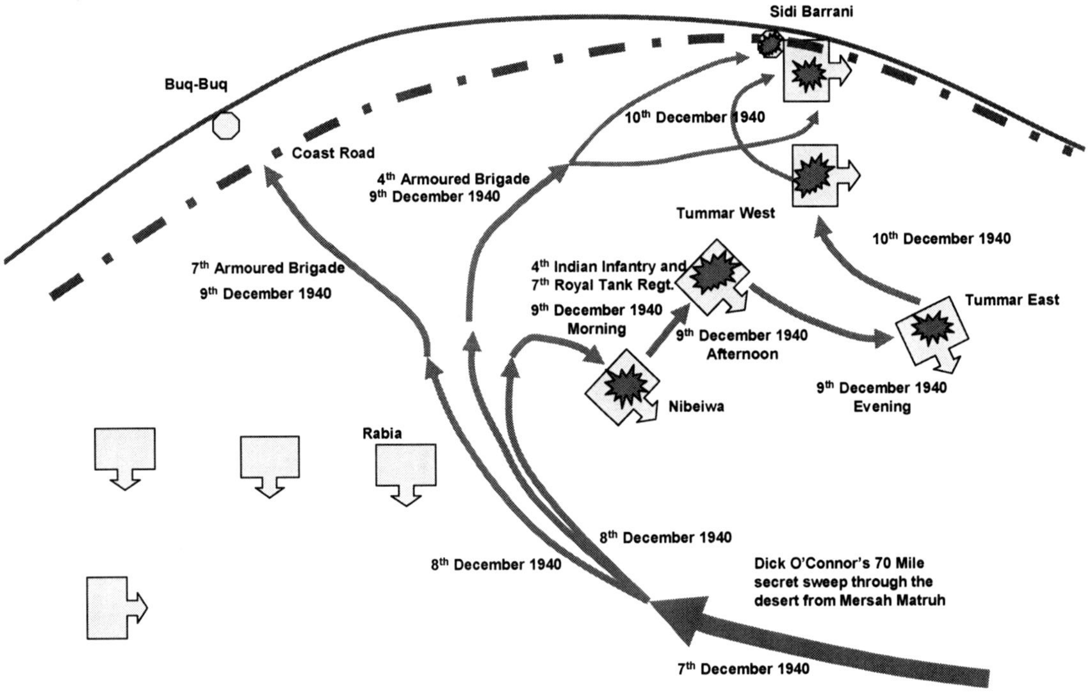

7. As a finale the retreat of the main enemy forces is intercepted and overrun by much smaller British outflanking Mobile forces.

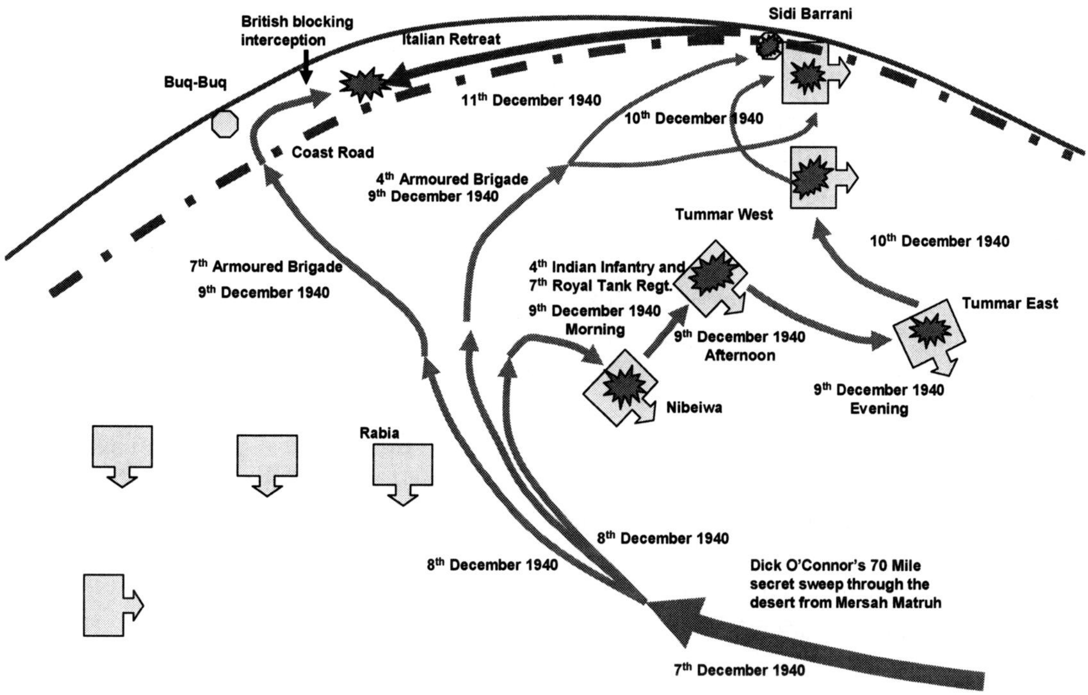

Besieging a Strongpoint

In 1098 the First Crusade was fully underway. Noblemen and their retinues from all over Western and Southern Europe had gathered to try to recapture the Holy land from the Moslems (and generally pick up as much plunder along the way as possible). The first major city they encountered after leaving Christian Byzantine Territory on their way to Jerusalem was Antioch.

Antioch was an “impregnable fortress”. Its walls stretched for 25 miles making it utterly impossible for any army of the time to completely surround it. It had 400 fortified towers along its walls making an attempt at physically storming the walls doomed to failure. It was garrisoned by warlike Turks under the leadership of a competent, but maverick leader called Yaghi Siyan. To top it all, contained within its walls was a secure water supply and pasture for herds of livestock, so the hope of starving the garrison out was not a possibility.

From the Crusaders’ point of view the situation was not promising. They didn’t have enough men to storm the walls, had no siege train, and there was no chance of starving the city into submission as it was better supplied than the besieging Crusaders.

The obvious thing for the Crusaders to do was to give up. After a period of encampment outside the city, that is exactly what Stephen of Blois, the leader of the French Crusaders did, he left and took the French contingent with him. He stopped on the way to tell the Emperor of Byzantium, who was leading a reinforcing army to the Crusaders that the siege had failed, and that the Crusaders had perished. What he didn’t know was that by this time the City had actually fallen to the Crusaders!

How could this have happened? It was due to a charismatic blond giant called Bohemond. He was the son of a Norman Count from Southern Italy and an Italian Lombard Princess. He had a formidable reputation in the Eastern Mediterranean as a cunning warlord, and had almost captured the Byzantine Emperor a few years earlier at the battle of Durazzo.

Bohemond had an intellect to match his huge frame. He understood the politics of the lands the Crusaders passed through, he knew that the population of Antioch was actually largely Christian, and had only fallen to the Turks fourteen years before due to treachery within the garrison. He conjectured that if it had worked for the Turks with a Christian garrison, it must stand a good chance of working for a Christian army with a Turkish garrison, faced with a semi-repressed Christian populace within the walls.

Bohemond realised that numbers weren't the crucial factor here. If the city were taken its spoils would be divided amongst the victors, so the fewer there were, the greater the individual rewards, and food was in short supply amongst the Crusaders. There would never be enough crusaders to storm the walls, or completely blockade all ways in or out of the city, but conversely the garrison wasn't strong enough to sally out and drive his forces off on their own. Because of these factors Bohemond calculated that it was in his interest to actually encourage other crusading factions to give up the siege and leave. .

Cities under siege were never hermetically sealed, especially not one as large as Antioch. Many people moved in and out of the city for their own reasons, usually for the basest of motives, providing they didn't offer an obvious threat, civilians had little difficulty in moving in and out in this fashion individually. In this permeable situation Bohemond infiltrated his spies into the city.

To make matters worse a Syrian army was on its way to lift the siege under Kerbogha the Emir of Mosul. It was this fact that caused Stephen of Blois to take his Frenchmen and head for home. Fortunately for Bohemond Kerbogha spent three weeks besieging Edessa, a crusader stronghold, but the walls were immensely strong, and held. This proved to be an immense error, although one that couldn't have been foreseen at the time, for it gave Bohemond three weeks to find a way into Antioch.

Bohemond needed a "key to the door" and that is what he charged his spies with finding. To this end his spies made contact with an Armenian Tower Guard called Firouz. Firouz had gone to the trouble of converting from Christianity to Islam to improve his position with his Turkish overlords, but had found himself repaid by being fined for hoarding grain, and to add insult to injury, his wife had been seduced by his commanding officer. He was not a happy man; Bohemond had found his key to the city.

With his key tucked safely in his pocket, Bohemond set about negotiating with his fellow leaders of the crusade. He made a deal that if he could capture the city then in exchange for a share of its spoil, they would acknowledge him as its lord. What did they have to loose? They weren't going to take the city anyway; it was just a boastful Norman bragging. They agreed.

Bohemond bought Firouz with a bag of gold and the prospect of revenge against his wife and Turkish Commander. That night Bohemond with sixty knights climbed up ropes Firouz had lowered from an opening high in a tower in the Western Walls, minutes later they opened the Great Bridge Gate, and five hundred fully armed Frankish knights on foot rushed in.

Bohemond had his men blow trumpets loudly from the tower's ramparts and raised his standard to give the impression that a much greater force had stormed the city. The ruse worked, all hell broke loose in the city, with Moslem and Christian civilians joining in on their respective sides, adding to the chaos, favouring the Crusaders. The previously sleeping Turkish garrison were taken completely by surprise and Bohemond's men killed ten times their number of Moslem defenders.

Yaghi Siyan the Turkish commander panicked and fled through a gate with his personal bodyguard when he was told, inaccurately, that the Crusaders were blowing their trumpets from the captured Citadel, the strongest part of the fortress. Hearing of Yaghi Siyan's flight, his second in command fled through a separate gate effectively leaving the remaining garrison with no chain of command.

Bravely Yaghi Siyan's son managed to rally enough of the defeated garrison troops to defend the Citadel, and resisted the immediate Crusader attacks. Some Christian Syrians in the hills killed his father during his attempted escape and his head taken back to Antioch. The son held out grimly in the Citadel, whilst the rest of the town fell to Bohemond and his Crusaders.

Then the tide seemed to turn, for the relief force under Turkish Emir, Ker Bogha, arrived to besieged the town. Ker Bogha replaced the tired Turkish garrison of the Citadel with his own men, and attempted to storm Antioch via the Citadel as entry point. The Crusaders managed to beat them off, the Turks unable to match the Crusaders man for man on the ground and unable to bring their numbers to bear in the cramp surroundings of the Citadel, or mount a surprise attack.

Facing stalemate and a protracted siege by a more powerful army Bohemond decided to risk all and marched out of the town to take on the greatly bigger Turkish force in straight combat. A reckless move? Maybe not; Bohemond seemed to have gambled through luck, judgement, or perhaps because of information from his spies, on political discontent in the Turkish ranks. Sure enough faced with the sheer bravado of the Crusader attack various factions of the Turkish army deserted their leader, and weakening the Turkish army enough for the Crusaders to drive them off. Seeing this, the Turkish garrison still holed up in the Citadel surrendered to Bohemond and converted to Christianity.

Many legends grew up amongst the Crusaders as to what had contributed to their final victory at Antioch, including the "manufactured" discovery by a particularly scurrilous, drunken, womanising pilgrim, of The "Holy Lance Head" which had supposedly pierced Christ's side when he was on The Cross, and the alleged ghostly appearance of a heavenly horde lead by St George during the battle with Ker Bogha, Bohemond publicly scorned such stories and their propagandists.

However the truth of the fall of Antioch was almost as unbelievable as the myths; a bagful of gold to a disgruntled husband had secured Bohemond a kingdom and an "impregnable fortress".

Summary: What to do

Summary of Rules

1. **Identify Pattern of current Campaign:**
    a. Linear Engagement
    b. Area Engagement
    c. Siege Engagement

2. **Asses your forces' for suitability to Campaign.**
    a. Liner Campaign, Defensive Arm must be predominant.
    b. Area Campaign, Mobile Arm must be predominant.
    c. Siege Campaign, Siege Arm must be predominant.

3. **Turn Linear Engagement into an Area Engagement:**
    a. Find and turn a flank.
    b. Create a flank via a Break-in and Break-through.
    c. Administer (Manage) Mobile Arm to the point of decisive victory.

4. **If Siege Engagement; either bypass and seek a more lucrative campaign, or attempt the following order of engagement:**
    a. Subvert strongpoint by treachery from within.
    b. Use approach that negates the defences.
    c. If you have adequate numbers storm the walls.
    d. If you have inadequate numbers, cover main information accesses and counter any attempts to supply the account with information from competition, until account surrenders.

Mnemonics

Identify Pattern

Linear, Wide Area, Siege

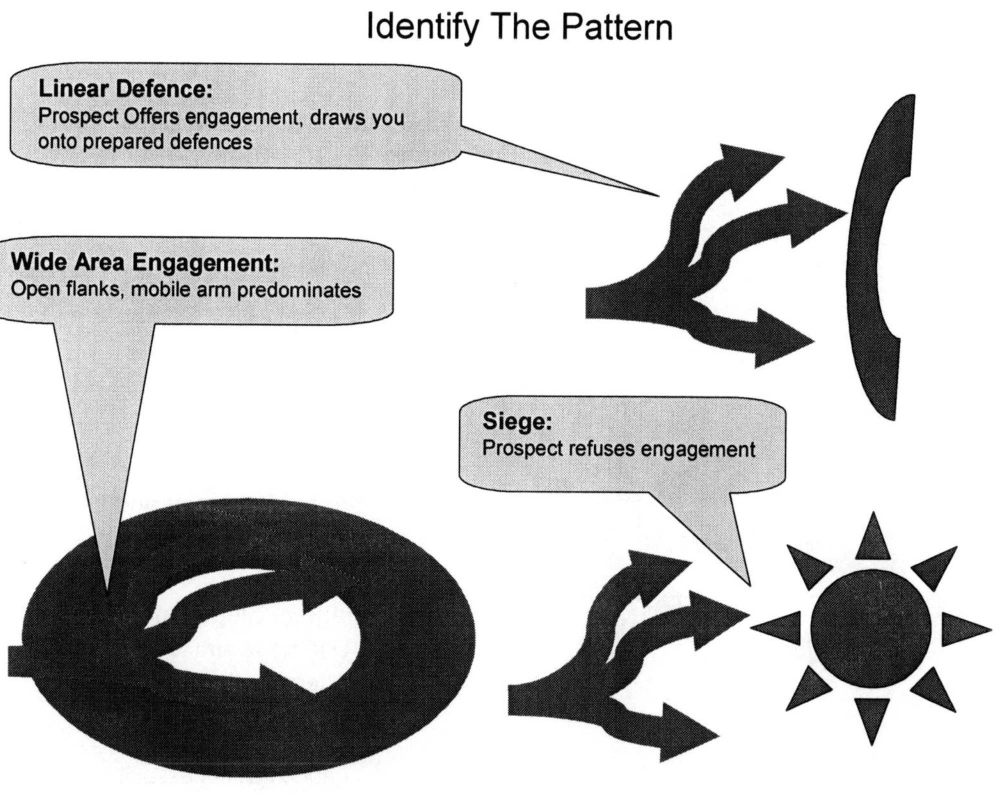

Linear Engagement

- **Either**
- Engage with Defensive Arm
  - Must fight on defenders ground
  - Lack of ability to control engagement
  - Will take a long time
  - Will focus on lowest price
- **Or**
- Use Mobile Arm to turn into a Linear Engagement
  - Find flank
  - Or create flank with break-in and break-through

Siege Engagement

- **Either**
- Bypass strongpoint and seek easier target
- **Or**
- Engage in Siege Operations
  - Use siege arm to engage
  1. Attempt subversion
  2. Use approach that negates defences
  3. Launch all out assault
  4. Attempt to invest account and control information flow and access
- **Expect**
  - Very protracted time periods
  - May never be successful

Wide Area Engagement

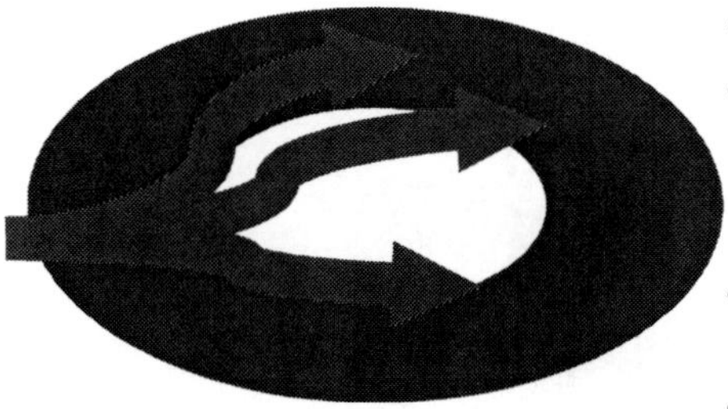

- **Mobile Arm must predominate**
- **Flanks must be Open**
  - Find and turn a flank.
  - Create a flank via a Break-in and Break-through
- **Manage the Mobile Arm to the point of decisive victory**
- **Expect**
  - Need for decisiveness
  - Need for boldness
  - Very fast result for good or bad

Pattern for Field Manual

If you have a Campaign Map you can use this to help identify the approach, for example if a department or individual has a propensity to buy of -1 then you are in for a siege at that point, if or +1 and +1 for their lack of hostility towards you then you have a chance of a free ranging Area engagement, in very general terms these opportunities roughly have the following pattern:

	P = -1	P = 0	P = +1
H = -1	Siege	Siege	Linear
H = 0	Siege	Linear	Linear
H= +1	Siege	Area	Area

If this is applied to the example used earlier on the Campaign Map the following would be the rough assessment:

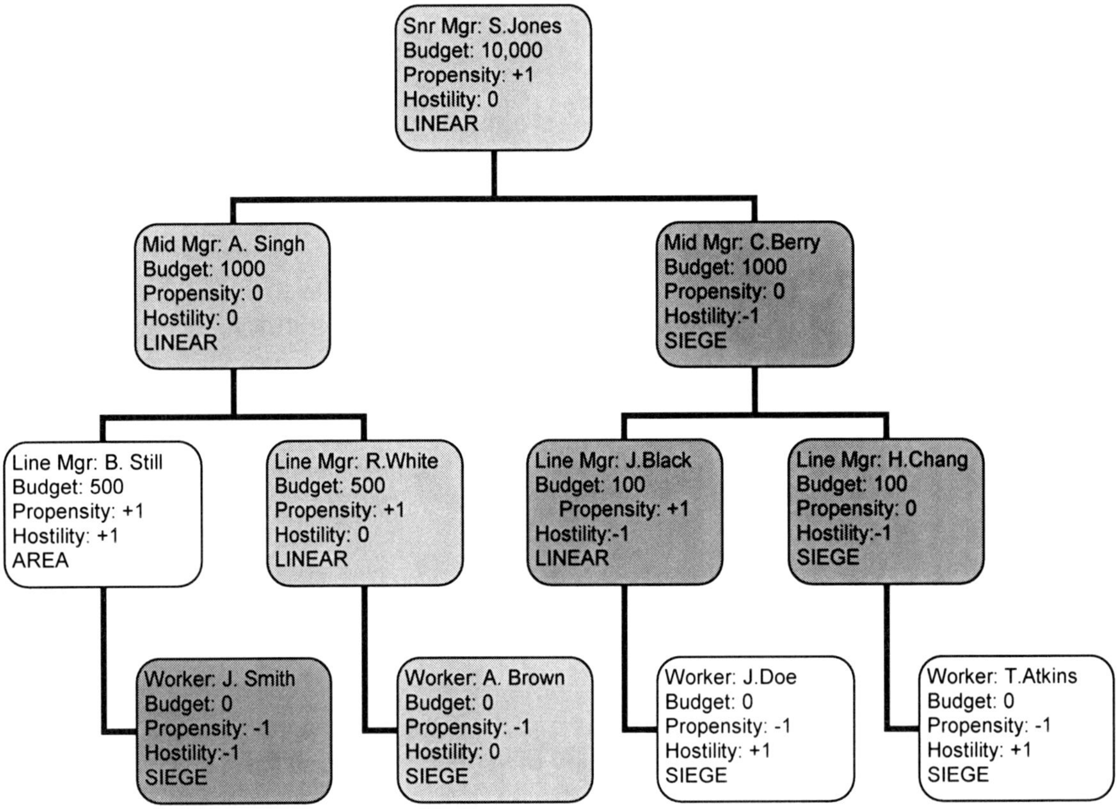

Where can I read more?

The Pattern of War
Lieut.-General Sis Francis Tuker K.C.I.E., C.B., D.S.O., O.B.E.

Cassel and Company Ltd
1948

ISBN

Summary
A simple, and easy to read book, very hard to get hold of.

The Indirect Approach

Based on
The Works of
Captain Sir Basil Liddell Hart (1895-1970)

Introduction

Who was he?

During the later stages of the First World War, amidst the trench bound slaughter, British army Captain Basil Liddell Hart observed the initiatives of the Allies and Germans to break this deadlock, took the essence of the successes of both sides, and formulated his Theory of The Indirect Approach.

During the 1920s he worked with JFC Fuller on his Principles of War until Fuller's fall from grace, he then had a varied career; British Army Captain, Military correspondent for The Telegraph and The Times. Appointed personal advisor to The British War Minister in 1937 he resigned in protest at the slow pace of preparations to the growing threat from the Facist powers in Europe. Ironically his theories, largely ignored by the allies, were exploited by the Germans in WW2 and lead to their Blitzkrieg successes in Poland and France. He personally interrogated the surviving German Generals at the end of WW2, and gave their accounts of why they believed they had succeeded and failed militarily.

What does The Indirect Approach Teach?

Out of the tactical methodologies he studied during WW1 Liddell Hart developed his theories of The Indirect Approach and The Expanding Torrent. The Indirect Approach described how to engage the enemy for greatest advantage, and The Expanding Torrent described the way of exploiting the positional advantages achieved via The Indirect Approach.

His basic tenant was that The Principles of War can be boiled down in a word to **“concentration”**, in a phrase to **“concentration of strength against weakness”**, and in a sentence to:

Concentration of Strength against weakness depend on the dispersion of your opponent’s strength, which is brought about by the distribution of your own strength that gives the appearance of dispersion; the sequence is your apparent dispersion, followed by your opponent’s actual dispersion, followed by your concentration against your opponent’s dispersed weakness.

True concentration is therefore the result of calculated dispersion.

He taught that simply trying to overwhelm an opponent in a head on collision is at best a costly approach, and at worst will prove disastrous. Even if you are stronger than your opponent, taking an Indirect Approach as described by Liddell Hart will bring success at less cost. Conversely utilising the Indirect Approach, you can take on and beat a much stronger opponent when a direct approach would only lead to defeat.

Using the Expanding Torrent shows how to fully exploit the initial successes of the Indirect Approach for maximum effect. The Expanding Torrent shows what to do in order to overrun an opposing area once the initial penetration is achieved.

Liddell Hart's Axioms

Liddell Hart boiled The Strategy of The Indirect Approach down to a list of principles, both positive and negative, or in modern terms, Do's and Don'ts:

Do's

1. Adjust your **ends** to your **means**.
2. Keep your **Objective** always in mind.
3. Choose the **Line of Least Expectation**.
4. Exploit the **Line of Least Resistance**.
5. Take a line of operation which offers an **alternative objective**.
6. Ensure that all plans and dispositions are **flexible and adaptable** to circumstances.

Don'ts

1. Throw your weight into a stroke whilst your **enemy is on guard**.
2. Renew an attack along the **same line** (or in the **same form**) **after it has failed**.

Liddell Hart's Synthesis of these Axioms in Practice

From these basic principles Liddell Hart developed his theories of The Indirect Approach and The Expanding Torrent Effect.

The Indirect Approach advocated the avoidance of simple frontal attacks in favour of the use of surprise and flanking manoeuvres to overrun the command and control centres of enemy positions, thereby rendering their fighting forces ineffective and potentially demoralised by surprise approaches from flanks and rear. These attacks were managed at battlefield level involving a good deal of delegated decision making, with the axis of attack being decided by Intelligence and on the spot probing to produce a battlefield lead initiative.

The Expanding Torrent effect was a description of the phase of engagement after the initial penetration of enemy lines, i.e. the phase where troops fan out to attack soft targets such as command and control centres, supply dumps, and lines of communication. During this phase speed of movement, use of initiative, and the ability to act without direct guidance are crucial. Once total confusion and disruption are achieved, it is time to regroup to overrun enemy troop concentrations, which by now should at least be greatly reduced in effectiveness, and may be utterly demoralised, so taking them out will at worst be much easier than via frontal assault, and at best will be a simple matter of engagement to allow them the excuse to run away.

The Indirect Approach consisted of a number of stages;

1. Gather Intelligence to look for potential areas of strength and weakness especially joins and gaps.
2. Probe enemy frontage to test intelligence, and distract enemy from guessing true objective, thereby approaching along a line of least expectation. Do not advertise your line of approach.
3. Use the line of least resistance to penetrate an exploitable weakness, throw the weight of the main forces against it, to widen and hold the gap.
4. Pour fast moving troops through the gap and drive as deep as possible as quickly as possible to cause as much dislocation as possible by cutting lines of communication.
5. Aim to overrun the enemy centre of gravity (Schwerpunkt as the Germans called it) this is generally represented by the main command and control centre. Doing this separates the centre of thought from the centre of action or metaphorically the head from the limbs.

The Expanding Torrent;

1. Disruption: Push out along lines of least resistance behind enemy front to extend the area of damage and disruption, hit as many soft targets as possible especially centres of command, and communications.
2. Protection: Cut off concentrations of enemy resistance, avoiding direct engagements with strong positions.
3. Destruction: Attack enemy concentrations once they show signs of a collapse in morale.

Axioms Explained

Do's

Adjust your ends to your means.
In determining your objective clear sight and cool calculation are required. Liddell-Hart likened the ability to achieve any given target, i.e. the confidence of your forces to the current in a battery, and your resources themselves like the cells in a battery, so the power available will depend on the number of cells and how well charged (with confidence) they are.

Keep your Objective always in mind.
Never loose sight of your objective whilst being able to adapt your plan to changes in circumstances. There may be more ways than one to your ultimate objective, and each action and minor objective along the path to your overall goal must be considered in relation to their possibility of success with their contribution to the overall objective if achieved.

Choose the Line of Least Expectation.
Put yourself in your opponent's mind and calculate which approach they are least likely to foresee or forestall, and make this your chosen approach en route to your objective.

Exploit the Line of Least resistance.
Attack where your opponent is least able to defend, but always in an area that leads to your ultimate goal. Tactically this means where to throw in your reserves, and Strategically it shows where to exploit tactical advantages.

Take a line of operation which offers an alternative objective.
March divided but fight united is an old military axiom. There are likely to be a number of lines of operation you could choose when engaging in your actions within an account, the best ones to choose are those that allow more than one end point or objective to be gained. These tactical objectives must be both feasible and valuable in terms of moving you towards your overall goal.

Do not confuse a single line of operation with a single objective at each stage of the action. A single line of operation in harmony with your overall goal is a good thing, alternative objectives, when engaging tactically with your opponent, are what will help you to further your aims. This forms the basis of infiltration tactics.

Ensure that all plans and dispositions are flexible; adaptable to circumstances.
It has been said that few plans survive contact with the enemy. There are simply too many unknowns that will be encountered in campaign to fully plan for which ones will be encountered, and therefore the effect they are likely to have on your plans. Therefore you must make sure that plans can be changed and resources reallocated to take account of this.

Don'ts

Throw your weight into a stroke whilst your enemy is on guard.
Do not attack a prepared defensive position. Make sure that any attack is against an opponent who is either not ready to, or not expecting to, receive it.

Renew an attack along the same line (or in the same form) after it has failed.
Once you have failed in a certain type of approach, do not repeat it. Doing so invites failure. There must be a substantial change in any such approach in the same campaign, either with the amount of resources, the types of weapons used to attack, or a substantial change to your opponent's situation. But in general it will be better not to even attempt such a repeat performance in the same campaign, look for an easier route.

Why is the Indirect Approach important to you?

Do's

Adjust your ends to your means.
Using Liddell-Hart's battery analogy, if you use up the current in vain action you will exhaust the confidence of the cells, and once this is exhausted your own confidence will prove inadequate in re-charging them.

If you attempt an objective that requires more power for a longer time than your battery is capable of, then you will never achieve your goal. Conversely if you aim too low in setting objectives, you will not gain all that could be achieved with the power available to you.

Keep your Objective always in mind.
To wander off track is bad if it is not the most direct route to your goal, but to find yourself at a dead-end which gives you no way forward towards your goal is much worse. So by keeping your ultimate objective always in mind when you take actions you will ensure that all actions lead you closer to fulfilment of the objective.

Choose the Line of Least Expectation.
Choosing the Line of Least Expectation will give you the initiative, and prevent your opponent countering your moves in a timely fashion.

Exploit the Line of Least Resistance.
Exploiting the Line of Least Resistance will enable you to push against your opponents weaknesses, and therefore gain momentum towards your ultimate goal.

Take a line of operation which offers an alternative objective.
This will put your opponent on the horns of a dilemma, and gives you the chance to gain at least one of the possible objectives, and possibly both in succession. Choosing such an approach gives two advantages; firstly it allows an alternative success strategy to be achieved even if one objective fails, and secondly it keeps your competition from fully understanding what your objective is.

In short having alternative objectives gives a much greater chance of gaining an objective, having a single objective may ensure that you won't achieve it once your opponent is aware of it and able to defend against it.

Ensure that all plans and dispositions are flexible and adaptable to circumstances.
The reason this is important is because by building flexibility into your plans and dispositions, you can absorb, counter, or bypass unexpected turns of events. Lack of flexibility will ensure that when the unexpected does hit you, it will so disrupt your plans that recovery may not be possible.

Don'ts

Throw your weight into a stroke whilst your enemy is on guard.
Attacking a prepared defensive position is at best wasteful of resources, and at worst a recipe for disaster. To successfully attack a prepared defensive position with similar offensive weapons to your opponent is traditionally seen as requiring a three to one advantage in strength. It can only really succeed if you have either a tremendous advantage in resources or you are facing a competitor who is unskilled.

It is always, without exception, better to compete with an unprepared or surprised opponent. This gives you the advantage of the initiative, allowing you to be much more conservative in the amount of force you need to deploy, and reduces substantially the amount of time required to achieve a result.

Renew an attack along the same line (or in the same form) after it has failed.
If you do, your competition will be prepared for you, they will have learned how to deal with your approach, and having been educated in your weaknesses, will be in a much better position to exploit them. If you know that a certain approach has already failed it is ridiculous to assume that it will work on subsequent occasions.

It is very important that failure is analysed and not ignored. The importance of this is twofold; firstly so that it can be understood and thereby avoided in the future, and secondly to prevent a myth of enemy invincibility growing up due to a lack of understanding of their actual strengths and weaknesses.

How to apply The Indirect Approach to Sales Situations

Do's

Adjust your ends to your means.
It's far better to have a plan than not to have one, however, there is no point in having a plan that is unrealistic. Look at your objective, then look at your resources, then look at your objective again. Be bold in formulating your plan, but not reckless, be cautious in formulating your plan but not cowardly, assuming that everything that could go wrong may go wrong, but be prepared to exploit your advantages, and never doubt your luck.

The hardest thing at the start of any campaign is to say is "NO!" to an enterprise; the account that has the problem your solution fixes and the money to pay for it but has already been penetrated and controlled by your competition, the account that makes all the right noises and the need for your solution but lacks the money to purchase, and the account that has the money but not the problem that your solution solves. You must not be tempted by these, always weigh up the potential reward, then work out the likely time and resources that will be required to achieve the reward, is it both realistic in terms of effort, and achievable in terms of time scales?

Keep your Objective always in mind.
Once you have your plan, stick to it as long as it stays ultimately realistic. Don't deviate from it unless circumstances have changed substantially, if they are the same as when the plan was formulated then there is no logic to changing it. Put all of your efforts into reaching that ultimate goal, think of every move leading to that objective.

Don't be lead astray by adventures in areas that don't move you on further towards that goal. The easiest way to loose your objective is to dissipate your efforts piecemeal, with members of your team being drawn into doing what they enjoy or feel confident with rather than what is required to move towards the objective.

Choose the Line of Least Expectation.
Look for an approach that you haven't advertised to your opposition. Don't let marketing broadcast your intent. Attack a spot that offers no resistance and you are sure to win. Understand what your solution can do outside of what the manual says, understand what your customer wants not just what he needs, and understand your competition's weaknesses better

than they do. Use the element of surprise to give you an advantage in terms of time, and to multiply the effect of your efforts.

Once the initial defences are penetrated it is possible to generate lines of least expectation by controlling lines of communication, thereby preventing the opposition being able to gain intelligence as to your plans and actions, they will never know where your next move will take place.

Exploit the Line of Least Resistance.
The line of least resistance is often brought about as a result of an approach along the line of least expectation; you aren't expected, so you aren't resisted, you take your opponent by surprise.

It is essential that the advantage provided by surprise is exploited to the maximum, and the first successes along the line of least resistance, if exploited quickly, can have a domino effect allowing the line of least resistance to be extended along the vector of your thrust.

As you are adhering to the line of least resistance, you should not deviate along a line of greatest resistance, i.e. should stiff resistance be met along the vector of your thrust, an alternative line must be chosen.

Take a line of operation which offers an alternative objective.
Plan in advance the possible outcomes of proposed actions en route to your ultimate goal. Approach down parallel lines so that whichever offers the easiest route can be taken if heavy resistance is encountered on the alternate route. When taking an action to achieve a new position think of more than one way to utilise this new position in case the obvious outcome is not as expected.

Ensure that all plans and dispositions are flexible and adaptable to circumstances.
Think of as many alternate outcomes to actions as possible, both good and bad, and have back up plans to allow you to continue to move forward towards your ultimate goal, without loosing momentum not matter what fate may throw at you. You must be prepared to quickly transfer resources to suit the new circumstances, and must have put plans in place to logistically achieve this before the event.

Don'ts

Throw your weight into a stroke whilst your enemy is on guard.
Threaten to attack in such a place, but only to hide your true intentions, make the right noises, but do not engage simply because it is the obvious thing to do or is "expected" of you.

Renew an attack along the same line (or in the same form) after it has failed.
You must analyse why your approach has failed, and what can be done differently to ensure that the next approach is successful, or what new approach can be attempted to bypass the difficulties of the previous failure.

One of the most common failures in businesses is a fear of admitting the true reasons for failure. There is only one reason for loosing a deal, and that is because you've been outsold; full stop. The key is to find out how you were outsold, it will be because your competition fulfilled a personal "want" of your prospect better than you did. Find out what that "want" was, and make sure you don't get beaten in that way again.

Theories In Practice

The Indirect Approach consisted of a number of stages;

Gather Intelligence to look for potential areas of strength and weakness especially joins and gaps.
Intelligence should be gathered from as wide an area as possible, on all factors affecting the account. Preconceptions and assumptions must be challenged, and if necessary discarded, trust the evidence not the myths, no matter how ancient. Use expertise and take the advice offered, do not reject advice simply because it doesn't fit preconceptions.

Intelligence should be gathered about weakness (needs and wants) not strengths (areas of stability), as you will not be attacking strengths unless you are stupid. Look for legislation that puts pressure on your prospect's industry that offers an opportunity to you, look for business drivers in their market place, look for competitive edge you can help them with, look for people within the prospect who are ambitious and can use your solution to further their ambitions, look for areas of discontent with competitive solutions. All of these factors offer you a point to exploit.

The only reason to gather intelligence is to use it to verify or modify your plan, if you don't intend to do this don't gather intelligence; charge on blindly, you may get lucky (not very likely). If it is from a reliable source but is so unpalatable that to acknowledge it would mean abandoning your plans, then that is exactly what you should do. Generally it doesn't amount to this, more likely that you can test the water by trying to negotiate a better position when the potential snags have been identified, often if you explain your concerns to the prospect they will comply with at least some of your requests if indeed they don't have an ulterior motive.

Above all Intelligence must be acted upon, decisively and whilst it is still fresh and accurate.

Probe enemy frontage to test intelligence, and distract enemy from guessing true objective, thereby approaching along a line of least expectation. Do not advertise your line of approach.
Probe as many points as possible with your available resources; all things in sales are fluid, and intelligence has a limited shelf life; don't trade old misconceptions for new ones. No

areas should be overlooked, your intelligence may help to pinpoint likely targets to probe, but it should not be accepted as fact until forces on the ground have tested it.

Probing in many areas will help to confuse your opposition as to your true intent, this will help protect your efforts, and delay your opponents' ability to counter attack. It may also open up more than one area of opportunity to penetrate the account.

Look for areas of weakness, note and avoid areas of strength, don't spend time on areas of strong resistance. Once an area of weakness is found, this needs to be communicated to reinforcements in order to exploit a line of least resistance.

Taking the intelligence as your starting point look for "Gaps and Joins" in these vulnerable areas. A Gap is a problem seen by higher management which lower level people are either unaware of or are unable to solve, a Join is a problem area for which responsibility is split between groups. The Gaps offer immediate routes to senior management without recourse to lower levels, the Joins offer perhaps less immediate access to higher levels, but generally a way in and the possibility of exploiting political tensions to accelerate the way to the top.

Use the line of least resistance to penetrate an exploitable weakness, throw the weight of the main forces against it, to widen and hold the gap.

Always attack weakness, never attack strength, act like a bully not a hero. The bully looks for quick easy targets with maximum return and minimum risk, heroes look for glory and challenges, they want difficult wins, and will put everything at risk for the sake of personal recognition. Selling is about money not glory.

Having studied the Intelligence reports, and probed the defensive frontage to test and confirm them, it is now time to look for the Line of Least Resistance. Lines of Least Resistance are often generated by taking the Lines of Least Expectation, most sellers approach an account along lines of Greatest Expectation, and thereby Generate Lines of Greatest Resistance. They do this by leading with their solution, which they will have advertised well in advance, and thereby proclaim exactly where their blow will fall, and ensure that all resistance will be marshalled to thwart it. To take the Line of Least Resistance, the true object of your thrust must be concealed from your opposition, and rather than leading where your solution immediately dictates, attack the customer problem (Gaps and Joins) by looking for ways in which your solution can address it. You must adjust your solution to the customer weakness, don't expect your solution to prove to be an adequate one where there is no customer weakness.

Pour fast moving troops through the gap and drive as deep as possible as quickly as possible to cause as much dislocation as possible by cutting lines of communication.

It is essential to reward success, and thereby go from initial success to greater success. If this isn't done you are left with the alternative of rewarding failure, this is the sin of pride. The inability to accept failure and either retreat from it, outflank it, or isolate it, in the early stages of an engagement, is usually a result of a fear of losing or a need to prove you are better than the opposition at every stage, and pride comes before a fall.

So when a success is achieved, it must be grasped, exploited, and used as a springboard for other actions; advertise the success to other areas in the customer hierarchy, promote the ideas and opinions of the customer personnel who made it possible credit them with all your good ideas, grind your enemy underfoot, make it impossible for your enemies to mount a counter attack by destroying their presence, discrediting their performance, rooting out their allies and isolating them; Shock and Awe. Bring in the necessary personnel to make your solution works exceptionally well, invite the customer to sponsored meetings with your other customers to reinforce what a good idea it was to have decided to go with your solution, sponsor them to speak at trade shows about the solution, widen the breach in the customer defences with as much personnel activity as possible.

The unsettling part of this is that unless you get really lucky, you can't be entirely sure where, or perhaps in what form the breakthrough will take, but you must be prepared for it. Worse still, it may come in outside of where you want it; put your pride aside, let the success draw you where it wants to go, let your customer decide what he wants to pay and for what, then deliver it.

The German Commander Ludendorff in the First World War refused to reinforce his successes if they failed to conform to the abstract plan he held in his head, this lead to a brilliantly conceived tactical system being sacrificed to a poorly conceived strategic ideal. Unless strategy and tactics are in sympathy with each other you cannot win.

Aim to overrun the enemy centre of gravity (Schwerpunkt) generally the main command and control centre. Doing this separates the centre of thought from the centre of action or metaphorically the head from the limbs

This is the centre of gravity, the Pearl in the Oyster, your target. It equates to the thing that you need to control in order to win control of the account. It is the nerve centre of the organisation or management structure; it may be a person, a department, a problem area, or a personal win.

The Expanding Torrent;

1. **Disruption: Push out along lines of least resistance behind enemy front to extend the area of damage and disruption, hit as many soft targets as possible especially centres of command, and communications.**
From a business perspective this means exploiting your breakthrough to find more areas of opportunity behind the front line engagement areas. There is no point standing still after making your breakthrough, at that point the work really begins. Momentum is everything; soak up every area of opportunity available as quickly as possible, don't wait to be invited, announce your successes and use them to make your next targets easier to overrun. This will make you look more powerful than you may actually be, you need a psychological advantage over your opposition.

2. **Protection: Cut off concentrations of enemy resistance, avoiding direct engagements with strong positions.**
Momentum = Mass x Acceleration. If you stop to attack strong points you instantly, and obviously, loose speed, but you also loose mass in terms of concentrating activity against these strong points instead of effortlessly overrunning weak points which would cost less in terms of momentum.

Unfortunately sales people are encouraged by inexperienced managers to attack centres of strength when the greatest and experienced sales people appear to win victories with ease. They do this by avoiding centres of resistance, and attacking areas of weakness, i.e. areas where the customer actually favours them and facilitates the selling.

3. **Destruction: Attack enemy concentrations with collapsed morale.**
The time to attack pockets of resistance is after they are completely isolated. Their psychological weakness is far more important than their physical state. Once an individual or group believes that they are defeated, then they will be defeated, unless their opponent makes the mistake of sparing them. Defeat is a state of mind, destruction is a state being. Napoleon said that the average British soldier cannot be defeated he can only be killed, the converse is that any group no matter how strong is defeated if it believes it can't win, when this happens it is the time to overrun them. Morale is everything in selling as in warfare.

These pockets must be alienated, dispersed, and destroyed. If they are left they will coalesce and forms centres of resistance. Many pockets will disintegrate due to pressure of acceptance of your fait accompli in the rest of the account, and gradually it will be seen that resistance is useless.

Sales Example

Conventional Sales Approach

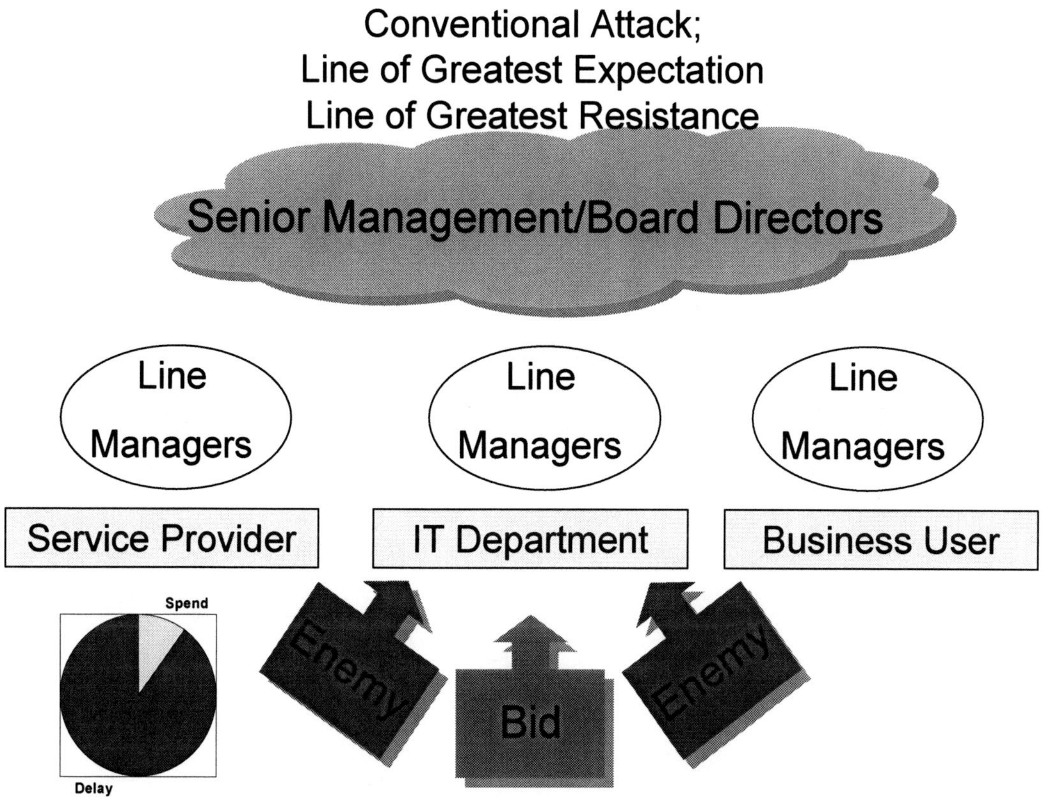

In a conventional sales approach most antagonists are drawn, by invitation (requests for tender etc) to concentrate along the line of greatest expectation, and therefore the line of greatest resistance. This is an area where the approaches are expected, anticipated, and countered. The result of this is that there is an inordinate amount of delay involved in this route.

Conversely the expected reward is low because operationally these projects are delegated as low down the organisation as possible, with decisions being made as to what is or is not acceptable being left with very junior technical people. This may all be pulled together by a management committee, but at this low operational level in the organisation the ability to spend is also low. So in effect a lot of time is spent fighting over a low potential prize in financial terms. Completely the opposite to what is required from a sales situation.

The Indirect Approach

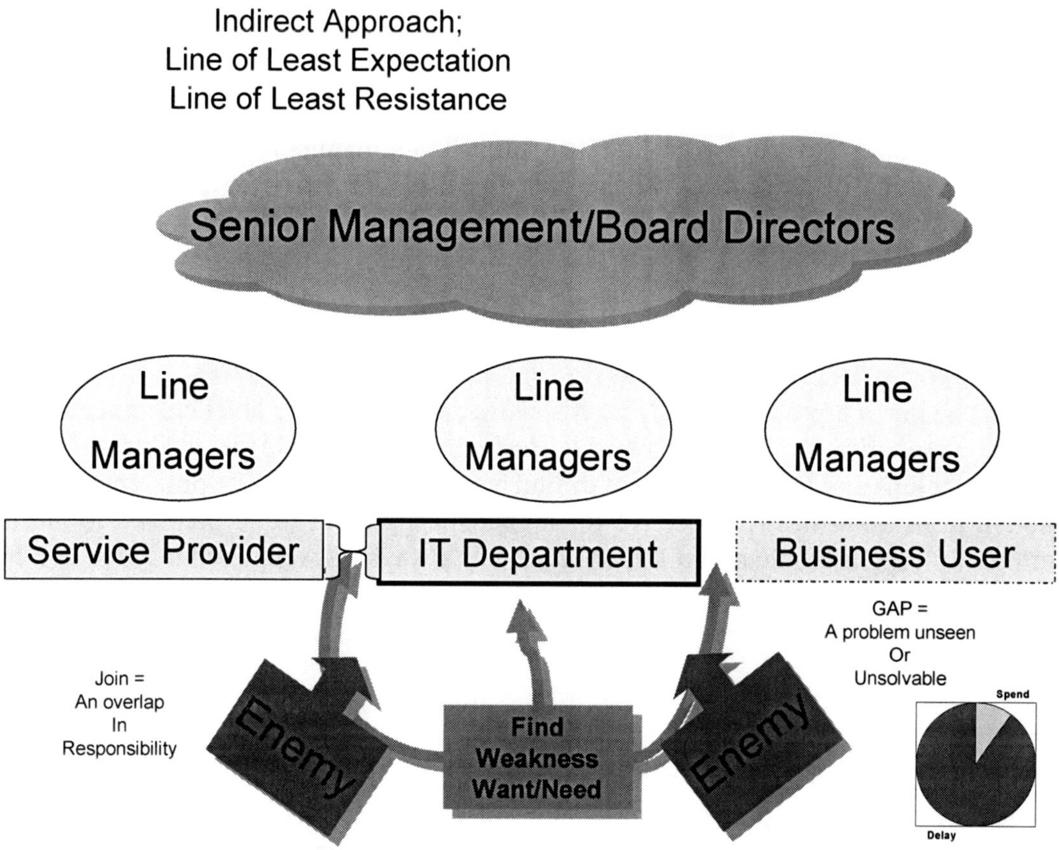

With the Indirect Approach, instead of simply engaging in the same manner as everyone else i.e. along the line of Greatest Expectation and Greatest Resistance, it is necessary to gather Intelligence to look for potential areas of weakness and strength in the defences, as no defences are ever homogenous, no matter what assurances are given by the customer.

In our definition a defensive weakness is basically an area where the customer has a want or a need over and what may be apparent within any strict guidelines defined in a tender, or known to the low level or technical staff who may be managing the tender, therefore the line of least expectation and therefore least resistance. A defensive strength is an area where the customer has nailed down narrow criteria which tend to be shared with all contenders, allowing an advantage to none of them, i.e. the line of greatest expectation and therefore greatest resistance.

So it is essential that the customer frontage is probed to test intelligence, and distract competition from guessing true objective, thereby protecting the line of least expectation. Under no circumstances advertise your line of approach, and maintain a presence on the line of greatest expectation in order to cover the real object of the activity. You must look for "Gaps and Joins" in the defensive front.

So what are joins and gaps?

Gaps

In this context a Gap is a problem which is either *unseen* by the lower level customer staff, or is considered *unsolvable* by them, conversely such problems should be visible to the top management echelons and they should want to find a solution to them. The problem should be grave enough from a business perspective for higher management to be prepared to pay for that solution. Solving a problem at a senior level will always outweigh solving one at a less senior level.

Joins

Tend to be more complex. They are areas of overlapping responsibilities between disparate groups. These groups could be within the same organisation, or be composed of two or more separate organisations. The reasons that these areas of overlapping responsibility offer opportunities for penetrating past the normal line of engagement is because there is a very good chance that where there is an overlap in responsibility that each responsible partner will assume that the other is taking responsibility, and therefore no one will actually take responsibility. This is a very common repeatable psychological trait. This is especially true where there is a contentious or unpopular area of joint responsibility, in these cases none of the groups involved will want to take responsibility for such areas.

Joins often lead to a build up of frustrations between the responsible groups, which in turn leads to one group acting recklessly in their decision making process. From a sales perspective this is the kind of join that should be sought, as someone prepared to act recklessly can speed up the sales penetration process, by being prepared to sponsor short cuts to the normal procedures. Conversely if a group involved in a join tries to you're your sales efforts by a reckless reaction, you have the opportunity to exploit this by highlighting it to your allies within the account who can use it against your competition, however it is usually better to be backed by a reckless group than to be opposed by one, as reckless behaviour is often an outward sign of power and confidence, and less often of outright stupidity. Joins are therefore areas of instability which can be exploited to advantage.

Most of these exploitable tensions will come down to interpersonal issues, poor management, and geographic separation. The greater the harmony between the overlapping groups (often as a result of functional similarity), the less is the likelihood of reckless action, although there is still scope for areas of missed/ignored responsibility. The greater the functional diversity between the overlapping groups, the greater the disunity of aims from a management and personal goals perspective, the more there is a likelihood of irrational action and blind spots.

It is highly likely that you won't know what or where the Gaps and Joins are when you first start probing, so you must maintain a flexibility of approach, don't assume you know what they are and dogmatically attack that point, let you intelligence and probing provide the answer, maintain a flexibility of approach, let your customer tell you what their wants are. Look for an alternative Gap or Join in case your advance gets block on the initially identified weak point; time is of the essence, if you meet significant time consuming resistance, exploit your alternative approach (if you have one). However once you have identified what you see as the critical point to attack, attack it single-mindedly until it is either breached or abandoned. Knowing when to attack and when to retreat differentiates the good sales people from the poor ones.

Having found the Gap or Join use this line of least resistance to penetrate and bypass the line of greatest resistance. Adjust your resources to concentrate the correct resource to attack the problem effectively and efficiently, pour fast moving sales staff through the gap and drive as deep as possible; to board level is ideal, as quickly as possible to let you take control of lines of communication from the board down. Throw the weight of your main forces against it the gap, i.e. your sales and marketing, and technical staff, and customer references, to widen and hold the gap open in order to allow you to bring in more resources in a timely fashion.

Examples of Gaps:

Personal pressure/personal wins

Any way your solution can help a senior individual gain a personal/career advantage, or remove a personal pressure. It is a fact of human psychology that people will go further to remove a personal pressure than to gain a personal win, however the higher up the tree within an organisation you operate, the more likely you are to find people who ignore personal pressures and are driven mostly by personal wins.

Legislation
New legislation which will change the way the customer needs to operate or report on their business.

Return on Investment
Pressure from share holders for the business to change in a certain fashion, usually associated with the need to increase profits, or reduce costs.

Competition
Pressure from competition, and the need for the business to find a way to beat the competition.

Fashion
A new trend or recommendation from Industry analysts, politicians, business leaders etc. that appears to senior management to be worthwhile, but has not been taken up at lower levels in the organisation.

Routine
An accepted way of doing things that has outgrown its usefulness as far as senior management is concerned, but is generally stilled adhered to by lower levels in the organisation.

Examples of Joins:

Contractual Obligations
Areas where there is a contractual agreement between two groups, such as occurs with an outsourcing or facilities management contract, where there are likely to be disputes over fulfilment of service levels. There will be a tension between the service provider trying to deliver the minimum service to the lowest budget whilst looking for areas outside of the contract for which additional charges can be made, and to mitigate an areas of failure within the contract which could result in penalties, and the customer who receives the service who will wish to maximise the return for their investment, and withhold payments where they believe contracts and targets have not been met.

Tenders

Any tenders which are to be managed by a committee of disparate groups, each which their own petty rivalries and agendas. Such tenders should be viewed as an amalgam of different wants and needs, some of which will carry a much higher value to powerful groups than others. It is necessary to deconstruct such a document and work out what these areas are. The other adage to remember is that if you receive a tender from a customer which you didn't help to write, then you may already be too late as one of your competitors will probably have helped to construct it.

Organisational Tensions

A business process which has input from two or more areas, e.g. a sales area and a technical area, or a research area and a development area. Any decision being driven by an inward looking core controlling group, often from a central corporate part of the organisation and often with some specific technical or administrative function, and an outward looking customer facing, often field based group, often with a sales/marketing background. The central group will be interested in conformity, control, and long term stability, the field group will be driven by the need for quick results, and competitive advantage.

The Ultimate Target

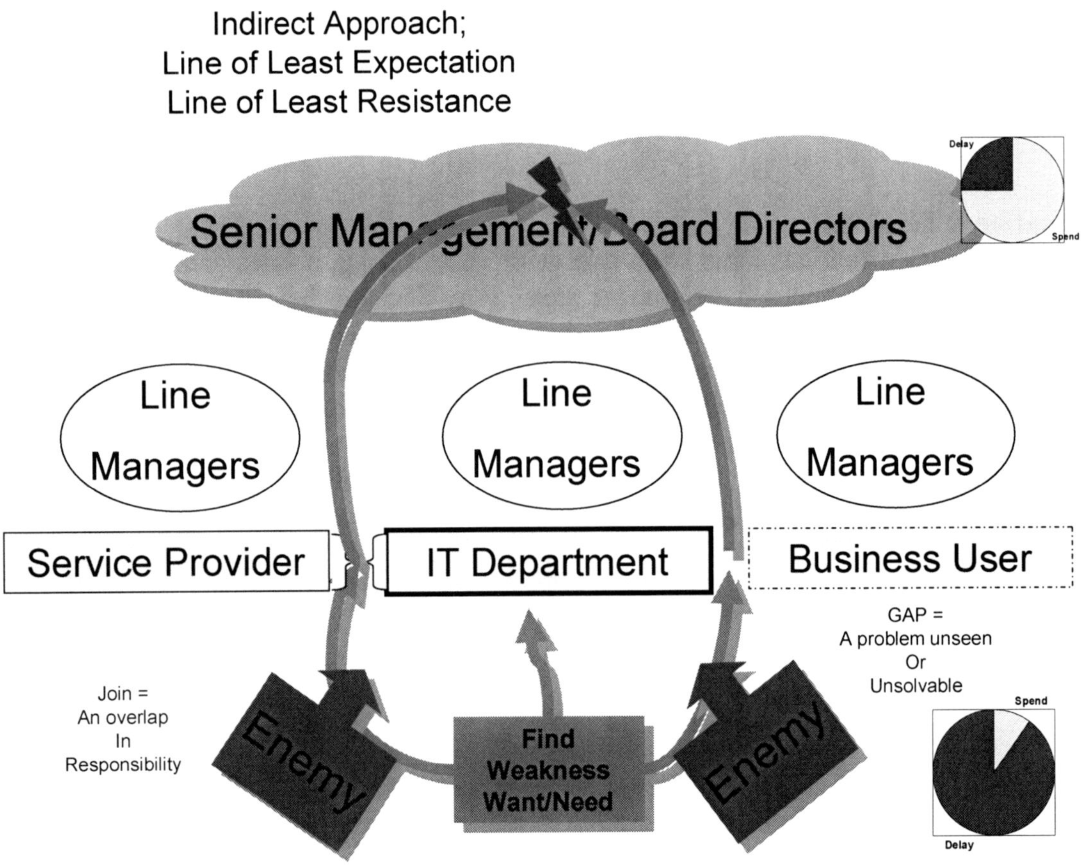

Remember your aim is to gain control of the customer centre of gravity (Schwerpunkt) The board or at least senior management. You do this by showing an ability to solve their problems. Doing this gives you control of the customer centre of thought which in turn gives you control of the centres of action (the head and the limbs).

The big advantage conveyed in working at this level is that you are working with people who are in a much better position to make quick decisions, it's one of the things they are paid to do, and also own or control a large budget, so are in a position to be able to pay to buy a solution to their problems.

The upshot of this is that your competition is working to a longer timescale lower down the food chain, and is competing for less budget, you however are operating to a much shorter time frame and can command a much higher budget for your solution.

At this level, even if you are rejected, you will be rejected much more quickly than at the lower level, so will waste less time fighting a battle that you can't win. It is a fact that you should only fight battles you can win tactically or strategically, the worst position to be in is to spend all your time tilting at windmills.

The Expanding Torrent

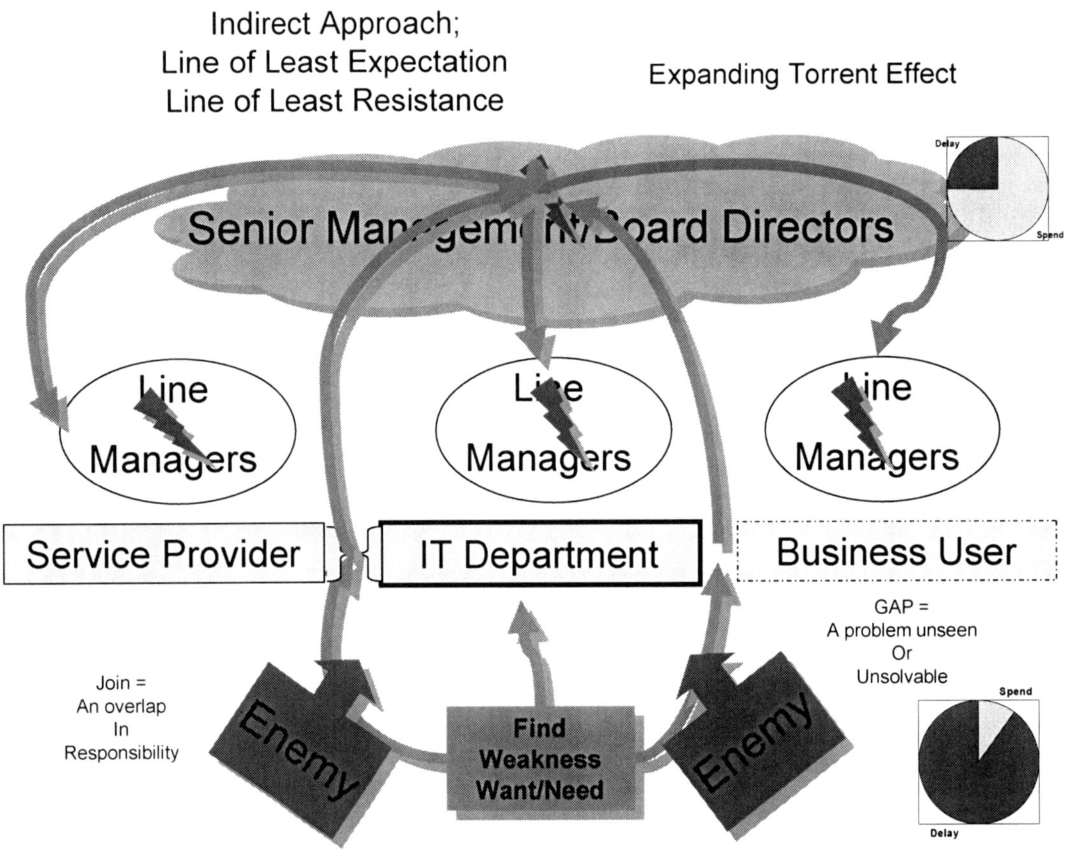

Once the centre of gravity is gained it is essential to push out along lines of least resistance behind the customer front line of conventional engagement to extend the area of control, convert as many subordinate management areas as possible as quickly as possible. This is the "Expanding Torrent Effect".

Where strong resistance is encountered, this should be cut off and isolated from the main impetus of engagement, and you should avoid direct engagements with such strong positions until they weaken or you have time to concentrate on them. Attack them once they show signs of a collapse in morale.

So in effect The Expanding Torrent is where you curtail senior management's ability to coordinate actions to resist your sales attempts by winning them over, you then have a free reign to overrun subordinate areas in detail from behind their lines. Senior management will communicate to the ranks below them what a good thing your solution is, because they have chosen it. Although some pockets of isolated resistance may be encountered, they can always be mopped up and overrun at your leisure with the backing and collaboration of the powerful senior managers. With no chain of command in place to apply control, checks and balances, subordinate areas down the command chain are left feeling cut-off, and can, at worst, only hold out in isolated pockets.

The Ultimate Result

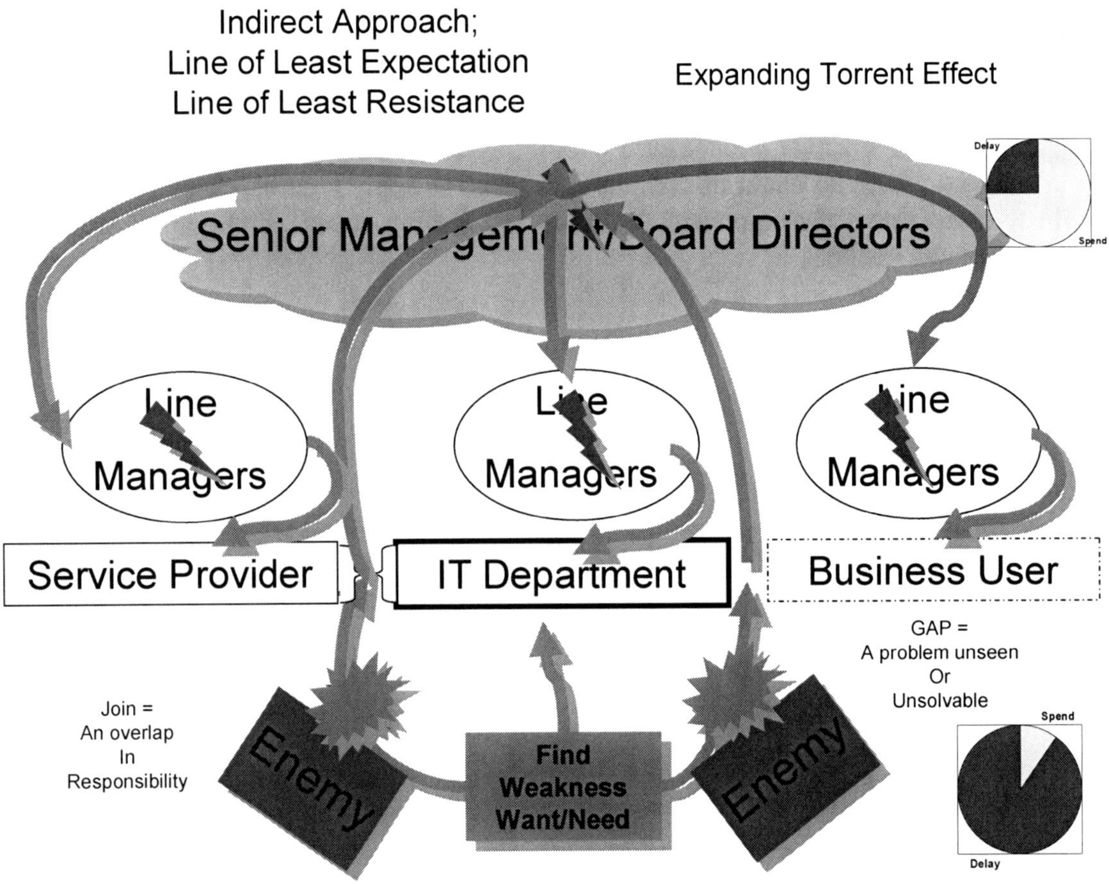

Further down the chain the story is the same with line managers compelling their subordinates to drop their current selection actions and adopt the solution chosen by senior management. This may be disheartening and frustrating for the guys at the coal face who had been going through their slow selection process with their limited budgets, but that isn't our concern, as long as we get their acquiescence as quickly as possible. Interestingly just as in battle, it is at this lowest level that the most niggling resistance can be encountered.

As for your competition, they will be cut off with no where to go. They have spent their time engaging at a level where the aim is to avoid making a wrong decision and a fear of risk, rather than a craving for innovation and excellence. The defence here is based on fear, a natural aversion to spending money, and a probable dislike of people who don't have a proper job, i.e. salesmen.

Differences in the two approaches

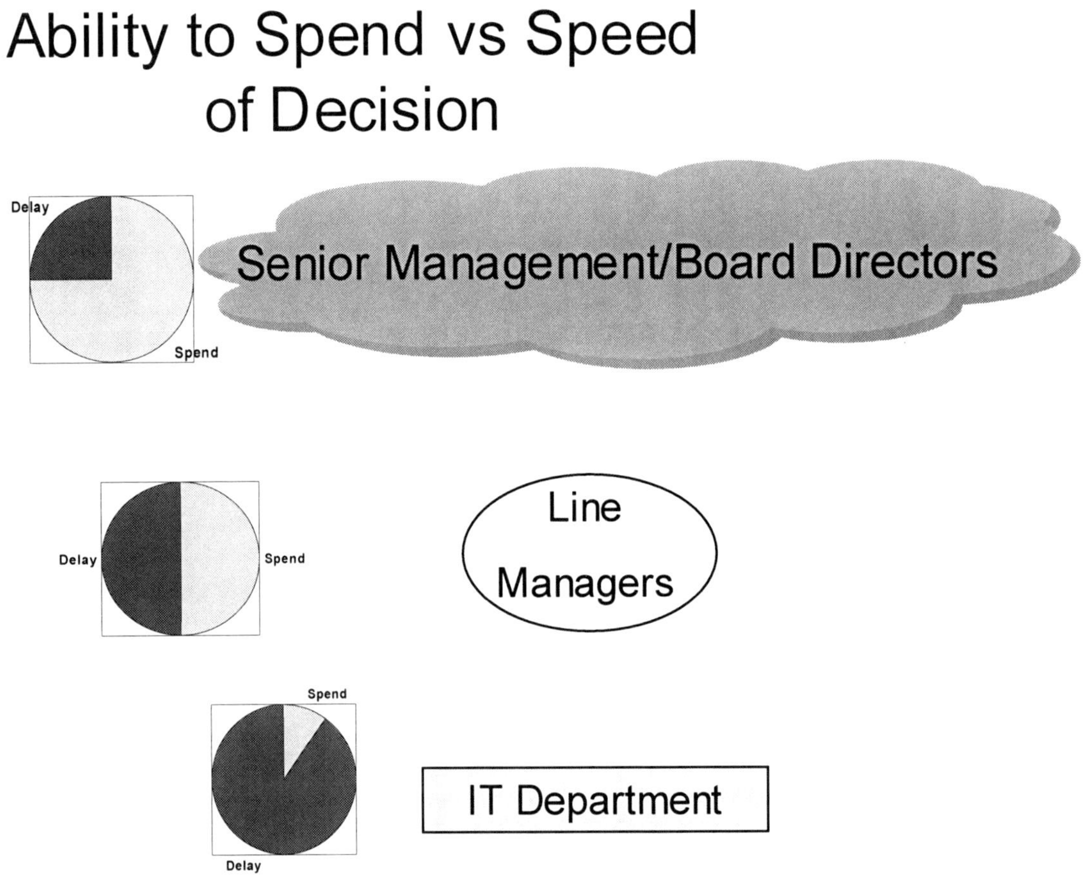

The contrasts between different levels of an organisation are in direct proportion to each other. At the highest levels the speed of decision making is short, and the ability and amount of spend large, whereas at the bottom of an organisation the speed of decision making is slow and the amount and ability to spend small. Therefore it is much better to spend your time at the top of a hierarchy rather than at the bottom of it.

Further, if your competition stays within their comfort zone at the lower levels of the organisation, then they will be forced to work to the long time scales at that level, making it impossible for them to effectively compete with you.

Effects of Working "From the Bottom up"

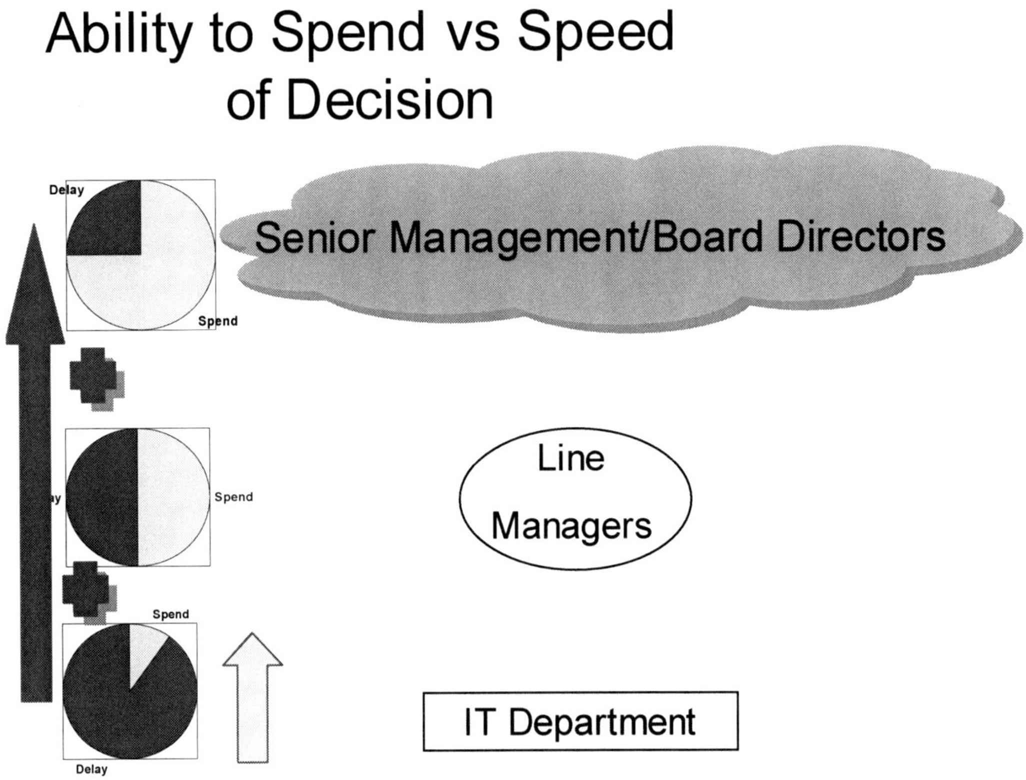

If working from the bottom up, each successive advance to the next management group up compounds the delay to closing a deal as each successive layer of management will go through its own decision making processes with associated delays.

In contrast, the amount of budget being fought over does not increase at each level, as it is only the budget at the lower level which has been justified. So the delay is compounded whilst the expenditure stays static, and in fact may actually reduce as the additional layers of management apply their own negotiations to the deal.

Effects of Working "From the Top Down"

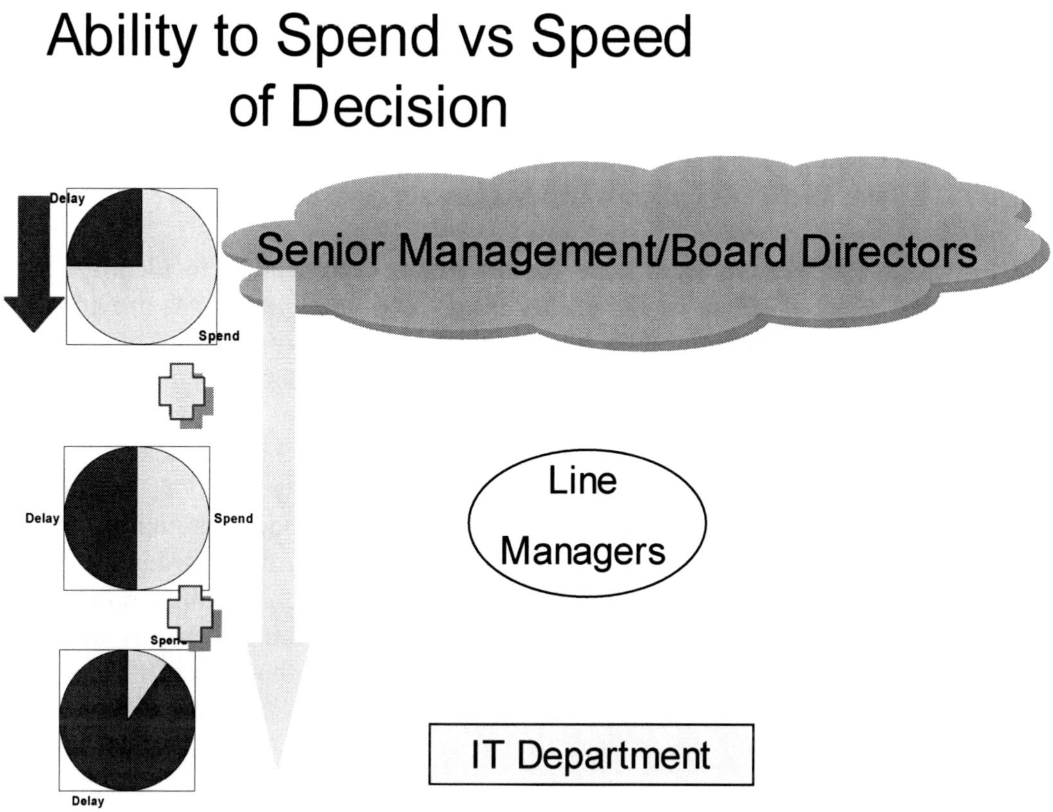

By contrast if you work from the top down, the decision gets made immediately by people who make fast decisions as part of their everyday jobs, therefore there is no need to go through the sales process for approval again at each subsequent layer, other than for reasons of courtesy.

The bonus is that because the decision has been endorsed at the highest levels, all the subsequent budgets in subsidiary levels are added to the win on the way down.

Military Example

Liddell Hart's theories were born out of the carnage he witnessed during the first world war, and two innovative attempts to break the deadlock on the western front in Belgium and France. One set of tactics which influenced him was the German Storm Troop Infiltration Tactics of the German Commander Luddendorf which will be discussed below; the other was the British Plan 1919 Tank Tactics of Fuller, which has already been discussed.

The standard tactics on the western front were for the senior commanders to identify from intelligence a potential point of attack on the enemy front. The intelligence was provided by aerial reconnaissance and night patrols, both of which could be costly in terms of the men involved in gathering the intelligence, and in the risk that it was inaccurate by the time that it was acted upon. Once the point of attack was decided upon that point was placed under an artillery bombardment to cut the enemy barbed wire, and force the defenders to take cover. It then became a race; the attacking infantry trying to reach the enemy positions before the defenders could re-emerge from their dugouts and shelters, the defenders attempting to get back to their positions and cut the attackers down with machine gun fire. Invariably it was a very close run thing with enormous slaughter on both sides. If the attackers won, a minor gain of territory would probably occur before the defenders could get reinforcements in place (forewarned by the artillery bombardment) and plug the gap. If the defenders won the attackers would be driven back and both sides would resume their previous dispositions. Either way the situation would soon revert back to one of stalemate. At the Tactical level a change in thinking was required.

The first change to these tactics came from the Germans. Their commander Luddendorf hit on the idea of infiltrating the allied lines with small Infantry Units called "Storm Troopers"; handpicked volunteers, independent and self reliant. Armed with a potent trench clearing cocktail of machine guns, mortars, flame throwers, and grenades, these units were the cutting edge of the German advance.

The role of these groups of Storm Troops was to; probe the allied lines for weaknesses, penetrate any found, communicate successes back to the main units waiting behind their advance, and attack command points and lines of communication. They were also trained to retreat from, work around, or try to bypass, any points which turned out to be strongly defended.

A weak point was defined as any point that they could penetrate quickly without taking too many losses, the judgement call on this being left to the Storm Troops themselves. The general area of attack was chosen by the higher command based on intelligence, and was based around the idea of "Gaps and Joins" in the enemy line.

A Join is an area covered by a "Join in Command", usually between two army groups of different nationalities, e.g. French and British, sometimes between two army groups of the same nationality, but always between two areas of command. The reason gaps were sought as potential points of attack was because it was often found that where there is an area of overlapping command, the possibilities for confusion and ineffectiveness are very high. This is based around a general principle that where no one person takes responsibility for carrying out specific actions, the assumption is that someone else will, even if that person is not clearly identified. The result being that no one takes responsibility. Where this is the case there is no coordination of action or reaction.

The definition of a Gap is an area where the strength of defences have been neglected, where there is no expectation of attack, or where it is difficult for the enemy to defend against the results of any attacking initiative due to problems in intelligence or lines of communication.

Once an action was started the main point of the attack was decided not by the Generals behind the lines, but by the experiences in real time of the troops on the ground. Because the attack was not preceded by an extended artillery bombardment, the enemy were not forewarned long enough in advance to get reserves into place to counter the attack when it came. This type of approach was termed by Liddell Hart as "The Line of Least Expectation", as opposed to the standard approach which was termed "The Line of Greatest Expectation".

When a soft spot was penetrated it was the job of the storm troops to get word back to the main body of troops, so far held in reserve, so that they could move forward to exploit the breach, and potentially change a join into a gap, or make the gap wider.

Once it was confirmed that the reserves were on their way, the Storm Troops would move on to penetrate further, but would specifically aim to knock out command centres by killing or capturing Senior and Staff Officers. Whilst searching out these centres of command they would attack lines of communication by cutting telegraph and telephone lines, and attacking soft targets such as supply and transport units.

These actions prevented the allies from sending orders to their front line troops even if they did realise what was happening when the line started to get penetrated, so it became impossible to stop the German initiative, and the killing and routing of transport and supply units spread confusion in the rear of the front line, clogging lines of potential movement for the defender's reinforcements, further isolating the front line units, and spreading panic and disorder to surrounding units, thereby multiplying the effect of the attacker's actions.

Advancing along "The Line of Least Expectation", the main German forces could penetrate behind the Storm Troops exploiting what Liddell Hart called "The Line of Least Resistance" as opposed to normal engagements which often consisted of attempting to penetrate via "The line of Greatest Resistance".

The Allied front line units were now cut off from supply and command, unable to communicate with other parts of the line, outflanked, and possibly surrounded. It was almost impossible for units in the vicinity of the breakthrough to take any effective action against it, and equally difficult for reserves to be brought in. Communications having been destroyed intelligence as to what was going on in the critical area around the breakthrough would have been lacking.

Ludendorf's tactics are exemplified in the German offensive launched on 27th May 1918. It started badly in as much as it was due to start on 17th May, but was subject to a ten day delay due to Ludendorf using his reserves in another part of the front. The problem with this was that it gave the allies time to study intelligence reports, and in fact American Military Intelligence predicted with a fair degree of accuracy not only the place of the offensive but also the date, but these warnings from the Americans were ignored by the French and British until they were confirmed by the interrogation of a prisoner captured on 26th, the day before the offensive, which didn't allow time to move reserves into place to counter the attack.

Undercover of smoke shells and an early morning mist the Germans made their move, penetrated the allied line and sent the allies reeling back across the Aisne, and in three days back to the Marne, the allies failure to heed the warnings from the Americans, meant that the Germans managed to get almost a 3:1 advantage over a twenty four mile front.

Stage 1
Identify the gaps and Joins

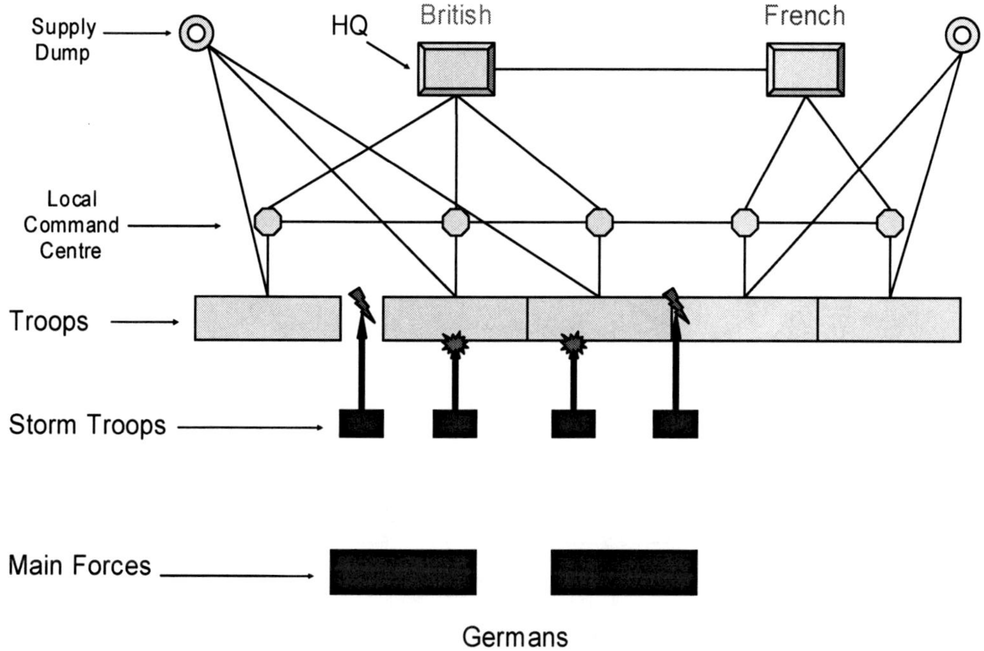

Mistakes made by the allies were amplified by the German tactics; French commanders bunched their infantry into compressed spaces to resist the expected German massed direct attack, which never came, making them cannon fodder for German gunners.

Worse still, once the German infiltration tactics had created a gap in the allied line and the German main forces and reserves poured through, they were able to overrun the allies command centres, artillery and local reserves very quickly because all of these were positioned in close proximity to the front, the speed of the German breakthrough taking them by surprise despite the warnings.

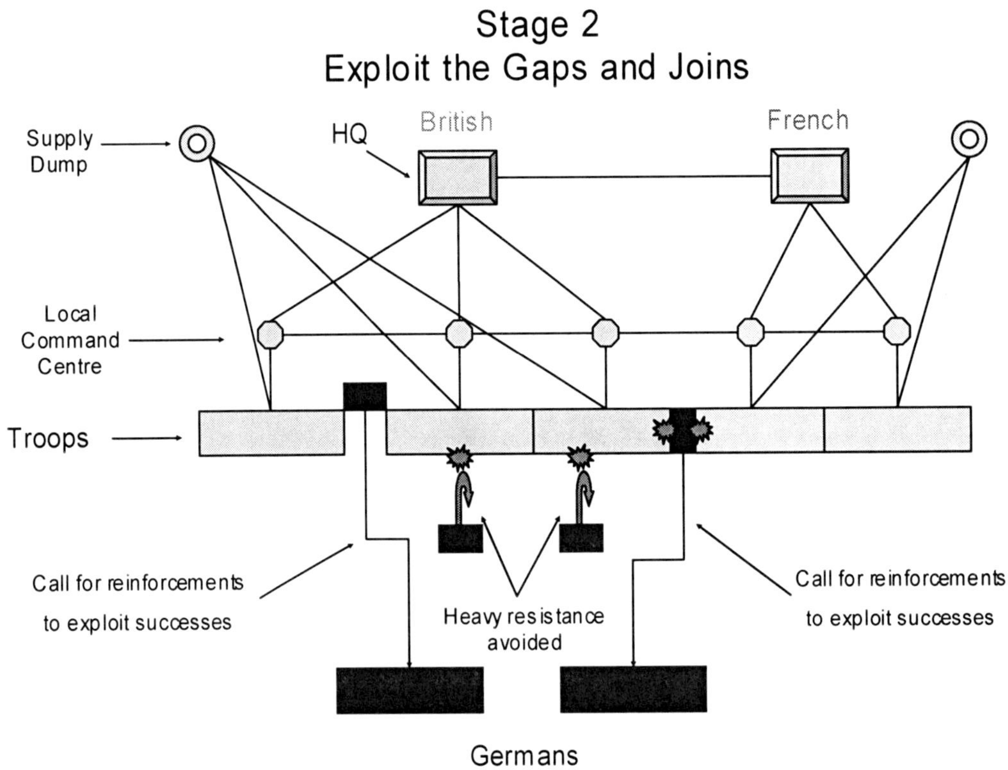

Lethargy invites surprise, even where surprise is expected, and inaction provides a line of least resistance. Surprise is a psychological state of mind that prevents an enemy from taking effective and timely action. If the enemy can react quickly and effectively enough then surprise is negated.

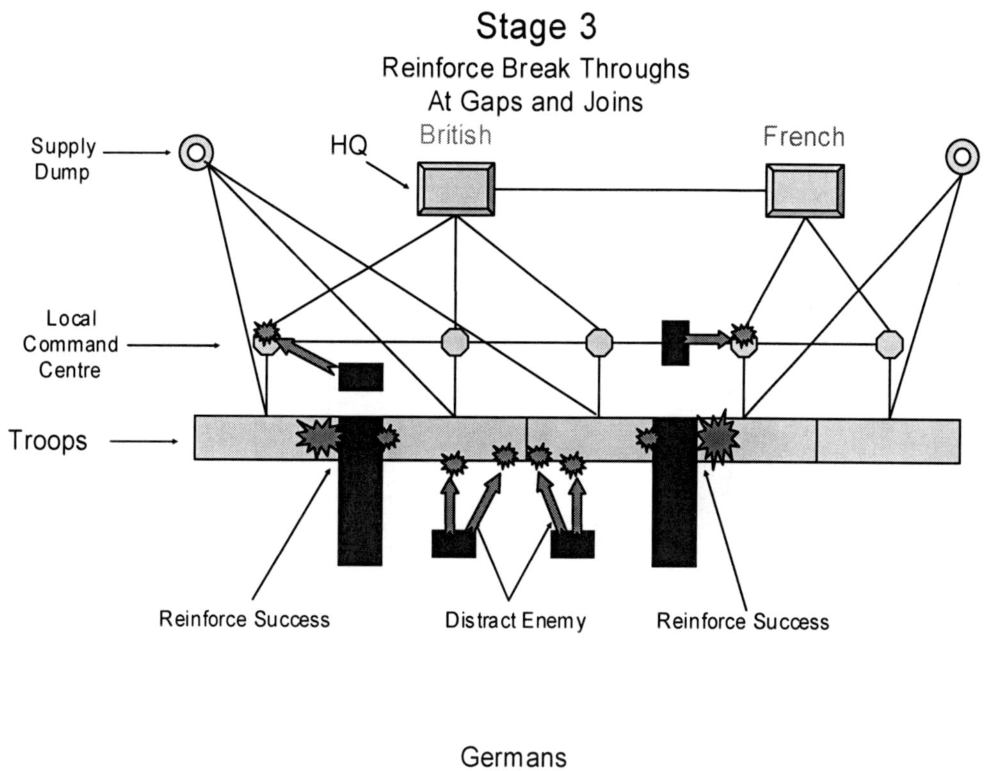

These tactics brought great initial success, with three huge bulges, called salients, being smashed through the allied lines. With large numbers of allied troops trapped in between them in isolated, but concentrated, buttresses.

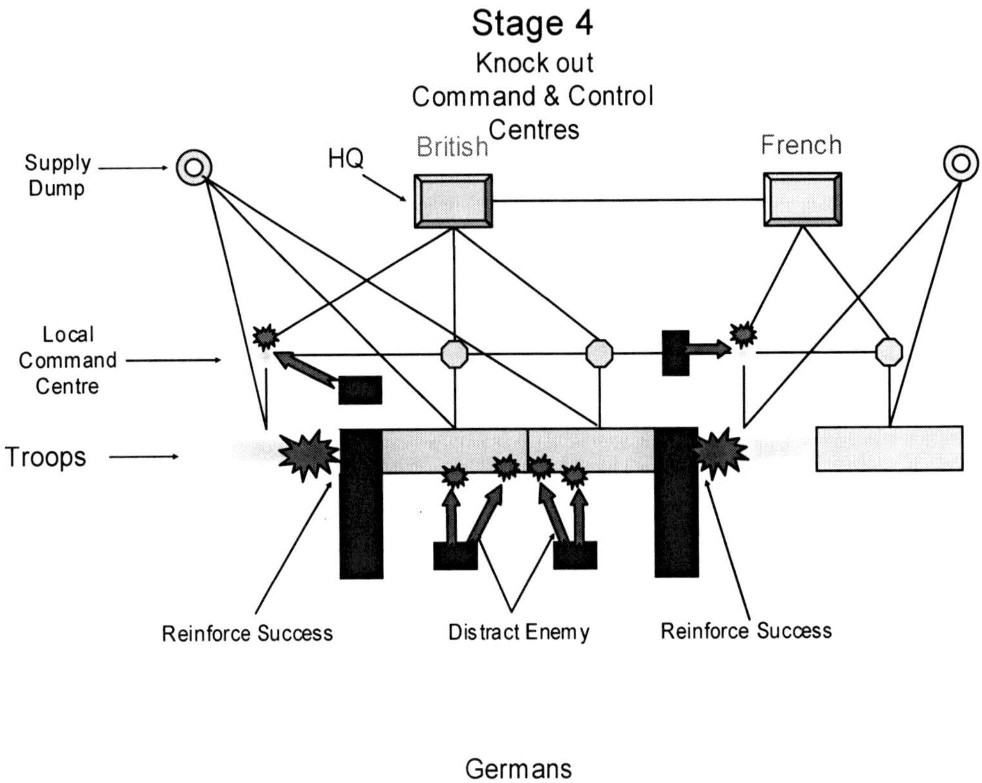

At this point Ludendorf decided to turn against these allied concentrations, and in doing so went from pursuing a line of least expectation to a line of greatest expectation, and from a line of least resistance to a line of greatest resistance. His first attempt on the allied buttress at Compiegne failed, so he decided to attack the other allied buttress at Reims, to do this he had to spend a month regrouping, unfortunately for him this gave the allies a breathing space to regroup and reinforce also. His attack came on the 15th July from two opposite sides of the buttress, and although it had some success where it met static allied defences on the Marne, it was ultimately held by the allies using a flexible defensive front, gradually grinding it to a halt over a period of three days.

Summary: What to do

Do's

1. Adjust your **ends** to your **means**.
2. Keep your **Objective** always in mind.
3. Choose the **Line of Least Expectation**.
4. Exploit the **Line of Least Resistance**.
5. Take a line of operation which offers an **alternative objective**.
6. Ensure that all plans and dispositions are **flexible and adaptable** to circumstances.

Don'ts

1. Throw your weight into a stroke whilst your **enemy is on guard**.
2. Renew an attack along the **same line** (or in the **same form**) **after it has failed**.

The Indirect Approach consisted of a number of stages;

1. Gather Intelligence to look for potential areas of strength and weakness especially **Gaps and Joins**.
2. Probe enemy frontage to test intelligence, and distract enemy from guessing true objective, thereby approaching along a **line of least expectation**. Do not advertise your line of approach.
3. Use the **line of least resistance** to penetrate an exploitable weakness, throw the weight of the main forces against it, to widen and hold the gap.
4. Pour fast moving troops through the gap and drive **as deep as possible, as quickly as possible,** to cause **as much dislocation as possible** by cutting lines of communication.
5. Aim to overrun the enemy centre of gravity (Schwerpunkt). Usually the main command and control centre. Doing this separates the centre of thought from the centre of action; the head from the limbs.

The Expanding Torrent;

1. Disruption: Push out along **lines of least resistance** behind enemy front to extend the area of damage and disruption, hit as many soft targets as possible especially centres of command, and communications.
2. Protection: Cut off concentrations of enemy resistance, **avoid direct engagements with strong positions.**
3. Destruction: Attack enemy concentrations once they show **signs of a collapse in morale**.

Mnemonics

Indirect Approach
Expanding Torrent

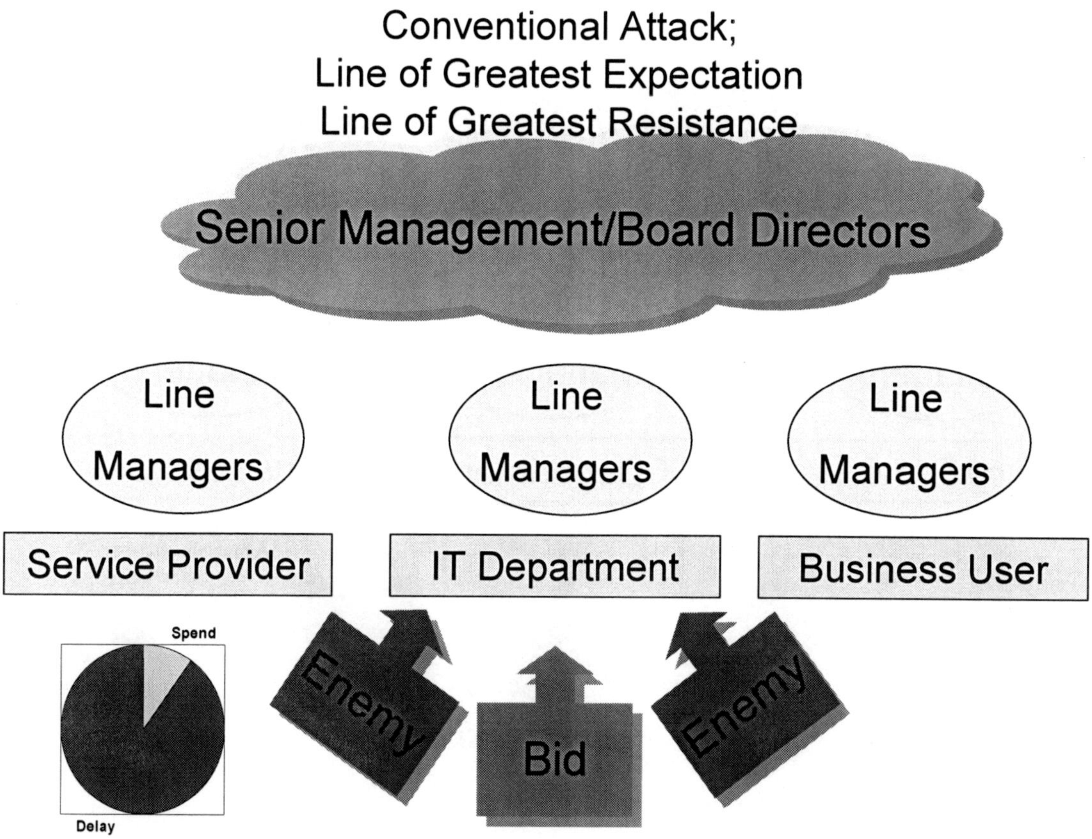

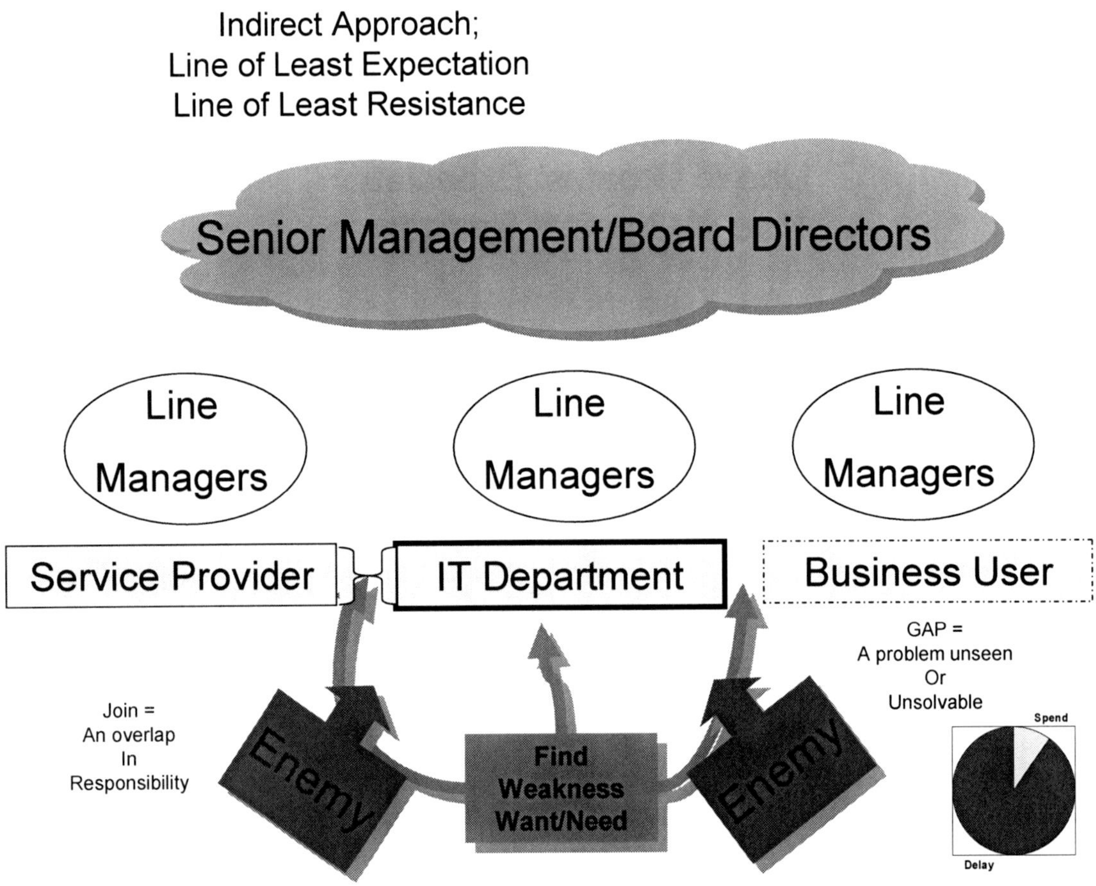
Indirect Approach;
Line of Least Expectation
Line of Least Resistance
Senior Management/Board Directors
Line Managers
Line Managers
Line Managers
Service Provider
IT Department
Business User
GAP =
A problem unseen
Or
Unsolvable
Join =
An overlap
In
Responsibility
Enemy
Find
Weakness
Want/Need
Enemy
Spend
Delay

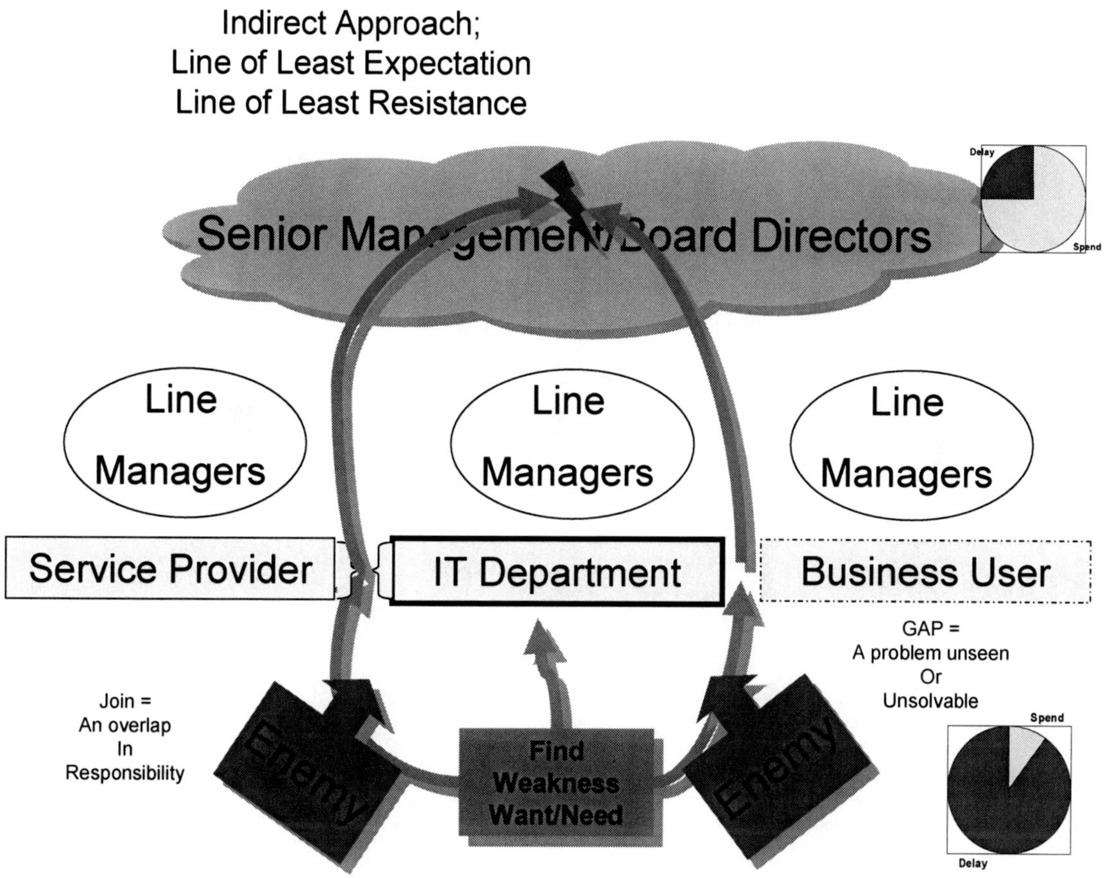
Indirect Approach;
Line of Least Expectation
Line of Least Resistance
Delay
Spend
Line
Managers
Line
Managers
Line
Managers
Service Provider
IT Department
Business User
GAP =
A problem unseen
Or
Unsolvable
Join =
An overlap
In
Responsibility
Enemy
Find
Weakness
Want/Need
Enemy
Spend
Delay

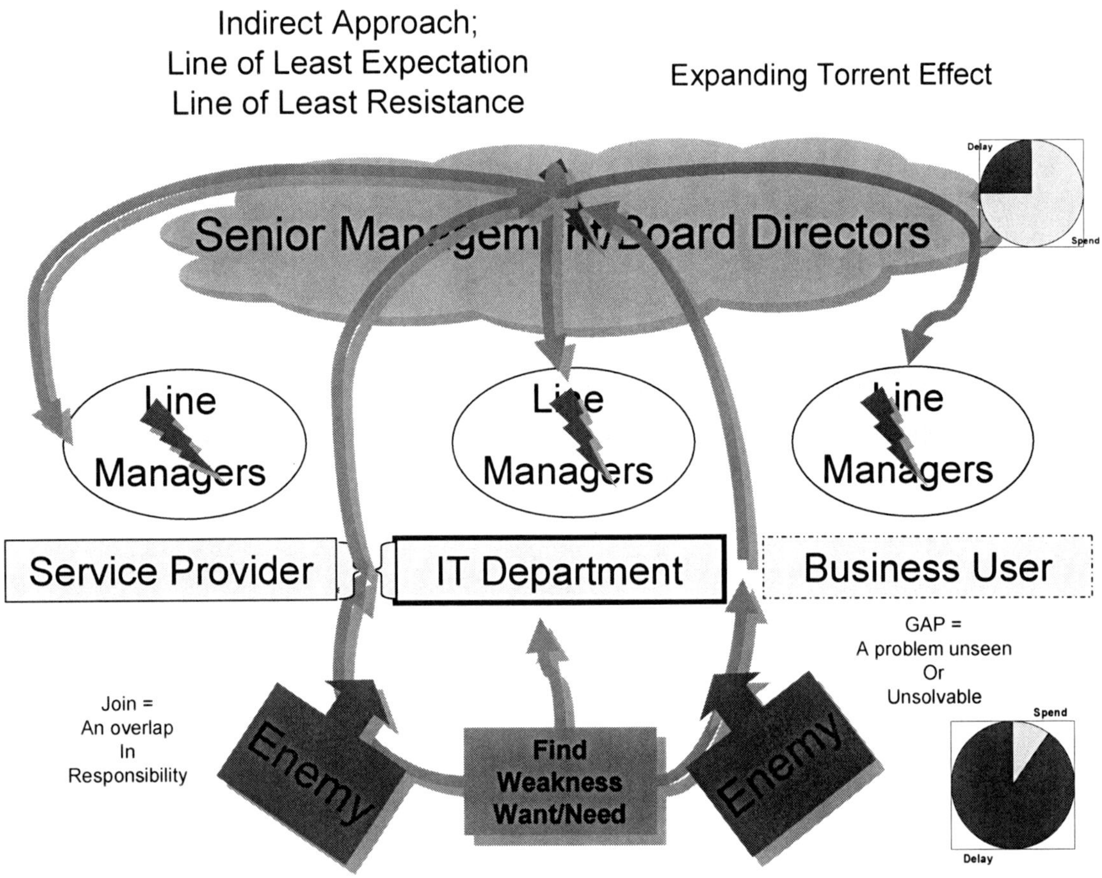
Indirect Approach;
Line of Least Expectation
Line of Least Resistance
Expanding Torrent Effect
Delay
Spend
Senior Management/Board Directors
Line
Managers
Line
Managers
Line
Managers
Service Provider
IT Department
Business User
GAP =
A problem unseen
Or
Unsolvable
Join =
An overlap
In
Responsibility
Enemy
Find
Weakness
Want/Need
Enemy
Spend
Delay

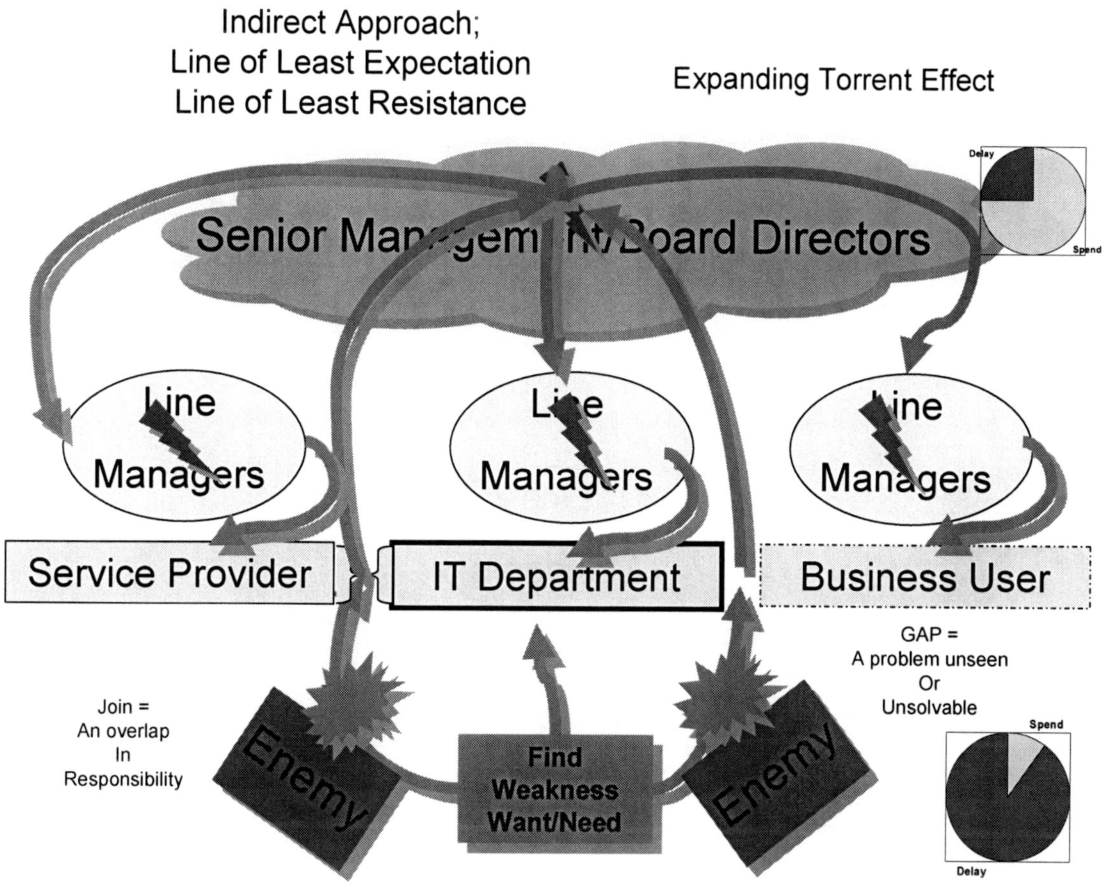
Indirect Approach;
Line of Least Expectation
Line of Least Resistance
Expanding Torrent Effect
Delay
Spend
Line
Managers
Line
Managers
Line
Managers
Service Provider
IT Department
Business User
GAP =
A problem unseen
Or
Unsolvable
Join =
An overlap
In
Responsibility
Enemy
Find
Weakness
Want/Need
Enemy
Spend
Delay

Ability to Spend vs Speed of Decision

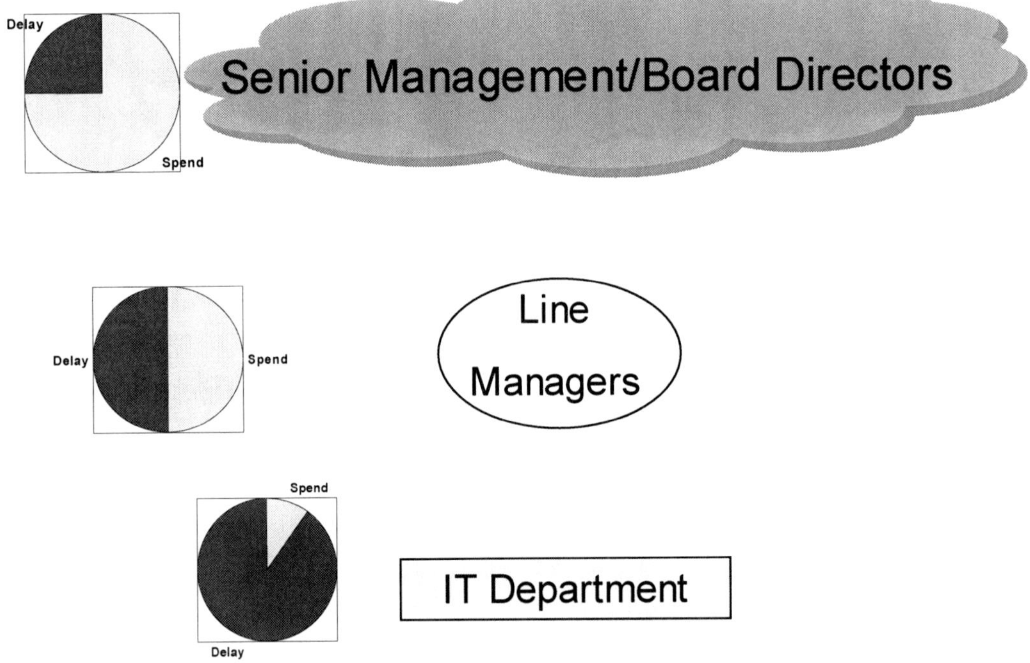

Ability to Spend vs Speed of Decision

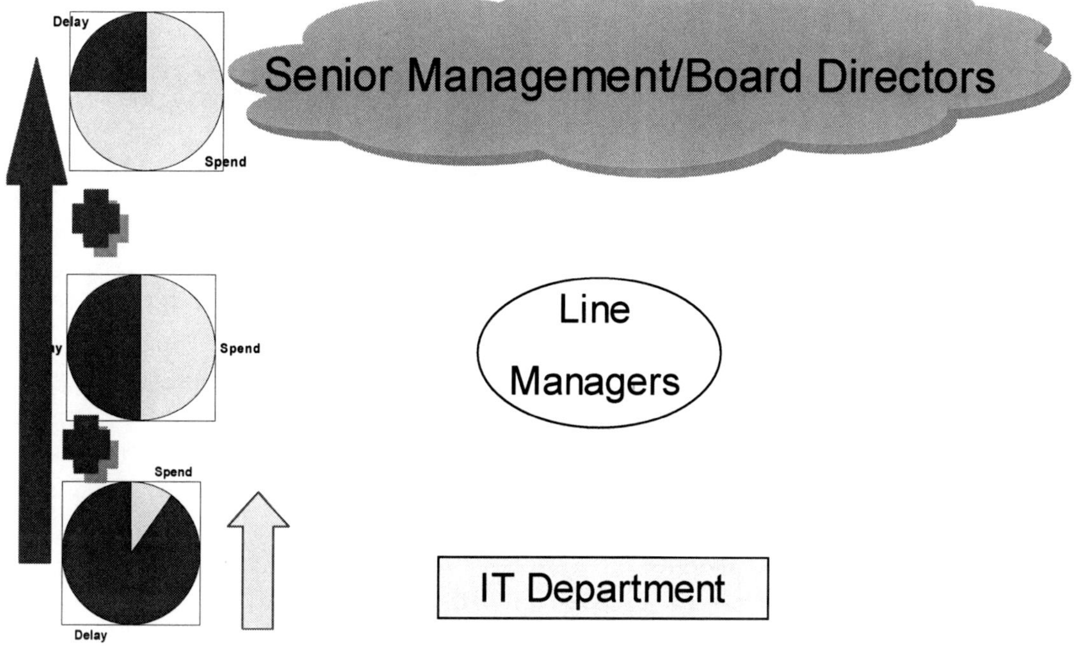

Ability to Spend vs Speed of Decision

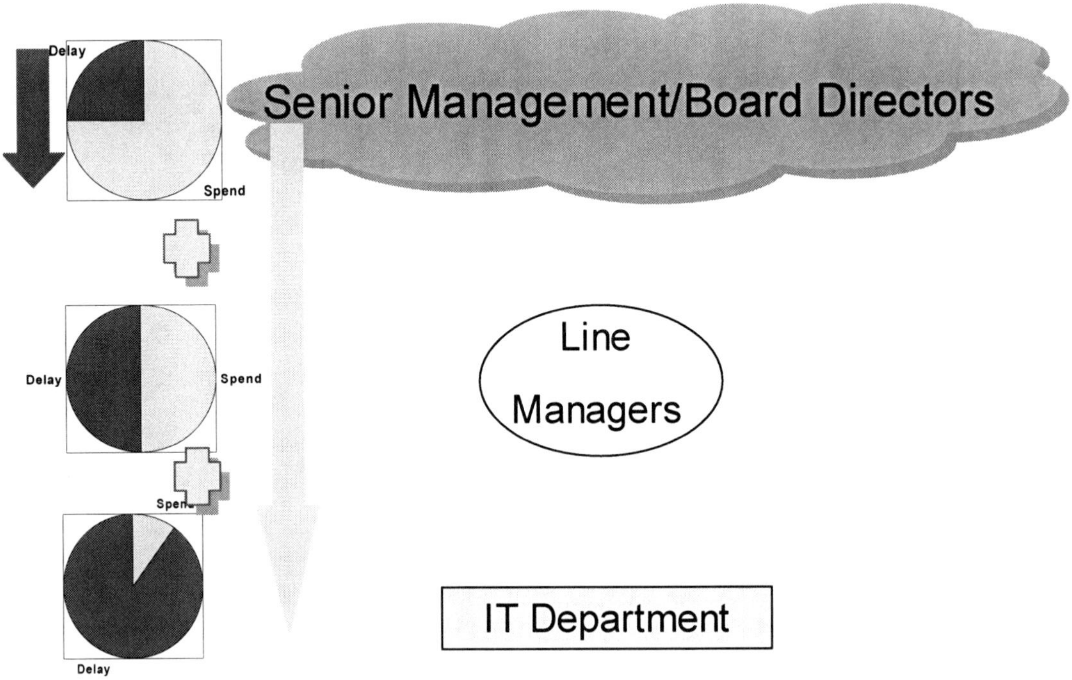

Where can I read more?

Strategy
First published 1929, revised 1954 and 1967.
Published by Meridian 1991.
ISBN 0-452-01071-3
Explains his teachings in the context of historical campaigns.

The Other Side of the Hill
First Published 1948, revised 1951
Published by Macmillan 1993
ISBN 0-333-60214 5
His interviews with the captured German commanders after WW2.

Lanchester's Laws of Concentration

Based on The Works of F.W. Lanchester (1868-1946)

Who was he?

Was an English inventor, who studied at Southampton University. By 1892 he had developed a theory of aerodynamics, but he was persuaded not to publish such outlandish theories (for the time) in fear of ruining his reputation and future career as a serious engineer.

By 1896 he had built with his brother the first petrol car in England. He went on to produce a car with a mid mounted engine, the first form of disc brakes, a water cooled engine in 1902, and a system of twin balancing shafts that are used today on modern designs, the crankshaft damper, fuel injection, turbochargers, steering wheels, the accelerator pedal, detachable wire wheels, stamped steel pistons, piston rings, hollow connecting rods, the torsional vibration damper, the harmonic balancer, and tinted glass.

Not content with this, on the outbreak of the First World War, he turned his brain to the war effort, designing engines, and developing theories of flight, which included the basic design for aircraft which remains the basic design to this day of almost all aircraft. On a more warlike level he developed theories for predicting the outcome of aerial combats, which is what will be discussed in this chapter.

His theories have been taken up by the USA, and renamed Operational Research, and were used against the Japanese in the Second World War, especially in encounters between aircraft carrier fleets. The Japanese went on to adopt his theories to help overrun many US and European Industries in world trade by applying his theories to Marketing operations.

What does Lanchester Theory Teach?

Lanchester developed two Laws, called, unsurprisingly, Lanchester's First and Second Laws.

The first law states that where combat effectiveness is equal and combats take place on an individual basis, the side with the greater number of men will destroy the side with the lesser number of men, and will have the difference in number between the two forces as survivors. So the smaller force will loose, and the difference between the two sides' losses will be arithmetic.

The second law states that where combat effectiveness is equal, but combat takes place where any number of individuals can engage with any number of opposing individuals, (called a Stochastic engagement) then the side with the greater numbers will destroy the side with lesser numbers at a geometric rate, i.e. the difference in kills between the two sides will be vastly larger in favour of the more numerous side than in an engagement fought under the first law of individual combats.

His formulas also show that where combat effectiveness is different between the two opposing forces, this relative difference will have a bigger relative effect on kill rates in individual combats than in stochastic engagements.

In Lanchester's own words he summarises individual combats as:

"...when weapon directly answered weapon, the act of defence was positive and direct, the blow of sword or battleaxe was parried by sword and shield....one man would ordinarily end himself opposed to one man. Even were a general to concentrate twice the number of men on any given portion of the field to that of the enemy, the number of men actually wielding their weapons at any given instant (so long as the fighting line was unbroken), was, roughly speaking, the same on both sides."

Again in his own words he says the following about stochastic combats:

"...the defence of modern arms is indirect: tersely, the enemy is prevented from killing you by your killing him first, and the fighting is essentially collective."

"With modern long-range weapons-fire arms, in brief-the concentration of superior numbers gives an immediate superiority in the active combatants ranks, and the numerically inferior force finds itself under a far heavier fire, man for man than it is able to return. The importance of this difference is greater than might casually be supposed."

Below is a mathematical breakdown of the two laws. If you are not into maths, then don't bother with this bit, just accept what I am telling you, i.e. larger forces win much more effectively by engaging in stochastic combats, and combat effectiveness is more important to smaller forces and to individual combats. This is shown simply and pictorially after the equations. If you are into maths; take a deep breath and dive in.

First law (Law of Single Combat)

The effect of numbers of combatants

Let's look at the result under this Law of a combat between army M with 5 men, and army N with 3 men.

The initial number of army M minus the survivors of army M equals the difference in weapons effectiveness times the initial number of army N minus the survivors of army N or;

$Mo - M = E(No - N)$
$5 - M2 = E(3 - N)$

If weapons effectiveness is equal i.e. $E = 1$, then we have;

$Mo - M = No - N$
$5 - M = 1x(3 - N)$

And if you wish to work out the difference in survivors when the smaller side is annihilated (so if N is the smaller side then $N=0$) you get;
$Mo - M = No$
$5 - M = 3 - 0$

You can rearrange this to show that buy subtracting the numbers of the smaller army from the numbers of the larger army, you end up with the number of survivors in the lager army when the smaller army reaches zero.

$Mo - No = M$
$5 - 3 = M$

Giving you the actual number of survivors in the victor's army;

$M = 2$

What this means that when a conflict takes place under the First Law between a 5 man army and a 3 man army, where their weapons effectiveness is the same, the 3 man army will be annihilated whilst the 5 man army will only loose 2 men.

Effect of increasing combat effectiveness (E)
The initial number of army M minus the survivors of army M equals the difference in weapons effectiveness times the initial number of army N minus the survivors of army N or;

Mo -M=E(No-N)
5-M2=E(3-N)

If weapons effectiveness is equal i.e. E =2, then we have;

Mo -M=E(No-N)
5-M=2x(3-N)

And if you wish to work out the difference in survivors when the smaller side is annihilated (so if N is the smaller side then N=0) you get;

Mo -M=E(No)
5-M=2(3-0)
You can rearrange this to show that buy subtracting the numbers of the smaller army from the numbers of the larger army, you end up with the number of survivors in the lager army when the smaller army reaches zero.

Mo –E(No)=M
5-6=M

Giving you the actual number of survivors in the victor's army;

M = -1

As you can't end up with a minus quantity in the real word it means that in actual fact M looses to N, and it is N that has 1 unit left when all of M is destroyed.

What this means that when a conflict takes place under the First Law, combat effectiveness "E" can radically change the outcome of the engagement, allowing a numerically inferior group to defeat a numerically larger group.

Second law (N Squared Law/Law of Stochastic Combat/Law of Concentration)

The effect of numbers of combatants

Let's look at the result under this Law of a combat between army M with 5 men, and army N with 3 men.

The square of the initial number of army M minus the square of the survivors of army M equals the difference in weapons effectiveness times the square of the initial number of army N minus the square of the survivors of army N or;

$$Mo2 - M2 = E(No2 - N2)$$
$$5squared - M2 = E(3squared - N2)$$

If weapons effectiveness is equal i.e. $E = 1$, then we have;

$$Mo2 - M2 = No2 - N2$$
$$25 - M2 = 1x(9 - N2)$$

And if you wish to work out the difference in survivors when the smaller side is annihilated (so if N is the smaller side then $N2=0$) you get;

$$Mo2 - M2 = No2$$
$$25 - M2 = 9 - 0$$

You can rearrange this to show that buy subtracting the square of the numbers of the smaller army from the square of the numbers of the larger army, you end up with the number of survivors in the lager army squared when the smaller army reaches zero.

$$Mo2 - No2 = M2$$
$$25 - 9 = M2$$

So if you find the square route of this result you get the actual number of survivors in the victor's army;

M2 = 16 so M (the survivors from the bigger army) = 4

What this means that when a conflict takes place under the Second Law between a 5 man army and a 3 man army, where their weapons effectiveness is the same, the 3 man army will be annihilated whilst the 5 man army will only loose 1 man.

The effect of combat Effectiveness "E"

The square of the initial number of army M minus the square of the survivors of army M equals the difference in weapons effectiveness times the square of the initial number of army N minus the square of the survivors of army N or;

$Mo2 - M2 = E(No2 - N2)$
$5squared - M2 = 2(3squared - N2)$

If weapons effectiveness is equal i.e. $E = 1$, then we have;

$Mo2 - M2 = No2 - N2$
$25 - M2 = 2x(9 - N2)$

And if you wish to work out the difference in survivors when the smaller side is annihilated (so if N is the smaller side then $N2=0$) you get;

$Mo2 - M2 = No2$
$25 - M2 = 2x9 - 0$

You can rearrange this to show that buy subtracting the square of the numbers of the smaller army from the square of the numbers of the larger army, you end up with the number of survivors in the lager army squared when the smaller army reaches zero.

$Mo2 - No2 = M2$
$25 - 18 = M2$

So if you find the square route of this result you get the actual number of survivors in the victor's army;

$M2 = 7$ so M (the survivors from the bigger army) = approx 2.65

What this means that when a conflict takes place under the Second Law between a 5 man army and a 3 man army, where the weapons effectiveness of the 3 man army is double that of the 5 man army, the 3 man army will be annihilated leaving approx 2.65 men in the 5 man army. So the 5 man army will loose about half of its strength, compared to only loosing a fifth of its strength where combat effectiveness was equal as in the first example.

So differences in combat effectiveness will have a greater proportionate effect on the outcome of an engagement in single combats than in Stochastic combats.

Simply and Pictorially under The First Law the following will happen:

Step 1

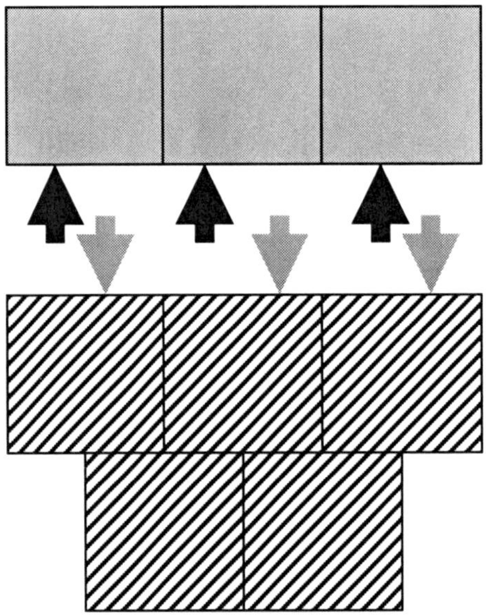

Step 2

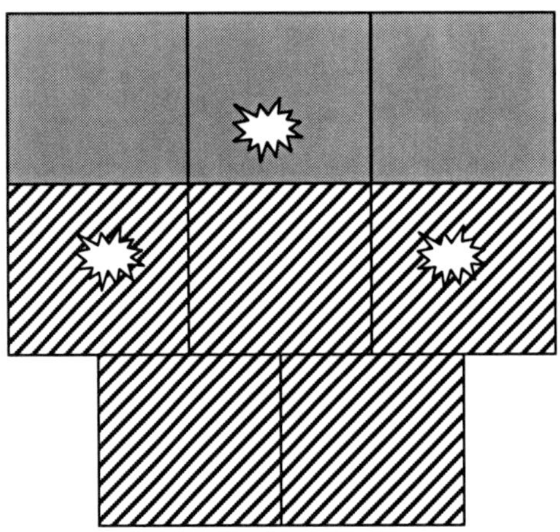

Step 3

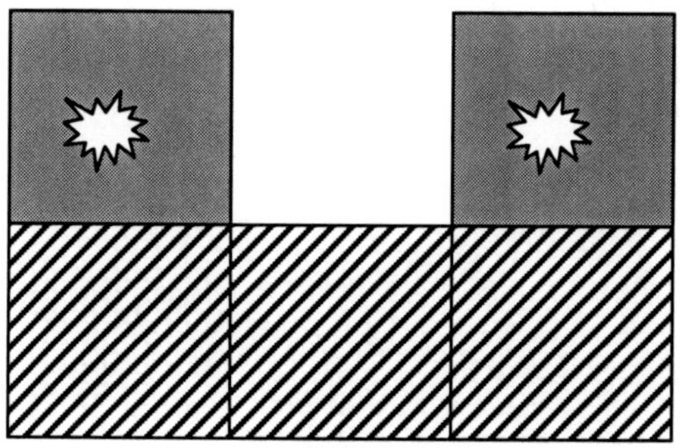

Step 4

Simply and Pictorially under The Second Law the following will happen:

Step 1

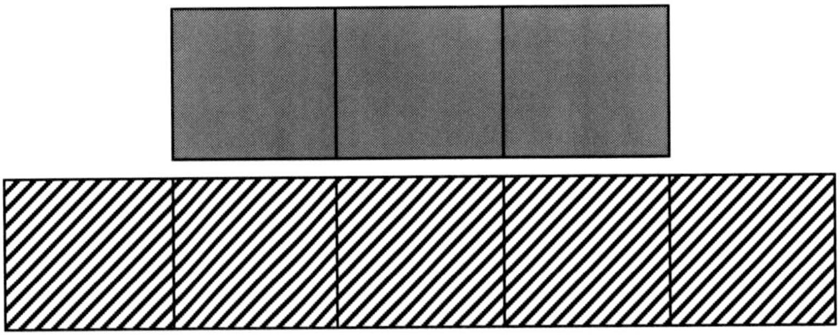

Step 2

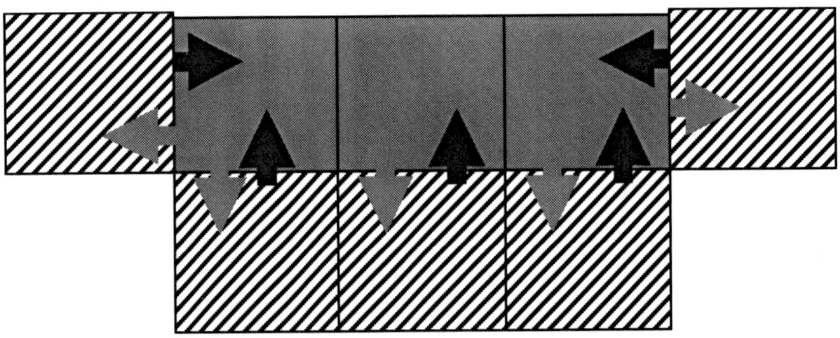

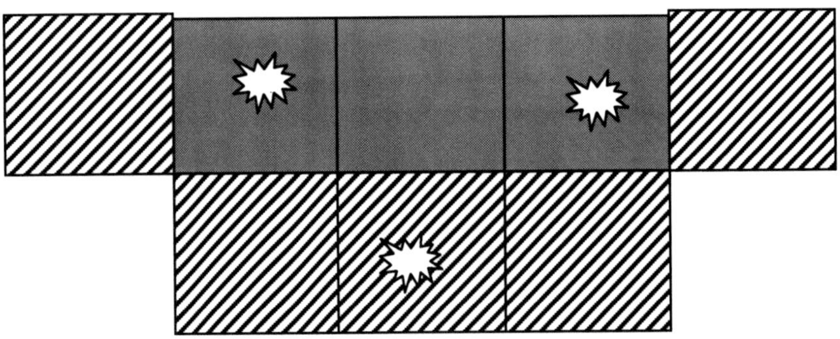

Step 3

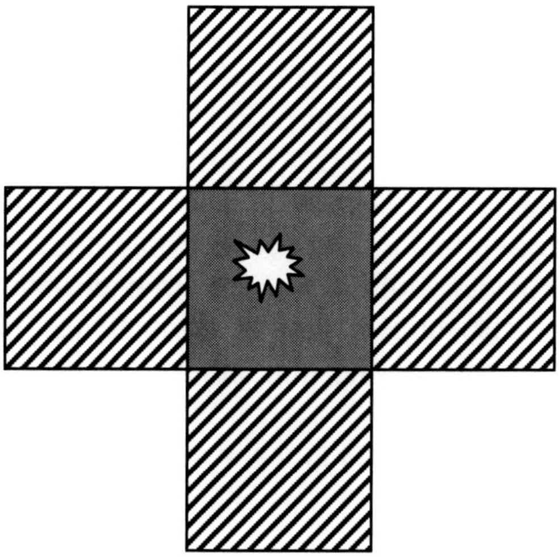

Step 4

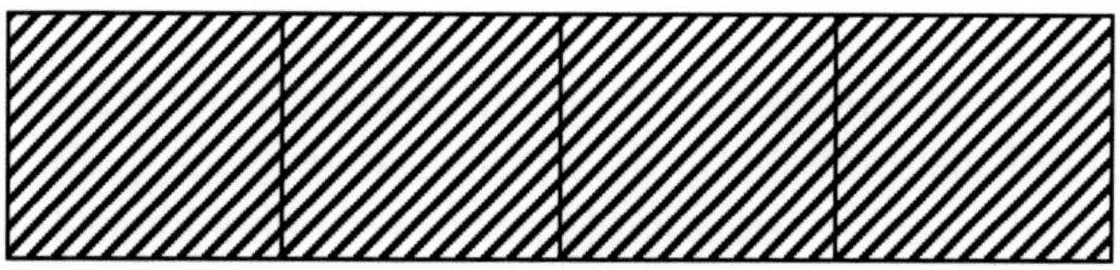

Why is Lanchester Theory important to You?

Because Lanchester's Laws allow you to decide whether to fight individual combats or stochastic combats depending on the relative strengths of your own forces and those of your competition, both in terms of numbers of participants, and combat (sales) effectiveness.

Therefore it is always in the interest of more numerous forces to attempt to fight Stochastic engagements, especially where their less numerous opponents have superior individual combat effectiveness ("E"). Conversely it is always in the interest of less numerous forces to fight local battles, especially where their E (combat effectiveness) is greater than their more numerous opponents. Where forces and effectiveness are more or less even, either both sides will slug it out indecisively for most of the engagement and it's ultimate outcome will come down to chance, or one side will manoeuvre it's opponent into a position where its forces can be split, locally outnumbered, and destroyed in detail, with far less risk and a much greater chance of winning for the side initiating such a strategy.

Why is this important in Sales situations? Because it allows you to calculate the relative strength of you versus your competition taking into account both numbers and effectiveness, and thereby dictates the type of tactics to adopt if you are stronger than you competition, or weaker than your competition. It also allows you to estimate the likely effect of your "weapons" efficiency in specific engagements, and whether this will affect your tactics.

You can also show you how to mathematically split an enemy force in order to be confident of defeating it.

In short it shows you the best way of concentrating your forces, or stretching your opponent's to concentrate your advantages or dilute any advantages your opponent may posses.

The conclusion is that if you can engage under the first law, you must ensure that your E is as high as possible in relation to your opponent.

To achieve an effective encounter under The Second Law, you must not only outnumber your opponent at the points of combat, but also must be able to bring your superior numbers to bear. If superior numbers cannot be brought to bear, a smaller force with a greater weapons effectiveness or E factor will be able to defeat a larger force with a lower E factor.

Conversely a larger force with a lower E can defeat a smaller force with a higher E if you can avoid one on one combats, and the larger force's advantage will be far more than the difference in numbers between you.

How you apply Lanchester's Theories to Sales Situations

In most cases I would recommend that you use the Simple Approach outlined below. If you are of a particularly mathematical frame of mind and are willing to give up your spare time to do the calculations, then the Complex Approach can be adopted.

Simple Approach

1. Decide if you are able to bring more resources to bear on the campaign than your competitor.
2. Decide if your E is higher than your competitor.
3. If both your resources and E are higher than your competitor then you should win quickly and easily no matter what you do, provided you do not make any mistakes, therefore fight a conservative campaign with the emphasis on not making mistakes or taking any unnecessary risks.
4. If both your resources and E are lower than your opponent then you will probably loose no matter what you do and should probably not choose to engage, look for a different engagement where you have some advantage.
5. If your resources are greater but your E is lower than your opponent then follow the Strategy of the strong, see below.
6. If your E is higher but your resources are lower, then follow the strategy of the weak, see below.
7. If you are roughly equal then follow the strategy of equals, see below.

Complex/Detailed Approach: Calculate the likely outcome

1. Decide which side will win. If you are not sure assume you will. This will decide who will be the M and who the N in the Lanchester equations (M is assumed to be the winner, and N the loser).
2. Estimate the relative numerical strength that you will apply to the opportunity, and that which your competition will apply. If you are unsure, estimate the relative strengths roughly. The point here is not to worry about absolute mathematical precision, because there are generally too many unknowns and chance factors to allow this, rather to get a feel of your account penetration or intended resources, compared to that of your competition. This will give you the Mo and No numbers from the Lanchester equations.
    a. Calculate the relative numbers of the sales teams engaged with the account.
    b. Calculate the relative numbers of the technical teams engaged with the account.
    c. Calculate the relative numbers of partner personnel engaged with the account.
    d. Calculate the relative numbers of outside influencers recommending the protagonists to the account (industry analysts etc).
    e. Calculate the relative numbers of internal advocates on both sides (who many customer personnel are in one camp or the other).
3. Estimate the combat effectiveness of your competition compared to yourself, this will give the "E" from the Lanchester equations. If you are equal in this area assume that E = 1. This takes account of things like:
    a. Is your perceived as cheaper than yours?
    b. Is their sales team who are in direct contact with the customer perceived as more effective than yours?
    c. Is their product perceived as better than yours for the customer requirements?
    d. Is their technical team who are in direct contact with the customer perceived as more effective than yours?
    e. What is the relative political strength of your backers versus your competitor's backers within the account?
4. Assume the looser ends up with 0 in the equation, and then do the math.
5. If the answer is that you would loose a Stochastic encounter, adopt the Strategy of the Weak (see below), if the answer is that you will win a Stochastic engagement, adopt the Strategy of the Strong (see below).

Caveats

Bear in mind the following when you make your estimates for the calculations:

1. In your estimates of relative numerical strength, only count people who will actually be engaging with the customer, anyone not directly interacting with the customer doesn't count.
2. Most companies believe they have the best product, not all of them can be right at the same time. Be objective about your claims and your competitor's claims. Don not believe all of your marketing or your competitors without proof, but equally your customer's perception of the relative truths will need to be managed by your, or you will find it being managed by your competitors, and remember for the sake of these calculations that; customer perception = customer reality. Objective truth is less relevant.

The Strategy Concentration

If you believe that you are weaker in forces then your opponent than adopt The Strategy of the Weak.

The Strategy of the Weak boils down to one thing: Single Point Concentration (SPC). If you are weaker in numbers than your competition you must do three things to increase your chances of beating them:

1. Compete on a narrow front, where their superior numbers are of no advantage. This is the Positional aspect of a Single Point Concentration.
2. Fight serial, local battles, where you can outnumber your opponent in the immediate engagement. This is the Temporal-Spatial tactical element of a Single Point Concentration.
3. Increase your combat effectiveness "E" to give you a significant advantage in local engagements. This is the Combat element of a Single Point Concentration.

The Positional tactical element of a Single Point Concentration.
The easiest way to negate the competition's superior numbers is to engage in a very specific narrow fronted area. This may be done by choosing a position within the prospect that forces your competitor to face you on a front fully filled by your forces, without an exposed flank or rear. This will force your competition to engage on equal numerical terms.

In terms of a sales situation, this usually involves taking up a position with an individual, team, or department, who are able to either grant the order, or veto the order on very specific narrow criteria, often containing a degree of self interest. In general terms the smaller this group of people is, the narrower the front on which you will need to engage your competitor, The optimum being a single person who can be targeted by a single person from your team.

They must be influential and politically strong enough within the account to prevent your competitor from outflanking your position by going to other individuals, teams, or departments, or if they cannot prevent this, they must have the power to block hostile decisions by these flanking attempts.

In this way, no matter how numerous your competition, their efforts will be wasted, because they will not be able to progress unless they can overcome your position on at best an equal numerical footing.

The absolute keys to be successful in this area are:

1. **Knowledge** of the critical pinch point.
2. **Initiative** to take that point first.
3. **Tenacity** to hold it until your competition's plans are thwarted.

The Temporal-Spatial tactical element of a Single Point Concentration.
You must attempt to break down overall complex parallel engagements into individual ones where you can outnumber your competition in each individual engagement one after the other, by choosing the timing of each engagement to ensure that you can concentrate your forces in space in order to have the advantage of numbers, or by collapsing time frames to preclude your competition from concentrating their forces at each decisive engagement.

This may well be tricky, and the more engagements required, the more difficult it will be to coordinate. The advantage that a small company has over a large one is that it is often very difficult for large over managed companies to bring forces together in a limited time frame.

So in general the best way to gain a Temporal-Spatial advantage is to pick out the most decisive engagements you can, and collapse the time frames to complete them, either by altering the expected timing of the engagement, or by collapsing the time to complete the crucial tasks. Usually your more numerous but less agile opponent will try to delay the engagement to fit their schedules, or attempt to buy time by lengthening the timeframes allowed to complete the task.

The keys to success in this area are:
Deconstruct the engagement to its basic parts
Urgency in delivery
Concentration of forces consecutively

The Combat tactical element of a Single Point Concentration.
As has already be seen "E" has a much greater proportionate effect in local combats than in Stochastic ones, and must therefore be made the most of in such encounters.

You need to ensure that your offering has a specific feature/function, i.e. a unique selling point (USP) that you can persuade the prospect is essential for the implementation of the project they are pursuing. If the prospect is convinced of this, and your competition cannot persuade the prospect that they can do enough in this area to match you, then you will win, but it is essential that your USP is matched to the requirements of the engagement.

In an SPC engagement, as opposed to a Stochastic one, the required "E" factor should also be reduced down to the minimum in terms of the factors affecting it, i.e. in general it is best to go for a quick win by focussing in on one very specific aspect of your offering as a USP, rather than looking to accentuate multiple factors and approaches.

Criteria should be set for a specific need
Unique ability to delivery must be demonstrated
Emphasise deficiencies and risks of less efficient delivery

The Strategy of Numbers

If you believe that you are stronger in forces than your opponent then adopt The Strategy of the Strong.

The Strategy of the Strong boils down to one thing: Prevent the smaller opponent from operating the Strategy of the Weak.

You must do two things:

1. Study your competitor's weapons and tactics then copy them. This will reduce any actual or perceived advantage of "E" they may posses. If E=1 in the equation, then your more numerous resources will win all encounters, as long as you can bring them to bear, and even if your E is inferior to your opponent's you can still win decisively if Stochastic engagements are sought. This is called a Matching Strategy, and forms the Combat element of the Strategy of the Strong.
2. Compete where your superior resources will stretch your opponent to breaking point, i.e. where their actual physical ability to respond to your initiatives is exceeded. This is called a Stretching Strategy, and provides the Positional and Temporal-Spatial aspects of the Strategy of the Strong.

Matching Strategy.
The primary strategy of the strong is to prevent the weak from operating the strategy of the weak. The fundamental tactic is to use your resources to dilute the individual tactics of the weak. The most basic approach is to attempt to reduce the waek's combat factor "E" to 1. This means that in an engagement you will be on equal terms with the weak in combat efficiency, and therefore, because of your superior resources you will win each individual contest. This is termed a "Matching Strategy".

To implement a Matching Strategy you must use the following tactics:

1. Match weapon (product) for weapon (product); by rearming to match your competitor's weapons (products).
2. Match propaganda (marketing) for weapon (product); if it is not possible in the short term to develop a similar product to your competitor, then announce that you will be developing such a product in the near future.
3. Match tactic for tactic; whenever your weaker competitor develops a new tactic, i.e. price cuts, vertical market concentration, etc, you must match them with the same or a similar offer.

Weapon (product) Matching.
It is not necessary to match exactly all the features of a weaker competitor's product. It is a matter of finding the balance between time to market, and product functionality.

The faster your product comes to market, the sooner you will be able to defend against a weaker better armed competitor, and even if your offering is inferior to your competitor's, just having some means of defence is better than none at all, and will prevent your competitor overrunning customers with an immediate need, and with whom you have a good relationship. The longer you delay before bringing a matching product to the market, the greater the number of consecutive attack points you will present to your smaller competitor, therefore the greater will be their momentum in the market. Coming to the market quickly will allow you to force your smaller competitor to try to fight a war on many simultaneous fronts thereby stretching their resources to breaking point.

The better your product's functionality, the more able you will be to beat your competition on the "intangibles" in a straight encounter, i.e. your customer's/prospect's perception of you as a bigger/safer supplier will make up for minor differences in functionality at neutral accounts, and for major differences at accounts where you already have strong relationships. However the weaker your product's functionality, the greater the number of encounters you are likely to loose, and the more your smaller competitor's morale and courage will increase. With a weak product you can only defend strong accounts; with a strong product you can defend all accounts, and win new accounts.

Worst case scenarios
The worst case scenario is where you do not come to market at all with a product and allow your weaker competitor to invade your territory and take your revenues.

The second worse case is where you come to market slowly with a poor product, which means that you will already have given your competitor enough momentum in the market to stop you from defending all but your most strongly allied accounts and these may only be defensible for a short time, and you will have used your own resources to have got you to a position where you fight battles that you can't win.

The third worse case scenario is where you come to the market quickly with a weaker product you can then defend your strongest accounts, but if you attempt to go on the offensive to a wider number of accounts in order to stretch your smaller competitor, you may find that if his offering is substantially better than yours, and his resources are not actually stretched to breaking point by your efforts, i.e. he can gain enough victories quickly and manage his resources to engage wherever you engage without reaching breaking point, you will have helped fuel the market demand for the smaller company's product, and strengthened them in the process.

Best case scenarios

The best case is where you come to market quickly with a stronger product, this will allow you to win every engagement other than where there are emotional customer reasons for not wanting to do business with you.

The second best scenario is where you come to market quickly with a strong weaker product, this will at least allow you to defend your strongest accounts and stretch your competitor to breaking point should you be prepared to pursue such a strategy.

The third best scenario is where you come to market late with a strong product. This will allow you to displace your competitor from accounts which are poorly defended, and to defend your own late adopter accounts, or go after and win new late adopter accounts.

Propaganda Matching

If you cannot bring a matching product to market quickly you must launch a Propaganda matching attack on your competitor. This involves announcing that you will be launching a matching product in due course; the due course should be in a short rather than a long time scale. The shorter the timescale you announce, the greater you will impact your competitor's momentum, and the larger the number of accounts that will choose to wait rather than engaging with your competitor whilst you have no defence against them.

At best this is a second best tactic, and the longer the time scale that you announce, or the more times you extend the timescale with later announcements, the greater the number of accounts that will engage with your competitor, until you eventually are left with only your most stubborn allied accounts.

Tactics Matching

Assuming that your competitor is smaller and has fewer resources than you, albeit with a higher E value, you can stretch them to breaking point by matching tactics. To do this effectively, the optimum position is to be aware of your competitor's tactical plans before they are able to implement them, and bat them to the draw on any announcements. The timing of this is important, as doing it too early will allow them to change tactics and wrong foot you, leaving it too late, will give them too much of an advantage with early adopters in the market. You must firstly gain knowledge as quickly as possible as to your competition's plans, and secondly launch your matching tactics at the point where they will still have to go forward with them, but seemingly behind you or in response to you. "Me too" is a tactic that generally will not work for smaller companies. By doing this, you can bring your superior resources to bear at the point where your competitor will be stretched to keep up with you.

Typical examples of this are:

Price matching; lower your prices to match your competitor, usually matching is good enough is you are a bigger market contender, and you may find that where the relative benefits of the two product offerings are seen as roughly on a par, a customer will generally be willing to pay on average 20% more for a larger company's product than one from a smaller less well entrenched competitor. Where you have greater financial resources to sustain such a pricing war for a long period, you will be in a position to drain your competition of revenue, wit a lower relative impact on your own company.

Market segment matching: where you know that your competitor is aiming to concentrate their resources on a particular market vertical, you should put in greater resources of your own to ensure that their resources are met with much stiffer competition from your own larger resources in this area, thereby slowing their momentum in their prime market, whilst you with greater resources can make greater gains in secondary markets which they do not have the resources to counter you in.

Mindshare matching: where your competitor attempts to get his marketing message to the market via analysts/press articles/advertising etc. you must destroy their attempt at thought leadership by countering with a campaign in such areas using greater resources, which will erode the market perception of any leadership they may have in this area. The best way to do this is to launch parallel campaigns, one of which mirrors your competitor's messages, and the other will offer either an alternative approach or even a counter argument to those put forward by your competition, you thereby appear to match them on their strengths, put also to beat them on their weaknesses, and spread fear uncertainty and doubt (FUD) amongst the more nervous accounts.

To summarise

Weapon (product) Matching is the prime tactic to counter your smaller competitor; you must balance the time to market of your matching product with the effectiveness of your product. It is intended to lower your competitor's E and thereby do enough to allow you superior resources to win in any engagement, and will give your resources the confidence to take the initiative in attacking accounts rather than just defending them.

Propaganda Matching is a secondary tactic, and is best employed in the period before you have a suitable Weapon Matching tactic in place. It is a defensive delaying tactic, and will allow you to defend strong accounts in times of weakness, but will not allow you to take the offensive or defend weak accounts.

Tactics Matching is a complimentary tactic that enhances your chances of winning where you have a suitable Weapons (product) matching Tactic in place. It should be used to counter and frustrate the tactics of your competitor and thereby stretch their resources to breaking point. It is primarily an offensive tactic to allow the attacking of new markets in areas that will force your competition to fight on uneven terms thereby reducing any localised advantage they may possess in E.

Stretching Strategy

The Positional Tactics of the Strategy of the Strong are based around the choice of customers and prospects who will form the field of engagement. It is necessary to use multipoint engagements to stretch your competitor's resources, so launch your campaign in main stream and late adopter prospects and customers, who tend to make up the largest part of the market, and avoid direct engagements with early adopters. This means using any matching products you have to engage over a large number of accounts that do not have deep requirements for more effective specialised products that would be on offer from your smaller competitor.

The Temporal-Spatial tactics involve Stochastic engagements , where superior resources form a much more important element than E factors. Stochastic battles are ones where probability is a major factor. It is necessary to confront the opponent on many and varied fronts and angles in the likelihood that a number of them will be effective through the smaller opponent's inability to defend all areas simultaneously, they are thereby overwhelmed by numbers despite their E factor superiority. Where there are many competitors pitching similar products into an account, it is likely that differences between will become blurred due to an overloading of inputs to the customer, and it therefore becomes probable that the customer will err on the side of safety or familiarity, and thereby taking the easiest or perhaps safest option of a larger or well established supplier.

Also where there are many competitors, the probability is that the smaller competitors will tend to negate each other with their efforts, and spend a large proportion of their resources on each other than on you.

By having slightly overlapping features in various products, a larger company can force a smaller one to compete on many different fronts on non-core issues which will erode their ability to concentrate their efforts on the main challenge.

Having a number of resellers or agents all pitching your product into a competitive engagement involving your competition will again force your smaller competitors to fight on many fronts on non-core issues, and may stretch them to breaking point.

Strategy of Division

If you believe that you are equal in forces to your opponent than adopt The Strategy Equals.

The strategy of the Equal is to turn the current situation into one where you can outnumber your opponent at the critical time. You must bring about an engagement at the time and place of your choosing in order to separate your opponent's forces into smaller chunks so that they can be defeated in detail.

1. Use very small detachments to distract larger portions of your opponent's resources in non-critical areas, use the rest of your forces to attack his now smaller portion of resources in critical areas.
2. Use superior speed to attack any separated units of your opponent's overall resources in detail, so that you can always manoeuvre larger numbers to attack his smaller numbers.

Sales Example

High E but low numbers
(Turning Failure to Stalemate to Victory)

Initial engagement

The campaign started with a betrayal by a partner company who we were supporting in a joint bid to a prospect. Our partner lead the bid and used the benefits of our product to help them win the tender, but then opened a competition between us and two cheaper, less functional, rivals for our part of the bid. As we had partnered previously with them, and were already being used internally by them, we were very confident that if we tweaked our price, we had nothing to worry about. We therefore marched into the campaign with flags flying and drums beating with every confidence of closing a deal. We knew we were far superior to our opponents in terms of our product's capabilities, and therefore did not take the kind of arrangements for battle that we should have, believing implicitly in our power of E.

So we were given the criteria of the comparative trial with our competitors, but rather than throwing some resource into it, we prepared little for it, thinking that our previous relationship would be enough, we also believed that our E was so great that we could not loose; unfortunately for us at least one of our competitors hadn't read the script, and we failed to bring our E to bear and were overrun by the numbers of our main rival, who pushed all his resources into coming up with a startlingly good demonstration of what they could do, even though they could do less than us in reality. They put so much resource in and acted so quickly that they appeared to achieve much more than us in the allotted time. They had also increased their numbers by courting the people we had ignored, so their greater number of backers effectively counted as extra resources for them, which allowed them to surround us and fight us stochastically despite their inferiority in actual E. Once close combat was engaged in a spear and shield could be as effective as a rifle with a bayonet, as a rifle without bullets is merely a stick. So, surrounded, and unable to bring our E to bear after the initial contact with the enemy, we were soundly beaten.

Their initiative after the first engagement.

Next our competitor attempted to use the momentum of their initial success as a springboard into the partner's internal systems where we were incumbent, albeit on a very limited scale.

This is where we were already showing our E in its concentrated form, where we were barricaded in a tightly defended area with people who were used to our product, and prepared to fight to the last to avoid being forced to use an inferior one. Here our competitor could not bring numbers to bear on the place of engagement as we were always able to show functionality and benefits, in a real world deployment, rather than the smoke and mirrors of a product demo. So we destroyed his arguments in droves, and their attempts to overrun our position left the ground littered with our competitor's broken promises and false claims. Simply put, our E was much stronger than theirs when properly deployed, and no matter what their numbers were in terms of resources and backers, as long as our few backers in the fortified position refused to break, they could hold them off indefinitely.

So after a vicious and bloody engagement, our competitor had to withdraw, to lick their wounds in the face of grim determination and firepower; the E of our forces. However we could not do anything immediately after this other than hold our position, as we did not have the numerical strength (internal backers) to pursue them at that stage. We would need to marshal our forces in order to fight them on a concentrated killing ground where our E would blow them away, despite their backers.

The final reckoning

But we bided our time, regrouped, and prepared a careful strategy, as it became obvious over time that our competitor could not deliver the benefits they had claimed for the tender they had been put into by our partner. This focussed the minds of the people within the partner company on the power of our E for their bids and delivery; it allowed us to take them on in other bids, where their obvious lack of E was exposed by their previous failure. In addition we had caused them to reduce their prices so much because of this difference in E (whilst maintaining ours), that they had become demoralised, and had lost the input of resources that had previously been available to them. Their internal allies had gradually dropped away as their lack of ability had become apparent. So although they could still muster more resources than we could overall, their E was so comparatively low that they were at an extreme disadvantage, and we could effectively fight stochastically from a distance and prevent them from even taking part in bids. This was the vindication of our superiority.

So we had a bitter taste and had learned a sore lesson, but it had paid off, by keeping our nerve, regrouping, and fighting a campaign where our obvious advantages in E could be brought to bear.

Example of Single Point Concentration

A business example from my own experience was were I had a very strong relationship with a Technical Manager in an account, shared a sense of humour with him, went to diner with him and his wife, made sure he was invited to all my company's trade shows, and ensured that he understood my company's philosophy of good support and after sales service for our customers. When tenders came up he was appointed as the "Technical Gatekeeper", i.e. the person who, irrespective of his actual position in the Management Hierarchy of the organisation, could veto a decision based on his own analysis of relative offerings. So he was not a budget holder, and could not decide unilaterally to go out and seek solutions, but he was the person who had the power of veto on decisions, so I identified him as the single entry point which must be traversed if entry into the account was to take place, i.e. if there was ever a tender for product he was the narrow pass, the holding of which would prevent a competitor of any size invading the account. So the Positional tactical element in this instance was identified as a particular individual.

Sure enough, when the time for a tender arose, we were invited to tender in the normal process, and did so, knowing that our competitor had not realised the strength that holding this one pass would give us. Our large competitor ran all over the account, and did a good job, through his superior numbers in reaching areas around us, but the flanks and rear of this particular position were unassailable, as all product offerings in the tender would need to be funnelled through the position effectively held by us.

Now, there was nothing untoward in this relationship, it was businesslike and professional, there were no undue personal incentives offered, nor was there any coercion, he was simply made to feel that, all other things being equal, he would have a better, and therefore more effective, ongoing professional relationship with us than our competitor. Indeed there was nothing to stop any our competitor from taking the same approach, unfortunately for them they just assumed that their numbers would prevail without understanding the value of an unassailable position at the decisive point of entry to the account, infarct so confident of their numbers were they, that they didn't even know that such a position existed until they marched up to it. Once there, they found that all their numbers meant nothing, they continued expending huge amounts of time in the account, probing for other paths in, and were successful up to the point where they found that all these paths ultimately lead back to the pass held by us.

We now had to collapse the time frames for testing the two solutions in both urgency and duration. Having spent the time "occupying the pass" we were already fully conversant and prepared for the tests, and persuaded him that if our competition was confident, then there was no time to waste in bringing this to a conclusion, setting a short maximum timescale and suggesting that a measurement of the time required to complete the trial by each company should be taking into account as an indication of efficiency of the relative solutions gave us the Temporal-Spatial tactical element of the engagement.

The last requirement to win the SPC was to ensure that he was fully briefed on our offerings USPs and therefore gave these a high rating in the comparison. We were also able to use our knowledge of his environment and requirements to ensure that our offering was tuned fully to his environment. These factors gave as an "E" factor that ensured that we would win the Combat tactical element of the engagement.

In summary you must identify the decisive pinch point in the account that will give you an unassailable defensive point on a narrow front, The Positional Tactical Element, and concentrate your efforts on engaging your opponent there. Next ensure that the start date and the duration of the engagement suites your forces, and forces your competitor to engage at a time and over a time period that will ensure that he is weaker numerically, this is the Temporal Spatial tactical element. And lastly when you do engage ensure that your "E" is narrowly defined and specifically tailored to the engagement, this is the Combat Tactical Element of the engagement.

Military Example of Strategy of the Equal

The "Nelson Touch"

The traditional way of engaging in combat for fighting ships in the age of sail had been in parallel lines of opposing ships, sails billowing, guns blasting, splinters of blasted decking flying, essentially individual combat with a very small amount of concentration of fire as chance and weapon skill gave either side a slight advantage. It meant that larger fleets would generally beat smaller fleets, but at great loss to themselves.

By the 1780s the French, generally outclassed by the weapons handling and general seamanship of the British Royal Navy, had started to introduce some defensive tactics allowing them to have a limited concentration of fire against the leading ships of a British fleet usually in Line abreast, by forming a column (Line Ahead) firing their guns, then veering away to another defensive position before repeating the process. This reduced their losses but made it very difficult for them to win an engagement, as the battle became one of limited engagement and maneuver, with the French attempting to "jab" and move aside, whilst the British would attempt to bring them toe to toe to knock them out. The French Admiral Suffren put French defeats by the Royal Navy down to "the introduction of tactics" which he called "the veil of timidity". Despite these comments, by an old sea dog feeling that honour was more important than expediency, the French did manage to protect their own numbers whilst whittling down their British opponents by such tactics, provided they did not try any complex maneuvers.

In 1782 a change in tactics was brought about by the actions of Admiral Rodney in the Battle of the Saints just off the Dominican coast in the Caribbean. Being outnumbered by the French and Spanish fleets, who had captured the island of St Kitts, and were about to attack Jamaica, Rodney, in best Royal Naval tradition, decided to attack. On the morning of the battle Sir Charles Douglas, Captain of the Fleet, memorably awakened Rodney with the report that "God has given us the enemy on the lee bow". Like the Knights Templar, it could be said of the Royal Navy that when necessity arose they never asked about the numbers of the enemy, just where they could be found.

It was what Rodney did tactically rather than just the bravery of him and his men that is instructive. Rather than coming to grips one to one in line as would normally have happened where the British had the advantage of the wind, and therefore the French couldn't adopt their defensive tactics, Rodney instead lead his ships directly at the centre of the Franco-Spanish line, cutting it, and separating the rear of the enemy fleet from the leading half. This allowed him to concentrate his guns against this rear section of ships and the rear of the front section of enemy ships, before the rest of the Franco-Spanish fleet could manoeuvre around to join the fight. The fact that it was mainly the rear that was attacked was not in itself important, it was the fact that only a fraction of the enemy numbers could engage at any given time that made the difference. It could actually take some hours for the front of a sail driven naval column, depending on wind conditions, to turn around and get back within range of the enemy.

This tactic of Rodney's set the tone for British Naval encounters for at least the next twenty years, and so in 1805 we come to Nelson and Trafalgar. Nelson was fully conversant with the idea of cutting the enemy line, especially if outnumbered, to allow concentration of fire on the rear of the enemy fleet. In fact this was such a well known British Naval Tactic that the French commanding Admiral, Villeneuve, at the Battle of Trafalgar, had briefed his staff on exactly what Nelson's tactics would be, he actually told them "The British Fleet will not be formed in a line of battle parallel to the combined fleet according to the usage of former day. Nelson, assuming him to be, as represented, really in command will seek to break our line, envelop our rear, and overpower with groups of his ships as many as he can isolate and cut off."

Villeneuve was absolutely correct in his foresight, but Nelson added his own refinements to the standard battering ram approach to the enemy line. His instructions to his staff called for his smaller fleet to be broken up into three sections, seemingly counter intuitive, the idea of dividing you force when already facing a larger enemy, but there was cold calculating method to his madness, displaying his tactical genius, and the confidence he held in his men. His plan was to divide his fleet into two squadrons of 16 ships and one of 8 ships. He expected to find the Franco-Spanish fleet in line ahead, and had instructed one of his larger columns to break the enemy line in the enemy centre, the other larger squadron to hit the enemy line about halfway from the back of the already broken line, thereby halving it again, and he instructed the small squadron to attack the rear of the front half of the enemy line, i.e. the enemy ships that had the best chance of turning around to help their rear ships.

If the numbers of ships involved are analysed using the N=square law, it can be seen that Nelson's 32 ships vs the enemy's 23, represents a two to one advantage i.e. 23 x square root of 2 = 32.5, this meant that once having finished off the rear ships of the enemy, he would then be on equal terms with the vanguard of the enemy force, and may even have slightly outnumbered them even if his 8 ship detachment had managed to inflict some damage.

If Nelson had engaged all of his ships against all of the enemy's the relative strengths under the N-square law would be Franco-Spanish 46 squared = 2116, British 40 squared = 1600, so the outcome of a Stochastic battle between the two would have been the square root of 2116 – 1600 = square root of 516 = about 23, so all other things being equal, the British would have lost all their ships whilst the Franco-Spanish would have had 23 of theirs left.

However by adopting his tactical plan he changed the odds substantially, by splitting the enemy their strength was now 23 squared + 23 squared = 1058, whereas his own fleet was effectively in two parts, two lines of 16 attacking the rear guard and one group of eight delaying the vanguard, so 32 squared + 8 squared = 1088. Under these conditions the difference between the two becomes 30 in favour of the British, so the outcome if the entire enemy is destroyed would be the square root or 30 or 5.5 ships remaining to the Royal Navy.

The other interesting fact about this, is that the splitting of the Franco-Spanish fleet into two equal parts, was exactly the in the right proportion to not only produce the smallest N-squared strength of the Franco-Spanish fleet, but also to produce an effect that would allow the British to fight both halves on equal terms, especially if the small 8 ship detachment could reek some havoc with the rear of the Franco-Spanish vanguard. As the N-square law would not be formulated for another one hundred years, Nelson must have made his own calculations based on experience, which went to confirm the maths of the N-square law.

There's an old saying that "No plan of war survives contact with the enemy" and Trafalgar was similar; although Nelson managed to keep enough of his plan in place to win a stunning victory. The Royal Navy attacked in two columns, more or less parallel, near the centre of the Franco-Spanish line, the third column of 8 ships nether formed precisely, but did harry the Franco Spanish vanguard, albeit in a less organized fashion than originally expected. Also the actual numbers of ships involved were very different from Nelson's original calculations; he had estimated a ratio of 40:46 or 1.15 in favour of the Franco-Spanish, whereas on the day, the actual ratios were 27:33 or 1.22 in favour of the Franco-Spanish, so the odds had increased in favour of the Franco-Spanish.

The Royal Navy lost 449 men killed, and 1241 wounded, the Franco-Spanish fleet lost 4408 men killed, 2545 wounded, and 7000 men taken prisoner. So the Franco-Spanish had ten times as many killed, and double the number of wounded, if the captured are included in the figures, the French and Spanish lost 13,953 to the Royal Navy's 1,690, this stochastic engagement shows that a smaller fleet, albeit with somewhat better fighting ability or "E" (in terms of seamanship and gunnery efficiency), if they are able to use the N-squared law to change the odds, can bring about a seemingly disproportionate victory. Losses of actual ships were 21 Franco-Spanish ships captured, and one blown up, with no losses for the Royal Navy.

Military Example

The Zulu Wars: Small numbers with high E (British), versus large numbers with low E (Zulus).

Introduction

In the later part of the nineteenth century British Colonisation of South Africa was proceeding at a fast pace. On the border of this outpost of empire lay the highly militarised and aggressive and expanding Kingdom of the Zulus under their King Cetewayo. The Zulus were seen as an imminent threat by the British, The White Boer Republics, and the Swazi tribes. Likewise the expanding British Empire was seen by the Zulus as an imminent threat, as were the incursions of the Boer settlers. Given this volatile situation, it was inevitable, despite various promises, treaties, and agreements that the situation would develop into warfare.

After some desultory border skirmishes by the Zulus, some tub thumping rhetoric and unacceptable demands with an ultimatum by the British, the real war started with mobilisation of an army by the British under Lord Chelmsford.

The aims of the British were three fold; firstly to destroy the Zulu Army formations (Impis) in battle, to capture the Zulu capital of Ulundi, and to capture the Zulu King Cetewayo. The Zulus had an army of about 50,000 well trained, disciplined, and brave infantry, but with a low "E" factor by comparison with the British due to being overwhelmingly armed with stabbing spears (Asegais) and shields, a few were armed with firearms but not many. Chelmsford had 5,000 British and other white troops, and 8,000 black Kaffiri troops, some Cavalry, all of these were armed with firearms, they also had 170 sailors and marines from HMS Active with two field guns, one Gatling gun, and two rocket tubes. So the Zulus had the advantage of numbers, the British and allies had the advantage of weapon's technology "E".

Chelmsford split his forces into five columns, three to invade Zululand, two to be held in reserve to defend against any counter attacks into British territory by the Zulus, or opportunistic incursions into British territory by the Boer Republics taking advantage of the British/Zulu confrontation.

Chelmsford leading the central column crossed the buffalo river at Rorke's Drift, and leaving a small detachment of engineers and about 100 men of the 24th regiment, plus a number of wounded in the hospital there, marched on to encamp the majority of his column on Isandhlwana Hill.

The Battle of Isandhlwana

Ignoring the protests of his white South African auxiliary troops, well experienced in border warfare with the Zulus, Chelmsford failed to fortify his camp and further split his forces in half, riding off to support some scouts who had run into Zulu scouts.

Right on cue, after Chelmsford rode off 20,000 Zulus appeared over the hill and descended on the small British force. Although the E of the British troops was considerably higher than that of the Zulus, they were limited to about 50 rounds of cartridges each, whilst the rest were sealed in wooden containers, only two quartermaster sergeants having the necessary tools to open them. This being the case the E advantage of the British quickly dwindled, and was further confounded by the quartermasters refusing to issue cartridges without the correct paperwork!

As the cartridges ran out the E factor dwindled to 1 as 20,000 Zulus armed with assegais were faced by a thousand British armed with bayonets, to top this, the battle became Stochastic as the Zulus broke into the British camp, thereby being able to attack the British from multiple sides simultaneously. The result could not be in doubt. All the officers and all but two of the men of the 24th regiment were killed. It was the single biggest defeat of a regular British force by native troops. The Zulu losses were not recorded, but in proportional terms, were far less than those of the British. So where this battle started as one under Lanchester's first law with a huge advantage in E to the British, once the cartridges had run out and the Zulus had closed, the battle continued under Lanchester's first Law, with an E value of 1, to be followed by the Zulus breaking into the British camp, and turning the battle into one fought under Lanchester's second law with an E value of 1.

Result; overwhelming victory to the Zulus. The British had assumed an overwhelming advantage in E, without accounting for their own systemic weaknesses, which couldn't be compensated for by the grim bravery of the redcoats.

The Battle of Rorke's Drift

Later that afternoon, a Zulu Impi of 4,500 men, fresh from their victory at Isandhlwana, swept down onto the tiny riverside hospital outpost of Rorke's Drift. Initially there were about 400 British and colonial troops there, but when the Impi was sighted, all the native troops fled, leaving about 140 Regular British soldiers of the 24th Regiment, engineers, and the wounded in the hospital. Unlike the troops at Isandhlwana, these troops had plentiful ammunition, and being in buildings with a compound surrounding were able to put up makeshift barricades prior to the Impi's arrival.

They defended their post for a full twelve hours from four in the afternoon till four in the morning, when the Zulus gave up the attack as too costly and withdrew. During that time they fired about 20,000 rounds of ammunition from their rifles, every single British soldier was wounded, and seventeen were killed. Against this the Zulus lost about 500 killed and wounded, plus an indeterminate number of walking wounded who withdrew with the rest of the Impi at the end of the battle, perhaps another 1,000.

Why the difference in this battle to Isandhlwana? Well, the British managed to keep the flow of ammunition to their fighters, thereby sustaining their high E factor, and fighting from behind, albeit makeshift, defences, they held the greater part of the Zulus beyond fighting distance whilst holding their ground and firing volleys into them at a distance, thereby getting a partial stochastic effect under the second law, and even when the defences were pressed, the British still managed to have a much higher E factor under the first law when fighting at close quarters. But it was the British soldiers' ability to fight stochastically at a distance that made the difference to the numbers of casualties; at close quarters the Zulus could inflict some casualties, even if they lost many more than they killed.

Result; a draw. The British could hold their position but could not leave it to exploit the superior E they possessed, the Zulus couldn't take the position without sustaining crippling losses, but could ensure that the British could not leave their position.

The Battle of Ulundi

The turning point of the war came with the battle of Ulundi, 4th July 1879. Lord Chelmsford march on the Zulu Capital with 5,000 men formed in one enormous square, Infantry forming the sides, Gatling guns and artillery at corners and centre of the sides, in the middle of the square were the Cavalry, irregulars, staff officers and supply train.

Slowly, ponderously, but with colours flying and the band playing, the square rumbled forward. There was o sign of the Zulu Impis, so the cavalry rode out and began burning the Zulu Kraals (barracks). After about three miles of the advance 20,000 Zulus appeared from all sides. The square stopped, the infantry closed ranks, the first two ranks kneeling, the second two standing. The cavalry withdrew as the Zulus attempted to surround them and cut them off, they gallop back to the square, the Infantry parted ranks and allowed them into the safety of the centre of the square, then reformed ready to meet the Zulu attack.

The Zulu closed at a run from all sides, only to be hit by volleys of fire, exploding artillery shells, and the steady thump of the Gatling guns. Despite all attempts at bravery, as long as the British could keep up their fire the Zulus couldn't effectively close to more than one hundred yards of the square. It was a hopeless situation, and eventually the Zulu Impis broke and ran; instantly the cavalry issued forth from the centre of the square, and pursued them "...cutting them down like grass before the scythe." according to one eye witness. The battle took 90 minutes. The British lost 82, the Zulus 1,500. Cetewayo fled, his capital was taken, and his army was broken. Shortly after Cetewayo himself and the last of his chiefs was also captured, the submission of the Zulus before the power of British E

At Ulundi the British E factor was vastly superior to the Zulus, the only casualties in the British ranks came from the few Zulu sharpshooters. This meant that the Zulus couldn't close, and the British weapons effectively allowed them to engage stochastically with the Zulus from a distance, there was absolutely no way that the Zulus could win without closing, and the British holding their ground and keeping up their rate of fire made them unbeatable.

Result; an overwhelming British victory. The British not only possessed far greater E than the Zulus, but could fight stochastically, which the Zulus could not unless they could break the British formation.

Summary: What to do

Stage 1 Decide on relative strength and Combat effectiveness

1. Decide if you are numerically stronger than, equal to, or weaker than your opponent.
2. Decide if your E is greater than, equal to, or less than your opponent.

Stage 2 Follow the relevant strategy

1. If you are stronger than your opponent and have greater E, engage in a stochastic engagement as quickly as possible, do not take any risks.
2. If you are stronger than your opponent, but lower in E, adopt the strategy of Numbers.
3. If you are more or less numerically equal to your opponent and equal in E, adopt the strategy of equals.
4. If you are weaker than your opponent, but higher in E adopt the strategy Concentration.
5. If you are numerically weaker than your opponent, and have a lower E, then do not engage at this time.
6. If you are uncertain of your relative numerical strength, and relative E factors, adopt the strategy of equals until a clearer picture is forthcoming.

Mnemonics

Tactics of Concentration, Tactics of Numbers, Tactics of Equals

Weaker, Stronger, or Equal

	Your E is Greater	Your E is Equal	Your E is Smaller
Your Numbers are Greater	Immediate Stochastic Engagement	Tactics of Numbers	Tactics of Numbers
Your Numbers are Equal	Tactics of Concentration	Tactics of Equals	Avoid Engagement, Use Tactics of Equals if forced to engage
Your Numbers are Smaller	Tactics of Concentration	Avoid Engagement, Use Tactics of Equals if forced to engage	Avoid Engagement

Tactics of Concentration

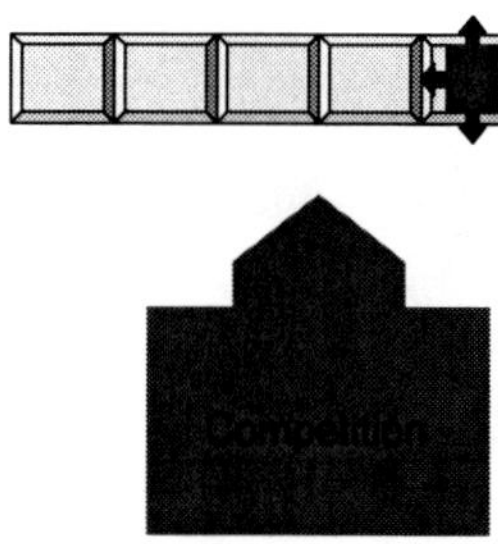

Focus on a
Single Point
Concentration

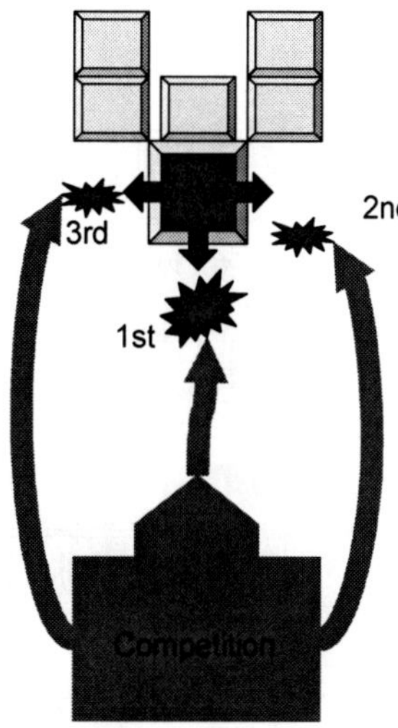

Fight serial
engagements
with local
superiority

Increase your
E as much as
possible

Tactics of Numbers

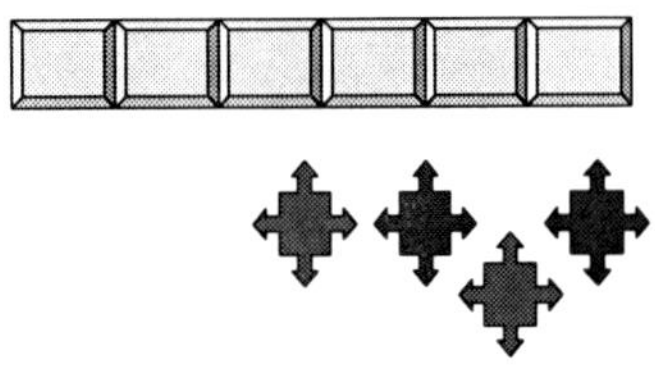

Use Matching Tactics
to copy your
Competitor's weapons
systems and tactics

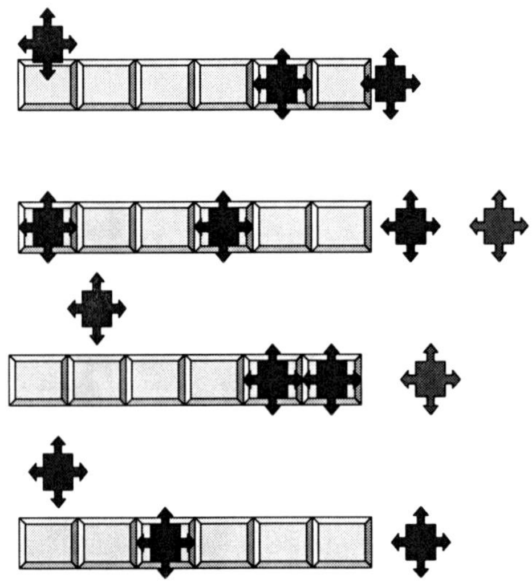

Use Stretching Tactics to
break your competitor's
ability to respond

Tactics of Equals

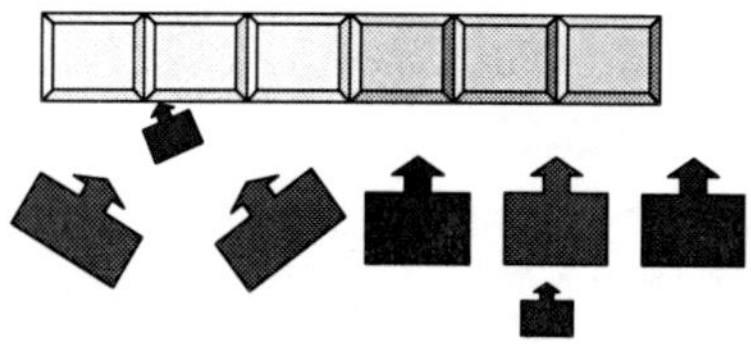

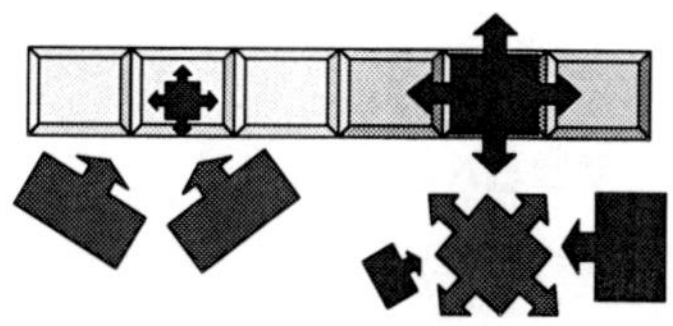

2. Use bulk of your forces to defeat his smaller force in critical area

1. Use Tactics of Division to split your opponent's resources to a non-critical area

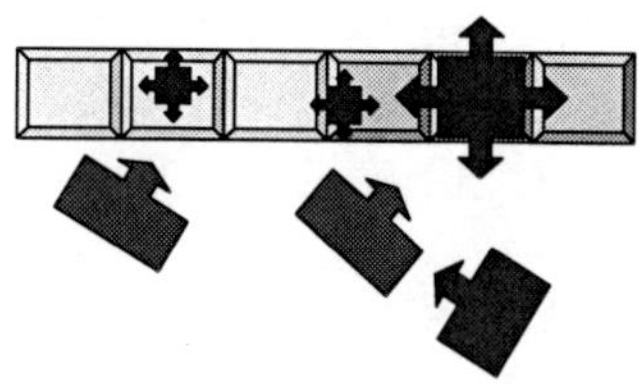

3. Use speed and numbers to isolate and destroy individual competitive initiatives

Lanchester Theory for Field Manual

As a general rule you can use the table below to calculate what is generally the best Tactical Plan against a Competitor:

Weaker, Stronger, or Equal

	Your E is Greater	Your E is Equal	Your E is Smaller
Your Numbers are Greater	Immediate Stochastic Engagement	Tactics of Numbers	Tactics of Numbers
Your Numbers are Equal	Tactics of Concentration	Tactics of Equals	Avoid Engagement, Use Tactics of Equals if forced to engage
Your Numbers are Smaller	Tactics of Concentration	Avoid Engagement, Use Tactics of Equals if forced to engage	Avoid Engagement

Where can I read more?

Aircraft in Warfare
(The Dawn of the Fourth Arm)

F.W.Lanchester

Lanchester Press Inc.
Sunnyvale, CA 94086, USA
1995

ISBN 1-57321-002-1

A classic and hard to find work, where Lanchester outlines his laws, and predicts the development of air warfare. Originally published in 1916 in London.

Leadership and Use of Ground

Henry V, King of England

Agincourt 1415

OR

"How to win a battle with an exhausted army suffering from dysentery when outnumbered ten to one by the finest army in Europe."

An idle boast

The battle of Agincourt was part of the "Hundred Years War" fought, as the name suggests, for just over a hundred years, between England and France. The policy behind the war was to settle the ownership of various territories on French soil, which were at the time, to a greater or lesser extent, legally owned by the English Crown.

In 1415 the young King Henry V of England had sailed across the channel to bolster the fortitude of his holdings in France, and take back a number of lost territories. He opened the campaign by besieging Harfleur, a port on the French coast. The French forces in Harfleur realised after a month of being held within their walls, they couldn't break out and drive the English away, nor was there any sign of the French King coming to help them, so a very civilized surrender was agreed, and Harfleur became an English port.

Henry was so encouraged by this quick victory that he rashly declared he would march on Bordeaux and Paris next. The only problem with this was that almost a third of his army had died of disease whilst besieging Harfleur. This level of loss was fairly normal during the mediaeval period; many more troops died from disease than were ever laid low by enemy action. The upshot was that Henry would loose a tremendous amount of face in front of both his friends and enemies if he didn't put up some further show of force. This could prove disastrous politically for the young King but obviously actually trying to besiege either Paris or Boulogne would have no chance of success, even with the whole of his original army, let alone with only two thirds of it. A compromise was needed, and so a more realistic plan was formulated.

It was decided to launch a raid across French territory, a Chevauchee, up to the English territory of Calais, and then home with the fleet to England by the shortest sea route. This would polish off a successful jaunt, and leave the King of France with the equivalent of a political black eye.

Sales Lessons

Just as Henry, once in France had no choice but to make an adequate show of force, so is the same for a salesperson entering an account. To mount a campaign within an account, and then spoil your efforts with inactivity is unacceptable. In Henry's case capturing Harfleur and then sailing home would have been fine, if he hadn't boasted about taking Bordeaux and Paris. You must remember that what is said can't be "un-said", and the words of monarchs were taken very, very, seriously in the middle ages. In the same way the boasts of a sales person in front of peers and management can come back to haunt you. So the march across country was absolutely necessary in order for Henry to keep a strong grip on his throne, and no doubt, in the back of his mind would have been the fact that his own father had started out as Henry Bolingbroke, and ended up as Henry IV after a coup d'etat against the unpopular Richard II. In sales situations delivery is everything, and a lack of delivery after an unwise forecast can mean the loss of a territory.

Chevauchee

On the 8th October Henry and his army set off on the 120 mile hike to Calais, maybe 12 days march away at the average march rate of most mediaeval armies. The first five days went very well, two thirds of the distance, rivers crossed, supplies replenished, and no enemy action. The following day the army needed to swing inland, away from the coast, in order to find a suitable crossing place of the River Somme. Unfortunately once the English found a crossing place, they found that the French were already on the other side of it waiting for them.

Trying to fight his way across a major river would have been disastrous. Going back the way they had come would have meant moving away from their goal of Calais with the French force in hot pursuit. The only option left was to push on, outmarch the French find another crossing point, and dash for Calais. In Henry's favour the French did not know Henry's intentions, and so couldn't second-guess his route. This was therefore the only option open to Henry that could bring success, albeit a slim chance of success. His other two options represented failure or at best an ignoble retreat and pursuit. Henry was a gambler, but in order to be a successful mediaeval monarch it was much more important to be a successful gambler than to risk nothing, and achieve nothing, an English monarch lacking in courage wouldn't keep the throne or their head for very long.

The English showed amazing endurance, marching without supplies, in driving rain, and with dysentery raging through their ranks, they outpaced the fit and well-supplied French army, found an alternative river crossing and got across ahead of the French. Having covered 200 miles in twelve days without a stop (nearly double the pace of most mediaeval armies) Henry allowed his troops a day of rest.

Over the next four days the bedraggled English army covered another seventy two miles subsisting on nuts and berries, they marched without stopping except to sleep and react to the symptoms of dysentery; and many were now only clothed in shirts, naked from the waist down having discarded their breaches due to having them round their ankles more than round their waists. All they wanted was to get back to England, Calais was at most two days away, Having managed to outpace the French and cross the Somme it is not difficult to imagine their dismay when they cross the tracks of a massive French army that had overtaken them and was now camped and waiting for them on the road to Calais.

Despite this Henry doesn't give up, he pushes on and manages to find a suitable venue to make a stand in the fields near the village of Agincourt. The fields were recently ploughed making for heavy going, and the recent constant rain had made them even more difficult to traverse. Woods, which would prevent a flanking manoeuvre by the French, protected both flanks, and better still would funnel the French down to the same frontage as the English, severely negating their advantage of numbers.

Sales Lessons

Sometimes you have to be a gambler, if the gamble is your best hope of avoiding an obvious disaster, even though the disaster may be the simpler option. The march was achievable if Henry could keep up a fast turn of speed and manage to avoid the French. He covered ground at double the speed of an average mediaeval army, and undoubtedly confused the French as to his whereabouts by this use of speed, so that he almost pulled it off. Likewise speed of movement within an account can confer security of movement.

Unfortunately the English had to traverse the river Somme to get to Calais, and this is where the French had a chance to catch them. Eventually the French did manage to find them and trail them on the far bank of the river, ready to pounce if they crossed it. Henry is not reckless, to refuses to cross on a number of occasions, despite his plight, as he knows he will be placed at a disadvantage by attempting this too soon. He holds his nerve and continues to do the "right thing", he doesn't accept the "hopelessness" of his situation and continues to seek advantage. Eventually the English out march the French and find a safe place to cross the river. This is key to the success of the whole campaign; Henry chooses not to fight from a position of weakness, Henry cannot win a Stochastic engagement against the French and knows it, he keeps his nerve in the hope that a better situation can be found. This is a key lesson; the job of the salesperson is not to engage with the opposition, the job of the salesperson is to achieve the objective, for Henry it was to get to Calais, for a salesperson it will be to win the account/revenue, taking on the competition from a position of weakness is stupidity not bravery. It is always better to loose walk away from ten possible engagements in order to win the one that counts, than to loose everything in an avoidable engagement.

It is important in sales situations to be like Henry, to keep a cool head in the face of adversity, and look at the situation dispassionately until an advantage can be found. Once cut off by the French Henry new that he had no choice but to fight, he therefore chooses his ground to the best advantage. Do the same in a sales campaign, if forced to engage when you would rather not, look for the piece of ground that gives you the best chance of success, "do all the right things" and you will put yourself in a position to take advantage of what fate, and the weaknesses of your competition may bring.

The Eve of Battle

The English spent the night sleeping and praying. The French had a jollier time of it, being better supplied with wine and beer, and being psychologically assured of victory due to their overwhelming superiority of numbers.

Come the morning of the 25th October 1415, and both armies faced each other at either end of a muddy field. The English priests heard confessions and gave communion to the troops, and in fact Henry himself took communion three times that morning, so great was the knowledge that they faced overwhelming odds. But despite this knowledge the English showed a very "English" trait. Knowing that there was a good chance that they would be defeated, rather than seeking terms, the English made their peace with their God, went down on their knees and then took a small scoop of earth into their mouths. The meaning of this was profound; they had by this act shown that they were dead men walking. Fear, pain, and death, mean nothing to dead men. Napoleon would say of English soldiers 350 years later that they could not be beaten; they could only be killed. Here was that spirit writ large.

The English waited, the French Knights jostled and argued, pushed and shoved each other to try to get the positions of honour in the front ranks, whilst their servants cooked their breakfast, no doubt the smell of roasting bacon wafted down to the starving English ranks. The English sat and watched this pantomime for four hours.

This gave Henry a dilemma. He couldn't sit indefinitely and do nothing; his men would starve. He couldn't retreat; the French would surround them and ride them down. He had only two options: Firstly he could surrender. Secondly he could fight.

Surrendering would be inconvenient for Henry as he would be taken prisoner and would have to give up his French possessions as part of any ransom, but he would be treated with respect, and would undoubtedly live in the lap of luxury until England was bled to provide the price of the ransom (Chivalry still in General held sway anywhere west of Austria, when it came to captured monarchs). The inconvenience would be little worse for his Knights; friends and family would ransom them in due course. The real losers would be his rank and file soldiers, no one would be paying a ransom for them, they would be kept in absolutely primitive conditions, and those who didn't eventually die of disease, would either be killed or mutilated, and even if ransomed, the archers would have their "draw fingers" amputated to ensure they could never use a bow again.

Sales Lessons

If you are prepared to fight every engagement as if to loose it would leave you with nothing, then you will fight much harder to win it than if you believe that it is a foregone conclusion. Pride goes before a fall, and it is essential that you do not enter into a competitive sales situation lightly, the English had no choice, and once that psychological barrier was crossed they could not be beaten; only killed. If you can instill this grit in yourself and your colleagues in a competitive situation all fear of failure will disappear.

The point of no return

So Henry decided to take "option B"; he would take on the cream of French knighthood whilst outnumbered 5 to 1. To his credit he decided to do it in style. Fed up with waiting for the French to make a move, he ordered his troops forward to within shouting distance of the French lines and ordered them to let fly with a volley of arrows, no doubt accompanied by displays of the English "V" sign (equivalent to the single "finger" used as an expletive in modern America) showing that they still had their draw fingers in place and were prepared to use them. This act of marching so close to the French knights and loosing a volley at them was an incredible psychological slap in the face for the haughty French aristocrats. The English archers were in the French Knights' eyes, their social inferiors (and the archers undoubtedly would have accepted this as a fact themselves), so to be goaded by them in such a manner simply could not be ignored. The French Knights promptly forgot about their arguments as to who should take precedence over whom in the battle line, and promptly thundered down from their elevated position on the high ground, towards the ragged, but defiant English ranks in the field below.

Sales Lessons

Having concentrated your resources in space, you must now concentrate them in time. If you have chosen the best place and time to force an engagement, given your circumstances, then you must make sure that engagement occurs, to delay may cost you your advantage and ultimately cost you the account. Be as audacious as you need to be to force a conclusion; Henry actually advanced on the French and understood enough of their psychology, to be able to predict that his aggressive move towards them and volley of arrows would tip them into a response. You must also be prepared to do this if the situation requires it, and it helps if you have studied and understand the sales psychology of your competition.

The Battle

As they came down from the ridge, the French entered the freshly ploughed ground in front of the English ranks, churning it to a mire as they did. The more Knights who rode over it, the worse it became. The trouserless, sick, hungry English let fly with volley after volley of arrows. Most of these would have done little more than bruise and aggravate the Frenchmen, although some would have found chinks in their armour, and many of the horses would have been hit and wounded. Some riders and horses went down, and others fell over these, but still they came on. The archers had failed to stop the Knights, and it seemed like their nerve was breaking, as they started to fall back, however they didn't run for the woods to their flank, which would have offered safety, their nerve held and they withdrew in an orderly way. The French finally closed the gap, but rather than unleashing the shock of their impact on the archers, they hit the sharpened stakes which the archers had hammered into the ground when they first took up their forward positions. The result was chaos; horses were impaled on stakes, tripped over them, and many fled either back towards their own lines or sideways to the relative safety of the woods. Riders struggled to control injured and maddened mounts, and many were pitched headlong to the ground. Archers battered prone Knights with mallets and swords, and loosed flights of arrows into the backs of fleeing French Knights and the rumps of their horses.

This disorganised rout hit and burst through the second line of French Knights, who had decided to dismount (having seen the state of the ground) and were advancing towards the English on foot. Battered but determined, they trudged on only to be hit by an arrow storm of five thousand shafts every ten seconds from the English. Many French men fell to arrows and mud. Heads down, shoulders hunched, and compressed together by the effect of the arrow storm, the survivors pressed on, and ignoring the archers positions, they made for the banners of Henry and his dismounted Knights, who were standing in three distinct places in the English line.

The French foot Knights met with some initial success, pushing the English Knights back through sheer weight of numbers. However this very advantage of numbers was to be their undoing. Because of the very narrow frontage occupied by the English Knights, the only way the French Knights could bring their superior numbers to bear was by the forward pressure of their rear ranks on their front ranks, preventing any chance of maneuvre. In contrast the English Knights could give ground and look for opportunities to fence with the French and wrong foot them. As the fighting progressed and the ground under the French was churned more and more into a mire the French rear ranks started to tumble over their fallen front rank comrades due to the continuing pressure from behind. The tidal wave of the French armoured advance crashed into the mud of the field.

The English archers on either side of the French columns compressed them further by pouring volley after volley of bodkin tipped armour-piecing arrows into the French flanks. Eventually running short of arrows the archers resorted to mallets, daggers and swords, flailing floundering groups of Frenchmen. For the French Knights, this was the ultimate indignity. To be held down by a couple of English peasants, whilst a Welsh peasant staves in your head with a mallet, had none of the chivalric dignity of death at the hands of a socially equal English Knight.

The French foot Knights were now a compressed mass. The front ranks and the flanks were mainly wallowing in the mud or dead, heaped in piles, forming a barrier to those on the inside of them. The rear ranks were still pushing against the backs of the Knights in front of them thinking to add impetus to the attack, and the inside ranks were caught between the pressure from behind and the wall of dead and floundering on three sides of them. Eyewitnesses stated that the French were packed so tightly that those in the centre of the mass who had been killed by English archery were literally unable to fall.

The situation was suddenly made even worse, as the third French line, seeing that the attack had ground to a halt, decided to tramp down and add their weight to the scrum, assuming that a good hard push from behind would engulf the English. Once this took effect a general panic seems to have set in in the French scrum. Some Knights tried to break back through their own ranks away from the battering they were taking from the English, and the crush from behind that was enveloping them. Some were dragged free by their squires and servants, and others simply gave up and surrendered.

By midday the English had possession of the field. The French who had attacked were, dead, captured, or had retreated back to the ridge. Despite this the danger for the English had not completely passed. A third line of mounted French Knights were jostling for position, in anticipation of raising the necessary courage to mount a charge, and in fact the Duke of Brabant, who had arrived late to the field, mustered his followers and launched a charge against the English line to try to turn the tide. Unfortunately for him he didn't have enough men with him to make an impression, but his action fortified the jostling French into considering a more serious attack, which if launched against the exhausted English could have had dire consequences. To compound the situation there were hundreds of fully armoured captured French Knights amongst the English ranks, representing a threat in themselves.

Whilst watching the prisoners and expecting the French Knights to come thundering down from the ridge again,the English were taken in the rear by a French force which had outflanked them through the woods and was now pillaging their camp and baggage. Fortunately for the English this force was a hotchpotch of peasants scratched together by the lord of the village of Agincourt, in an attempt to take advantage of the distracted English and make off with anything they could carry from the baggage, with perhaps the added enjoyment of being able to kill some of the wounded and non-combatants in the process. Unfortunately for the French prisoners, Henry, lacking definite information took this as a real threat, and ordered the massacre of the prisoners in order to stop them considering taking advantage of the situation. The attack on the camp was beaten off, and having witnessed the killing of the prisoners, the French Knights on the ridge lost their nerve, and the threat of a renewed attack disappeared. The threat having been removed, Henry ordered the killing to stop.

The battle was over, the French Herald Montjoie, officially brought hostilities to an end by recognising Henry as the victor, and named the battle "Agincourt".

Sales Lessons

Henry had chosen the ground on which to fight superbly. He had made sure that the French numbers could not be brought to bear, so had in effect produced a Single Point Concentration (SPC) to negate the French Stochastic advantage of ntheir numbers. In addition the fields were freshly ploughed, and soaked from recent rain, and it is no coincidence that this is the terrain chosen for a stand by Henry, and just to make sure, he had his archers carry wooden stakes during the course of the march, ready for when the moment came to add to the discomfort of the French, these factors had effectively greatly reduced the French "E", so what on paper had looked like an advantage in both numbers and E for the French, had turned into an even match in numbers, and an advantage to the English in E.

Even where the arrows of the English had failed to halt the charge of the French (French armour was to a large degree invulnerable to most English arrows) the stakes managed to destroy the French impetus, so both weapons systems had failed in this part of the engagement, but the English were much better able to exploit the failure of the French than vice versa. So the difference between success and failure in sales situations can be seen as "relative" i.e. if I fail to win a deal because for example the customer doesn't make a purchase, but the outcome is that you come off considerably worse than me in the account, then, even though I may not have achieved all that I wanted, I still gained the advantage over you, and you may have irreparably damaged your chances of further business at that account..

This engagement also shows the value of a mixed force, sometimes deals are not won by the "Sales Knights", it can be the "Technical Archers" for example, that decide the day if you can choose your ground carefully for an SPC.

If you can narrow the frontage on which the battle will be fought, i.e. restrict the parties involved from the customer side, then it is much more likely that weight of numbers of your competitor can be negated.

The French compounded their predicament by throwing in their reserves along a line that had already failed twice, this was stupidity, but is a commonly paralleled by poor sales teams and sales management, where the assumption is often that the failures before were because somebody wasn't good enough to achieve a result, rather than the approach being wrong in the first place.

The turning point of the battle, was the point at which the French morale breaks and uninjured and unengaged French forces become dismayed, and believe that they can no longer profit from the engagement. They were defeated because they chose to be. This is the point that you must get your competition to, they will only be defeated when they give up, you don't decide when that point comes, they do. What you must do is hold your own morale, and inflict enough pain to hasten them reaching the point at which their morale breaks.

Aftermath

The aftermath was that the whole of Europe was shocked by the performance of a backward island on the periphery of the civilised world, which, despite being completely outnumbered and supposedly outclassed by the cream of the nobility of arguably the greatest kingdom in Europe, had roundly thrashed them. Henry's victory was so thorough, that soon after the battle he effectively negotiated to take over the throne of France, once the French King died, and would have done so had he not died of dysentery, just prior to the death of the King of France; thereby ending the career of one of the greatest warrior Kings that England had ever produced.

Sales Lesson

Such a victory, can have far reaching effects in the sales world. It can open up an account, or a series of related accounts, and make your competition believe that they can't beat you, thereby destroying their morale before they even take to the field against you. But all success is transitory, and you must capitalize on it within an account and a market as soon as possible, otherwise fate may take a hand, and rob you of bigger rewards.

Summary of Lessons

1. You may not always have a choice in the course of events in a campaign. Henry's idle boast about taking Bordeaux and Paris forced his course of action because of the political risk of not, at least partially, living up to it. Taking on too high a target, or boasting of capturing a specific account may force the unwary sales person in to the same situation. The outcome of which could be fame and fortune as it was for Henry, or possibly something much less pleasant for a lesser commander.

2. Always work to a plan that has at least some chance of success within the abilities of your team and those of the enemy. If you find yourself facing a potentially disastrous situation like Henry, have a single simple objective. Henry decided that his one real objective was a march to Calais then shipping his army safely home, a single simple objective that everyone from the lowliest archer to the haughtiest knight could understand and adhere to.

3. If you meet unexpected circumstances or events, do not despair; carry on doing "The Right Things" to better the situation. Henry had the opportunity to cross the river Somme on a number of occasions, but chose not to due to the risks involved; he waited until the opportunity for an unopposed crossing presented itself. He did this despite the fact that it required him to head further and further *away* from his destination of Calais, but he pursued his slightly counter intuitive course because it was tactically "The Right Thing" to do. He stuck to his judgement and never let despair or panic influence his actions.

4. A well lead team will follow a respected leader irrespective of the hardships endured. Good leadership out weighs poor conditions. Henry could have surrendered at any time and received very good treatment and eventual freedom. Instead he chose to stay with his men and endure what they had to endure, a very powerful boost to the morale of his troops, guaranteed to win him enormous affection and loyalty. He also stuck to his objective, and showed no signs of wavering.

5. Do not rush into a confrontation; the idea is to win, not just to engage. Concentration of force in both time and space, is only a good idea if the concentration takes place in the right time and space.

6. Choose your ground as carefully as possible to improve your advantages, and reduce your opponent's advantages. It is far better to fight with a weak army in favourable conditions, than with a strong army in unfavourable conditions. Henry made the most use of all the advantages he could, choosing the ground and positioning of troops on that ground very carefully, and adding to his advantages where possible, for example by making his men carry stakes for some time prior to battle, and making them deploy the stakes, then take them up again, and redeploy them on the day of the battle when the archers were ordered to march up to confront the French.

7. Once you have chosen the best ground to fight on, force your enemy to fight, do not allow such an advantage to slip by. Be prepared to be unconventional and audacious if necessary.

8. Know your enemy's psychology use this against him to control his actions to your advantage.

9. Once you have an advantage pursue it to the limit. Punish your opponent without mercy.

10. Reduce in your enemy's mind the perception of value in continued resistance. Force the risk reward ratio to a limit that makes continued sustained engagement unprofitable.

11. Carry out actions, even distasteful ones, which will undermine your enemy's morale. Battles and sales are won when the enemy looses the "will to fight". Henry's mistaken belief that he was being surrounded, which led to the execution of his prisoners, filled the remaining French troops on the ridge with distaste and robbed them of their "will to fight".

12. Immediately wring as much advantage out of the settlement terms as possible, whilst the opposition morale is low.

13. Winning an account is very different from holding an account. Just as Henry's untimely death prevent the English and French crowns becoming united to form the

greatest nation Europe would ever have seen, chance and a lack of follow-up can turn a brilliantly won account into hostile territory.

General Nathan Bedford Forrest

Confederate States Army

Initiative and Flexibility

"Git thar first with the most"

Let's take a fantastic example of initiative turned into an art form. General Nathan Bedford Forrest was both, unconventional, and successful. He could act both independently and under direct orders, no matter what situation confronted him he expected to adapt his tactics to confront it and usually overcome it, and equally he instilled this attitude in his men. He was unconventional in the extreme, whilst dining with a group of European observers during the war, he was asked to adjudicate in an argument between two of the Europeans over which was the most effective cavalry weapon, one man arguing for the Lance, the other for the Sabre, Forrest's answer was terse and pragmatic; "Sawn-off shotgun."

Forrest as a man is a controversial figure; after the civil war he was a founder of the Ku Klux Klan, and during the war his men massacred the black Union troops who had bravely defended Fort Pillow against them. The Fort Pillow incident was more likely a result of the endemic racism in his troops than any orders of Forrest, but it was a war crime none-the-less. Just as with the other subjects of this book, we shall deal with his genius as a soldier, rather than his prejudices and failings as a man, I will leave that to other writers.

Siege of Fort Donelson

We start the story with the siege of this Confederate Strongpoint by Union General Ulysses S Grant. In command were three Confederate Generals, two of them Pillow and Floyd, were facing indictment and trial if they fell into Union hands. They slipped away upriver to avoid capture leaving the third general, the romantically named, but reliable and able, Simon Bolivar Buckner, to fight or surrender to the surrounding Union forces.

Buckner sent word to Grant asking for terms of surrender; Grant sent back the immortal lines: "No terms except an unconditional and immediate surrender can be accepted." Given that

Grant's initials were U.S. Grant, he would be forever known as "Unconditional Surrender Grant". Buckner knew Grant from before the war, they had been close friends, he knew Grant meant what he said, and so to spare the lives of his men he acquiesced to Grants demands.

One man had other ideas; Colonel Nathan Bedford Forest. The Confederate Cavalry Commander took his Cavalry and some units of Infantry who still had the stomach for a fight, out through the swamps between the river and the Union right flank. They would escape to fight another day.

Sales Lesson

You don't have to do what all the others do, it's OK to go your own way if you have confidence and ability, and your team will follow you. Forest's escape had enormous repercussions in later years for the Union Commanders. At the time, a small body of troops escaping under a dashing cavalry commander would have seemed annoying to the Northerners, but not important. As it turned out Forrest played a major role later in the war, probably helping to extend the war by months if not years, at the cost of many Union lives.

So the other lesson for sales here is, once you have your opposition in a trap, do not relax, make sure you punish them to the hilt, do not allow them a way of living to fight another day in an account, or you may end up paying the charges with interest.

Fighting in the West

Forest turns up again harassing Union lines of supply and communication. The Union was attempting to implement the "Anaconda" plan, i.e. the encirclement of the South by land and sea. Grant was pushing along the Mississippi Valley when Forrest crossed the Tennessee River, and proceeded to cut Grant's communications by tearing up railway track and cutting telegraph lines forcing Grant to abandon hope of reaching his objective of Vicksburg overland.

Forest's activities gained the grudging admiration of Grant who described him as a "brave and intrepid cavalry general". So much did Forrest impress Grant, that he paid him the ultimate accolade of copying his ideas by installing Phillip Sheridan as a Union equivalent of Forrest. Despite this, General Sherman described Forest's cavalry as travelling one hundred miles for every ten that the Union Cavalry could muster. Forest was described as the biggest threat to Union bases and communication between the Appalachians and the Mississippi.

Forest displayed great ability, not only as a long distance freelance raider, but also as a subordinate commander in a mixed force. At the battle of Shiloh a late charge by Forest saved the retreating Confederate Army, by deterring any further pursuit by Union forces. He was also more than happy to dismount his men and hold defensive positions on foot, as he demonstrated at the battle of Chickamauga.

Sales lesson

A small force can achieve results out of all proportion to their size and their relative lack of numbers compared to the enemy if they are well led and achieve speed of movement. By adopting an indirect approach when faced by a bigger enemy, i.e. attacking "soft targets" within an account such as command and control centres (senior managers) and lines of communications (thought leadership and personal relationships) you can do more damage to your opponent than with a head on collision.

The perfect Salesperson will not only be able to act independently and with initiative, but should also be able to act as part of a larger Campaign, and in a subordinate role if required, whilst still able to take the initiative within the framework of command. Too many salespeople are unable to do this, either lacking the initiative to act in isolation, or the self confidence to take orders from others. Being able to do both is a rare and prized gift. The key is to be able to show initiative, irrespective of the circumstances, and to the greater good of all concerned.

1864 Okolona Mississippi

In February 1864 Sherman with 20,000 men was marching through Mississippi to attack the Railroad hub of Meridian. 7,000 men under Brigadier General W. Sooy Smith were to sweep down the line of the railway from Memphis, join with Sherman at Meridian, for his move on the important Confederate arsenal of Selma Alabama. Sherman had realised that Smith's column was likely to act as a lure to Forest, and had instructed Smith to pursue and destroy Forest's smaller ill supplied force should they make contact.

By 20th February Smith's force discovered a part of Forest's force, probably no more than 1,000 men, south of Okolona. Rather than pressing home his numerical advantage with an immediate attack, Smith withdrew back towards Okolona in the hope of drawing Forest into the open away from the defensive advantage of the swampland. The plan worked, but not before Forest had gathered reinforcements giving him about 3,000 men, so he was a little less than half the strength of Smith.

Once Forest was within striking distance Smith drew his men up in order of battle, seeing this Forest held back and refused to attack, so Smith started to withdraw again towards Okolona, once he was once more on the move Forest attacked and fought a running battle with him, this state of having to perform a fighting withdrawal for the rest of the day, started to demoralise Smith's troops, and with nightfall approaching Smith decided to make a stand, and started to reform into line of battle. Seeing them in this disorganised state Forest pushed home his attack and made for the flanks of Smith's troops.

To buy time to allow his men to reorganise and draw up in proper battle formation Smith ordered a charge by his cavalry to drive Forest back, and bolster his men's sagging morale. Seeing this Forest's men held their positions on foot and poured a steady stream of rifle fire into the charging northerners. This drove them back in total confusion. This was the last straw for Smith who ordered a general retirement, which under pressure from Forest's mounted pursuit turned into a panicked rout towards Memphis.

In three days of fighting Forest killed 400 Northerners for the loss of 150 of his own men, and had driven twice his number back the way they had come, thwarting Sherman's plans to attack the arsenal at Selma, and also causing Sherman to withdraw back to Vicksburg. So for the loss of 150 casualties out of a force of 3,000 Forest had thwarted the plans of 27,000

Northerners, and saved a strategic prize from falling into enemy hands. It was described by one of his enemies as "the most glorious achievement of his career".

Sales Lessons

Three lessons here are, firstly the numbers of your opposition can be compensated for by , in Lanchester's terms the "E" of your troops, provided you can bring your resources to bear in the right place and time, and in the right manner. Don't compete with your opposition when it suits them, delay, and obstruct them. But as soon as they put themselves in a position of weakness, push your attack home, and again look for an Indirect approach, find the flanks of their formation, look for the poorly defended areas and make that the Schwerpunkt of your attack.

Secondly keep a cool enough head, that should they change tactics, as with Smith's cavalry charge, your forces can defend if necessary and drive them off from areas that you must hold.

Thirdly, the thing that must be broken is your opponent's morale. As soon as this starts to go you have success in the palm of your hand. And when the rout does start, do not sit back, harass your opponent in the account to make it so unpleasant for them that they take their offerings somewhere else.

Fort Pillow

Now we come to the most controversial incident in the whole of Forrest's career. The Union had control of the Mississippi North of Memphis, Union gunboats and supply boats sailing its length giving them a great communications route into the heart of the Confederacy. This great artery of communication was defended by various strongpoints manned by Union troops, Fort Pillow, having been captured in 1862 being one of them. It was basically a large earthwork, earthworks being extremely effective defences against cannon fire, garrisoned by 560 men of the Union army, about half of whom were black soldiers. Racial prejudice was rife in both armies in the civil war, overt in the South, and more subtle in the North. Black soldiers in the Union army in the early part of the war were given labour duties and kept in the less forward commands as their fighting ability was treated as suspect by the white northern commanders.

In this case Fort Pillow was a backwater far from the main theatres of operations. No doubt to the shock of its commander in 1864, two years after its capture, the fort found itself surrounded by Forrest. Forrest demanded its surrender, no doubt believing that its garrison of black soldiers would not dare to fight. But fight they did, supported by Union Gunboats firing from the Mississippi.

It must be credited to Forrest that his cavalry troops were prepared to dismount and attack a fortified position whilst under artillery fire, causing 70% casualties among the defenders, and their bravery and self confidence cannot be denied, but alas this must be weighed against the fact that when the battle ended there was testimony at the time that black soldiers trying to surrender were shot by Forrest's men. It is unlikely that Forrest ordered such killings; it is more likely that the endemic racism of the Southern troopers was to blame.

Sales Lessons

Just because your resources have one job title doesn't mean that you can't use them in a different way, you must use the resources to hand in the best way possible to deal with the situation you face. The ability to do this will come from your leadership skills, and the morale of your resources.

The other lesson here, is that no matter how great or how many your sales achievements, be responsible for one distasteful, immoral, or illegal incident in an account, and that is all you will be remembered for. The stain will not wash out, and if you value your reputation within your industry you should make sure you are beyond reproach.

South to Tennesse

After the Fort Pillow incident, Forrest fought two more battles against the Union forces in Mississippi, outnumbered in both he defeated the Union troops in the first at Brice's Cross Roads driving them off and capturing their supply train of 250 Wagons packed with food and ammunition, and was forced into a draw in the second engagement at Tupelo, where the confederates lost more men in the engagement than the Union, but the Union troops were forced to withdraw.

After these engagements Forrest made a raid that actually took him in the Union held command centre of the City of Memphis, and came within an ace of capturing Major General C. C. Washburn the Union Departmental commander. So close a shave was it, that Washburn was forced to flee in his night clothes, and Forrest rode off with the General's captured uniform. There followed a somewhat uncharacteristic display of good humour between the two men, when, under a flag of truce, Forrest returned the captured uniform to its owner, and not to be out done, Washburn had a new uniform made for Forrest by Forrest's old Memphis tailor, and had that delivered to the Confederate raider!

By October 1864 Forrest was called south to join General Hood in the proposed Confederate invasion of Tennessee. Pushing up to the Tennessee River Forrest appeared near Chattanooga, attacked Union Gunboats and transports on the river with small arms and artillery fire, capturing a Gunboat and five transports. Astonishingly he then manned the captured Gunboat with his troopers, and steamed off to attack the Union Navy on the river. Sherman later described this as "…a feat of arms which, I confess, excited my admiration."

Sales Lessons

Again the lesson here is to be audacious and prepared to do whatever it takes, no matter how unconventional, to achieve your goals. The essence of this is to have the morale of your resources and yourself so high that you will have confidence in all your actions, nothing should seem impossible if you can disencumber yourself and your colleagues of artificial restrictions, and you will find inspiration to feats that under a lesser leader would seem impossible. If a camaraderie and joint sense of purpose can be engendered in a tactical team, then nothing is impossible. The flair and style, and indeed cheek of Forrest played a great part in his charismatic leadership.

Subordinate Command in Tennessee

Having wreaked havoc on the Tennessee River, Forrest then took his command to join Hood in the last major Confederate offensive of the war, and took up the subordinate command to Hood of regular army light cavalry commander during Hood's offensive.

However the offensive, although off to a good start with Forrest forever putting the Union Generals on the back foot, was doomed to failure. Confederate leadership and fighting spirit their "E" as Lanchester would put it, was not large enough to offset the shear Stochastic numbers advantage, and "E" in terms of supplies and weaponry of the Union forces.

Worst still for the Confederates, Grant had learned from Forrest's example. He had seen and cultivated the potential of a young Brevet Major General of Engineers, James H Wilson, and had converted him through necessity into a Cavalry Commander to rival Forrest. It would be Wilson who would "out Forrest" Forrest.

After the Confederate invasion petered out, Forest found himself back at Selma covering the Confederate arsenal from Union attack. But now his numbers were depleted, and his attempts to deflect the relentless Wilson were brushed aside in Wilson's "Blitzkrieg" campaign against the southerners. Forrest took the only steps he could; he fought a holding action from a defended village to allow time for scattered units to concentrate at Selma, then withdrew himself to Selma, mustered the local militia to boost his numbers, and prepared to defend the town.

Wilson appeared before the town's earth ramparts the following afternoon, being an Engineer he quickly surveyed the town's defences, and decided on an immediate attack on one section of them. This has echoes of Guderian's crossing of the Meuse just over 75 years later, no one expected the Union troops to mount an immediate attack after a having recently fought and pursued Forrest's veterans, the Confederates sat back and awaited the dawn when the rule book said the Union troops would make their move, and with almost any other Union commander they would have been right, but not Wilson. Wilson was working to his own script.

After an initial bombardment, Wilson's dismounted troopers charged the ramparts, hurled themselves into the ditch in front of it, and formed a human rampart of their own like ants clambering across each other's backs and shoulders to gain the breach in the line. This took the defenders completely by surprise, and the speed of the attack and the inexperience of the Confederate Militia meant that they were unable to mount a spirited fire fight to repel it.

Once the Union troops were in, Wilson poured reinforcements into the breach to hold it open and effect a Rolling Torrent as Liddell-Hart would have called it. Well lead by Forrest the Confederates fought bravely in hand to hand fighting in the streets of Selma, but they were no match for the numbers of Union troops. Eventually Forrest had to admit defeat and make a hasty retreat with his veterans back into the wilderness to lick his wounds and hope to fight another day.

Wilson rested his men for a week at Selma whilst destroying the foundries, ammunition dumps and stores that had given the town its value to the Confederacy, then took up again his Blitkrieg through the south at a rate of 25 miles per day (two and a half times as fast as a normal Union Cavalry unit would progress) attacking and destroying centres of command, logistics, and communication, until ordered to cease fire by Grant, due to the Confederacy looking for terms of surrender.

Sales Lessons

Grant had the intelligence to look at what had made the Confederates under Forrest successful, and perform in Lanchester terms a matching strategy, but backed by far greater resources than Forrest had at his disposal. Undoubtedly not as great an innovator as Forrest, and definitely lacking his swashbuckling flair, the man Grant chose, Brevet Major General Wilson, showed energy and determination, and inspired this in his men, and with the backing of far superior resources was able to counter Forrest. Had the roles been reversed, had Forrest had the resources at his disposal possessed by the Union, he would have proved unstoppable, and Wilson would have been no match for him, but that is the difference between the power of E and the power of a Stochastic engagement.

The first lesson is always take the best from your competitor's tactics and use them against the competition, even if you aren't as individually talented as your opponent, you may not need to be, just improving with lessons learned may be enough.

Secondly don't think that you need the same background as your competition to do what they do, Wilson was an Engineer, not a cavalryman, and yet he became one of the most effective cavalry commanders of the war. Generally basic intelligence coupled with drive is what is really required in a salesperson.

The third lesson, is don't underestimate your adversary, once they have learned the trick of your tactics, be prepared for them, don't learn and emulate their original failings in return. Had Forrest had realised the drive of Wilson and taken account of it, he would have been better prepared for his speed of action, and although Selma would undoubtedly have eventually fallen, the taking of it would have been far more costly and protracted than it turned out.

Summary of Lessons

Forrest was undoubtedly a superb Cavalry Officer, charismatic leader of men, and brilliant tactician. He was able to work totally isolated, and was equally at home and effective in a subordinate role in a mixed force. He placed his art above his ego, did not cause trouble for superiors, but took decisive and fast action to make the most of any situation he found himself in, extending the boundaries of the capabilities of his men, and testing his enemies to breaking point, before melting away if overwhelming force was pitted against him. It took the Union's copying of his techniques, with Wilson one of their greatest cavalry generals, many years ahead of his time, and plentiful resources to finally contain him, if not completely defeat him.

The biggest lesson to draw from Forrest, is one of speed of movement, which delivers surprise, and the surprise was fully exploited by the flexibility he inspired in his troops to pursue as a cavalry force, engage as an infantry force, storm fortified positions under artillery fire, capture and man Naval vessels and audaciously challenge regular naval units, and finally to have a very mixed group of men with enough leadership to take on, albeit forlornly, the best the Union had to offer in hand to hand combat in a besieged town.

To have the confidence and self belief to do this, is way outside of one's normal comfort zone, this what sales legends are made of. Think like this yourself, see no obstacles only opportunities to change your approach and learn new skills, use your resources, whether human or product in ways that make them fit the situation, for you'll never make the situation fit your resources if the fit isn't already there.

1. Show charisma and leadership and people will follow you.
2. Have the confidence self belief, and desire to act outside of your comfort zone.
3. Believe that your people are capable of doing anything and they will too.
4. Place your art above your ego when acting as a subordinate, or in leadership.
5. Take decisive and fast action to exploit an advantage.
6. See no obstacles only opportunities for new ways of winning.
7. Make your tactics, people and products fit the situation if the situation doesn't fit your tactics, people, and products.
8. Walk away from hopeless engagements.

Bringing All the Lessons Together: Blitzkrieg

General Heinz Guderian

Intelligence
Speed of Movement
Concentration of Force

Heinz Guderian and The Fall of France 1940

Heinz Guderian, more than any other single individual, understood, developed, and enacted a Blitzkrieg strategy. By his own admission he studied and implemented the teachings of Fuller and Liddell-Hart.

Guderian, almost single-handedly, and to the point of insubordination, pushed through the necessary actions which lead to the defeat of France and the evacuation of British Expeditionary force from mainland Europe. He came close to delivering Hitler an outcome which could have ended the war with a negotiated victory on German terms.

If it is ever possible to attribute success in a campaign to a single soldier who actually took part in the fighting, then the fall of France in 1940 can be attributed to Heinz Guderian.

If as a salesperson you study the campaign that Guderian ran in France in 1940, you can learn many lessons on how to emulate his strategic and tactical approach with your own sales campaigns and with any others in your team. The essence is to emulate the mindset of Guderian in the parallels to his military campaign that you will see in your sales campaign.

He was famous for his "sayings" to his troops to cajole and inspire them to greater efforts, use them to inspire yourself and those around you to greater achievements in a sales campaign, and to inject energy into your actions.

Wit and Wisdom

Guderian's famous one liners, embody so much commonsense from a military point of view and as metaphors in the sales world, that it is worth including a few of his better known ones here:

"Klotzen, nicht Kleckern !"

"Bash them, don´t splash them" - Guderian's favourite quotation and one adopted by Adolf Hitler. Guderian used it to bang home to his troops that they must show courage and force home their attacks with the intention of inflicting as much harm on the enemy as possible, the epitomy of Fuller's principle of the expending of offensive power.

"Man schlägt jemanden mit der Faust und nicht mit gespreizten Fingern".

"You hit somebody with your fist and not with your fingers spread" – Meaning that you must concentrate your efforts in a combined focused impact, spreading your resources in the attack weakens that impact.

"Fahrkarte bis zur Endstation".

"Ticket to the last station" which he shouted to his Tank Commanders as they roared past him, telling them to push on as far as they could, and not to stop for anything until they reached the channel.

"Der Motor des Panzers ist ebenso seine Waffe wie die Kanone".

"The engine of the Panzer is a weapon just like the main-gun". In other words think of all your resources as part of your sales armoury and use them offensively.

"Es gibt keine verzweifelten Lagen, es gibt nur verzweifelte Menschen".

"There are no desperate situations, there are only desperate people". So all situations can be handled calmly and rationally, sales situations are just sales situations, and must be approached depending on how the cards have been dealt. They only become desperate when you do. Morale and a cool head are essential to a good sales person in order to turn the odds back in your favour.

"Der Kampf gegen die eigenen Oberen macht manchmal mehr Arbeit als gegen die Franzosen".

"It is sometimes tougher to fight my superiors than the French" – The lament of all experienced salespeople faced with inertia and lack of initiative from senior management.

The Plan
4th December 1939

The initial German Plan was same as the WW1 Schlieffen Plan, simply consisting of a sweep down through Belgium and into Northern France.

General Manstein argued that based on his and General Guderian's previous experience the hilly and wooded Ardennes was crossable by armoured columns, and that there would be weaknesses in the Maginot Line that could be exploited, and therefore put forward an alternative plan involving, in addition to the attack from the north, a thrust from the East with armoured divisions through the Ardennes, across the River Meuse north of the Maginot line, to cut the allied forces in half. The German High Command rejected this, and after Manstein argued his corner he was removed from his position and put in command of a third line Infantry Division.

Fortunately for the Germans, a courier carrying details of the basic plan, disobeying standing orders, lost his way on a night flight and landed in Belgium, where he, and his plans, were captured, this completely compromised the German plans.

The second stroke of good fortune was that Manstein managed to get an audience with Hitler to put his case direct. This resulted in wargames being carried out on 7th & 14th February 1940 to test the efficacy of the plan. At these wargames a mass argument ensued between Guderian and his few supporters who advocated a fast crossing of the Meuse by the Panzer divisions followed by a deep thrust through France to the channel coast, against the rest of the German high command, who wanted his Panzers to halt at the line of the Meuse and await the infantry to help with the crossing and protect their flanks, then to advance more slowly with an organised mass advance. The high command's version of the plan estimated that this operation would take ten days from the first Panzer crossing the French border, to the first troops landing on the far bank of the Meuse.

Despite the arguments the Germans managed to carry out some very worthwhile manoeuvres, trained for the crossing of the Ardennes by using similar terrain in the Black Forest, and for the crossing of the Meuse by the exercises on the Moselle.

Sales Lesson:

As Fuller said, first is at least to have a plan, and as Liddell-Hart added, give your plan a dual objective to place your opponents on the horns of a dilemma.

You may find many in high command lacking in imagination, they will have a tendency to "Do" one of Liddell-Hart's "Don'ts", i.e. repeat an approach that has already failed. A good salesperson will be imaginative enough to see an alternative, and brave enough to fight for its adoption by going all the way to the top if necessary. It may also be necessary to share key roles with other people who posses the ability to carry the plan out, there is no place for glory hunting when business is at stake.

The other important lesson is to train for the likely environment and obstacles that will be encountered, and the best way to overcome them, and make this as realistic as possible. This will take an experienced devil's advocate to represent the customer, and an impartial and equally experienced referee to make sure egos don't get in the way of practical lessons.

Reconnaissance
9th – 13th May 1940

Initial air photography showed strong fortifications covering the Meuse at Sedan, but a very close study by an Austrian expert showed that many of the fortifications were not yet completed.

The decisive point (the Schwerpunkt) had been found. The advance to the Meuse became a race to get there before the French could counter the move. This race was helped by the fact that Guderian was a "hands-on" commander and insisted on taking part in the leading units of his column so that he was able to make decisions based on first hand evidence. His vehicle of choice was an armoured half-track equipped with radio communications equipment. This enabled him to make decisions based on first hand knowledge.

Guderian's Panzer columns pushing through the Ardennes faced little resistance, as accepted wisdom suggested that the hilly and wooded Ardennes area was unsuitable for the movement of heavy equipment.

When they reached the Meuse, they had been supplied with aerial photographs and detailed maps of the French lines of defence, even down to individual fortified points, so knew exactly where to attack.

Guderian actually reached the Meuse on day 4, 12th May; so far everything had gone to plan.

Sales Lesson:

Just as advocated by Liddell-Hart you must look for the gaps and joins in your target's seemingly linear defences.

Don't accept conventional wisdom, especially when other people spout it in order to prevent you from taking a necessary action. Speak to the experts run through in detail and analyse the options challenges the conventional wisdom for weaknesses.

In order to control a campaign, you must be on the spot, if you don't hear it yourself you cannot be sure what was said, if you didn't see it yourself you cannot be sure what was done, and if you aren't sure what was said or done, then how can you make decisions that have any validity or guarantee of a positive outcome.

Make sure that you apply the knowledge of the situation you have gained, and that all parties involved use that knowledge to the hilt in the account and in detail, the devil is in the detail, and used correctly it may make the difference between winning and loosing a campaign.

Initial Bombardment
13th May 1940

Guderian decided not to stop at the Meuse to wait for the main body of Infantry to catch up and initiate the river crossing, instead he decided to force an immediate crossing to prevent the French from reinforcing the defences. Despite his reputation for reckless advance, Guderian was far from reckless, knowing that his engineers would be shot to pieces in their rubber dinghies by the French if he didn't provide them with cover, he believed that he could achieve a fast crossing if he could keep the defenders pinned down till nightfall.

His problem was that his commander had arranged for a short but intense bombardment during the afternoon that would have left him at the mercy of the defenders' artillery during the river crossing. So he had to make his own arrangements for air support with a contact he had in the Luftwaffe. Guderian's arrangements won through, and the Artillery and bombers carried out protracted bombardment of French defences opposite his main attack point through the night, giving him the cover he needed to attempt a crossing.

Sales Lesson:

Don't confuse speed with risk, speed can be achieved without risk if you use Fuller's second principle of security of action, the security being there to provide for the action.

If your circumstances are such that you will not have such security, then it is incumbent upon you as the leader of the campaign to think out of the box, and to use whatever influence or contacts you have to ensure the security of your actions, if you don't you will only have yourself to blame for a bad outcome.

Bridgehead
13th –14th May 1940

Under cover of the air attack Guderian sent over his Panzer Infantry in rubber dinghies, supported by fire from his artillery, bombers, and tanks.

The French defenders were reservists; older men without effective anti-tank or anti-aircraft weapons, and the combined assault proved too much for them. The riverside defences were soon silenced when Guderian moved his anti-aircraft guns down to the riverbank and enfiladed the French pillboxes from close range, finishing off what the Stuka dive bombers had begun.

By midnight the thrust had reached five miles from the river. Despite this success Guderian had only infantry across the river, no tanks, artillery or antitank weapons. Any type of counter attack by even a small French armoured force would probably have pushed them back into the Meuse. However French advanced artillery units, (artillery being by far the best defence against tanks) panicked and fled at the sight of their own Tanks believing them to be Panzers.

By the 14th Panzer Engineers had built a ferry for light vehicles, then a pontoon bridge for Panzers. German casualties on the 13th had been light due to the suppression of French defences by protracted German bombardment. Now on the 14th there was a potential exposure when the Luftwaffe were switched to another area, and this gave the allies air superiority which they duly exploited to try to destroy the only source of reinforcement and supply for the Germans; the scratch built bridge across the Meuse. Unfortunately for the allies Guderian was well equipped with 88mm anti-aircraft guns and a tremendous barrage was successfully put up to cover the bridge. Allied losses were put at 150 planes. The bridge held and the tanks poured across.

Sales Lesson:

If you get a small bridgehead in an account, exploit it ruthlessly, as it may only be there for a short period if you don't. Push resources through the gap you have formed, and hold that gap open for as long as necessary.

Speed of action can provide a defence in itself, and the element of surprise will often act as a "positive probability generator" or "luck machine"; destroying a less motivated opponent's morale without much effort from your resources. You cannot take an opponent's morale, he can only give it up to you, what you can do is to generate the right circumstances for your opponent to believe they are beaten, once that mind set has become entrenched your opposition will disappear.

Breakout
14th – 15th May 1940

The 1st Panzer Division crossed the Meuse via the Panzer Engineers' hastily constructed bridge, causing the capitulation of the remaining French defenders at the riverside emplacements. The French commanders were taken by surprise at the speed of the crossing, conventional military wisdom dictated that the German's would take anything up to a week to build up enough Infantry strength to force a crossing, and it wasn't till later on the morning of the 14th that they had managed to organise enough strength to pose a threat to Guderian.

The French sent a force of Infantry and tanks to counter the German bridgehead, and they managed to catch some of the German tanks unawares and refuelling. A few Panzers were knocked out, and the German Colonel in charge was wounded. The Germans reacted quickly, sending combat engineers to single handedly attack the French tanks' with explosive charges, and turning some of their 88 mm anti-aircraft guns against them. This bought enough time for Guderian to get more Panzers on the far bank of the river, and counter attack the French force, knocking out half of the French Tanks, and capturing the commander of the French Infantry force.

Despite the fact that more French armour and infantry were unengaged and nearby, the French commander, Huntziger, failed to re-launch an attack, instead sending back completely inaccurate reports saying that the German bridgehead had been held. In actual fact Guderian now controlled fifty square miles of territory in just over a day.

Sales Lesson:

Eventually your competition will attempt to counter you, when this happens, you must maintain morale and counter them vigorously. Compare the reaction of the French artillerymen on 13th, so low in morale that they fled at the sight of their own tanks, when they had in their possession a powerful weapon to halt the German attack, to the German assault engineers a day or two later, who, far from running away from the French Tanks, actually attacked them individually on foot with explosive charges, and played a big part in halting the French advance.

The difference was morale, self belief, this comes through leadership and training, and it is up to the salesperson leading the campaign to make sure this is achieved. At the end of the day, it was the French officers who were to blame for their men's actions, not the men themselves.

Taking the example of Huntziger it is important to avoid self delusion. Huntziger wanted to give a positive report back to Paris, and in doing so deluded himself into believing that the Germans were held, instead of going to the front seeing for himself what was happening, and arranging more counter attacks. Compare this to Guderian who had on the spot knowledge of the actual situations, and put all his efforts to ensuring the momentum of his plan was not interrupted.

Consolidate
15th May 1940

Guderian's plan was to swing his units westwards and race for the coast, thereby splitting the allied forces in half. To do this he had to secure his southern flank, and hold open the Meuse crossing to allow the following Infantry Units to catch up and consolidate the gains of his Panzers.

He allocated the 10th Panzer division plus the Panzer Grenadier Regiment "Grossdeutschland" to take and hold the high ground at Stonne, at a loop in the river Meuse and along the line of the Ardennes Canal; enough to keep the French from closing the hole in their defences on the Meuse. There followed ferocious fighting for the heights at Stonne, the ground changing hands on a number of occasions, the Germans finally emerging victorious and holding the ground long enough to both protect the immediate flank of the Panzers, and keep the Meuse crossing open, until reinforced by motorised Infantry units.

At this point the French Prime Minister phoned Winston Churchill and said "We are defeated; we have lost the battle."

Sales Lesson:

You beat the competition when you destroy their morale, and quite often the further away from the engagement your competitor's Management are, the quicker their morale can be collapsed. Often Sales Management who are "at the front" will wish to continue the fight in the face of adversity, whereas those less involved will give up.

The Breakout

15th – 16th May 1940

On the 15th May, Guderian decided on a "Klotzen, nicht Kleckern" (bash 'em, don't pat 'em!) strategy, moving the bulk of his Panzers westwards in two divisions, with their flank protected by the troops at Stonne. Again this was counter to conventional wisdom at the time, which would have dictated using the armour to mop up the defenders in the area, which was actually a substantial force, but Guderian decided on taking a bigger gamble, for a much bigger prize.

Risks there were; the further his advance went the more exposed Guderian's flank became. His columns had to cross numerous watercourses, and presented a potentially tempting target for any French commander with some initiative.

The commander of the main French armoured force in the area had split his tanks up and dispersed them to support his infantry, and continually failed to make a serious attempt on Guderian's extending lines of communication, preferring to claim that his pointless defensive positions had held; in reality this meant that he sat and did nothing.

Guderian rushed westwards to achieve his strategic aim of bisecting the allied forces in France and Belgium, largely ignoring French defences outside of his immediate path. A potentially high-risk strategy, but classic Blitzkrieg.

Sales Lesson:

Be prepared to take calculated risks, know your enemy and decide if surprise and your speed of action will be enough to provide you with the security you need to extend your advance within the account. But know the difference between a calculated risk, and recklessness.

Halt Commands

17th May 1940

With the whole of France lying within his grasp, the German high command ordered Guderian to halt and consolidate his position. They feared for his exposed southern flank, which was within striking distance of the French 3rd armoured division. On paper they were right, but Guderian was the commander on the ground, and had seen for himself the lack of initiative shown by the French, so he ignored the order, and continued his advance on the pretext of moving forward to make room for the following troops. General Von Kleist was infuriated, and Guderian was personally ordered to await the General who flew in to see him. This Guderian did, and after a furious discussion resigned his commission, Von Kleist accepted his resignation.

Fortunately for the Germans, General List was sent in to sort the situation out and immediately reinstated Guderian. List explained to Guderian that the order to halt had come from Hitler, so couldn't be ignored. However, he gave Guderian permission for a "reconnaissance in force", this Guderian was to interpret in a very liberal fashion.

Sales Lesson:

Sometimes it is necessary to stand on your principles, this won't always be necessary, and may not be the best option. It can be avoided if senior management, rather than hiding behind rank, and expecting blind obedience, actually do some management and look for intelligent compromises where appropriate.

"Reconnaissance in force"

17th – 19th May 1940

Instead of a simple reconnaissance, Guderian linked up with two other Panzer commanders, crossed the Oise then the Somme and captured several French Staff Officers and collapsed all French resistance for a further fifty miles.

To prevent interception of his communications and therefore his actual actions by army group HQ, Guderian set up a telephone line to his immediate commander rather than use radio.

Guderian had used the "reconnaissance in force" order to push into positions that would allow his units to sweep forward once the order was lifted, which was after two days when the flank units were in place.

Sales Lesson:

An intelligent salesperson will at least pay lip service to protect the feelings of less well informed senior managers. Guderian had realised that being openly defiant and having a stand-up row with a senior officer was not the most productive course of action, an d would do little to advance his plans. So he used cunning and did enough to keep the senior staff quiet, without spoiling his chances of victory.

French Counter Attacks

17th and 19th May 1940

On 17th May a French Colonel, Charles de Gaulle (later the President of the French Republic), launched his 4th armoured division against Guderian's forward centre of communications and supply lines. The Germans taken by surprise lost a number of supply vehicles. They did however manage to mount an ad-hoc defence; long enough for de Gaulle's tanks to run low on fuel and ammunition, forcing them to retreat.

The French 1st Armoured division ran out of petrol, and were surrounded and overrun whilst helpless, and the French 2nd armoured division had been split up by the higher command to defend bridges, and therefore was unable to offer any concerted resistance to the Germans, and as the French 3rd Armoured division had been left sitting behind their defensive positions near Sedan, there were no other forces to help de Gaulle in his attempts to stop the German tide.

On the 19th May, after re-supply De Gaulle again attacked Guderian's lines of communication, but this time the Germans had prepared their defences with land mines on the bridges, and anti tank guns in place, the French took severe casualties, and were finally beaten off by Stuka dive bombers.

Despite his bravery and DeGaulle had lost the initiative after the first failed attack when he had not been able to hit hard enough, and now the German's were forewarned and could effectively counter him. Had he been able to call on reinforcements from other units he may have had a fighting chance of disrupting Guderian's plans.

Sales Lesson:

Don't assume that your competition are all idiots, even if some of them are. Be prepared to meet and counter resistance, take such challenges seriously, and deal with them vigourously.

Advance Officially Reinstated

20th May 1940

On 20th the advance was officially reinstated. Guderian rushed forward with his tanks and both Abbeville and Amiens were taken. The allies were so taken by surprise by his speed of advance that some British Artillery troops were even captured with dummy rounds instead of real ones because they were still carrying drilling and practicing rather than digging in and preparing to fight. A British Tank column had been overtaken by the German advance, and covered in dirt and dust, audaciously joined a German Tank column, and attempted to make their way back to allied lines in the midst of their enemy! Courageous as this show of improvisation and initiative was, they were unfortunately discovered and captured.

By nightfall German units had reached the channel coast. Allied forces had been cut in half, and allied troops in Holland and Belgium were cut off from their command and supply bases.

Sales Lesson:

Speed of action leads to tactical surprise, tactical surprise presents you with the gift of good luck and unexpected advantages.

British Counter Attack

21st May 1940

The only serious threat to the Germans' thrust came on May 21st, when units from the 50th Northumbrian Division and two battalions of the Royal Tank Regiment launched a counter attack near Arras.

The Germans used their 88 mm flak guns to take on the heavily armed British Matilda tanks. One captured British officer complained to his German captors about their unsporting use of AA guns to knock out his tank, the German replied that the British shouldn't have been so unsporting as to use Tanks which only an AA gun could knock out!

This attack almost stopped the Germans to the North of Guderian in their tracks. Their losses were 600 men killed, wounded, or captured, and 30 Panzers destroyed. Rommel's Divisions were temporarily stopped; the confidence of German Higher Command was shaken, as there was a chance that the Panzers would be cut off before the supporting Infantry could arrive. However the allied opportunity was lost when both a lack of French support and a lack of British reinforcements prevented exploitation of the initial success. Given that such a small number of British tanks could cause so a great problem, shows what could have happened if more allied armour had been thrown against the Schwerpunkt of the Germans' advance.

So the immediate British threat ran out of steam, and left the way clear again. Fortunately for him, Guderian found himself lacking orders, so he took the initiative, turned north, and got his units into position to drive along the Franco-Belgian coast, his aim being to now cut the BEF off from the channel coast, and all chance of retreat by sea.

Sales Lesson:

Same lesson as that of the French counter attack under DeGaulle; not all of your opponents will be cowards or idiots, but you must keep your nerve and deal with such situations calmly and competently as they arise. In the case of the British counter attack at Arras, Rommel, one of the most highly rated commanders of the second world war, sent highly exaggerated claims as to the size of the British counter attack back to HQ, and indeed a so called elite division, the SS Totenkopf, almost broke in panic; the line only held because of the actions by more experienced troops in "subordinate" units, showing that shiny uniforms and the favour of senior management is no substitute for experience.

Boulogne

22nd – 25th May

Guderian's sweep up the channel coast caught the allies by surprise, and on 22nd May Guderian's panzers reached Boulogne and cut it off from allied reinforcements by land. But some enemy concentrations cannot be ignored, and again Guderian is not reckless, he understands the exposure of his flank if the channel ports are not taken, and the strategic advantage of having these in German hands to deny the allies the chance to reinforce or evacuate mainland Europe.

Fortunately the allies still had control of the channel, so reinforcements from the British Brigade of Guards were shipped in to bolster the non-combatant Pioneer Corps, and regular French forces who had been bravely holding the town, and evacuated their wounded.

Despite hostile fire from the Royal Navy and RAF, the Germans broke into the town and a fierce fire fight broke out with the British Guards, Pioneers, and French units. It soon became clear that the allied position was hopeless, so the bulk of the British troops were evacuated, leaving a rear guard unit of British and the remaining French troops, to cover the withdrawal until their ammunition ran out. The Germans took the town on 25th May.

Sales Lesson:

Ensure security of action, and always take actions that lead towards your overall objective. Force home your attacks powerfully and quickly.

Calais

23rd – 26th May 1940

On 23rd May, the day after reaching Boulogne, Guderian's troops reached Calais and cut it off from reinforcement by land. Again the port was reinforced from the sea by the British. The order came down to Guderian that should Calais prove difficult to take, it was to be left to the Luftwaffe. Not wanting Goering, the head of the Luftwaffe to steal his victory, Guderian sent in his troops against the British Tanks and Infantry who fought street by street against overwhelming numbers of German Tanks, Infantry and Stuka dive bombers. Despite offers to take their surrender, the British commander, Brigadier Nicholson, replied; "The answer is no, as it is the British Army's duty to fight as well as it is the German's." The British continued to fight until their ammunition ran out.

Unlike Boulogne, there was to be no evacuation by sea. Churchill had promised to fight to hold Calais "to the last man", and the British army duly did so. On 26th May Calais fell; 3,000 British troops were captured, along with 17,000 French, Belgian, and Dutch who the British had locked in cellars when they refused to fight the Germans.

Tactically Calais and Boulogne were both straight forward defeats for the allies, but according to Churchill, their staunch defence had bought a few extra days to help facilitate the coming evacuation at Dunkirk.

Sales Lesson:

If an approach works once, it may work again, i.e. if it works don't fix it, especially against an opponent who may not have seen it before, so Calais was a repeat of Boulogne, against a stubborn and brave enemy, but forced home with extreme vigour to achieve the strategic objective of cutting off the enemy from their means of withdrawal and reinforcement.

Dunkirk

23rd May to 2nd June 1940

Guderian reached the River Aa at Gravelines at about the same time that General Reinhardt's column reached St Omer and the canal there. The River and canal formed the last obstacle between them and the Allied line of retreat to Dunkirk, the last remaining accessible major port offering an escape route for the Allies.

Between 23rd and 25th May Guderian marshalled his available units to overrun Dunkirk in the manner of Boulogne and Calais. This would block the last escape route of 400,000 allied soldiers. A single British battalion defended the last obstacles; the River Aa and the Gravelines canal, and the bridges across the river were all intact. The Germans sent armoured cars across the canal and entered Hazebrouck effectively between the Allies and Dunkirk, this happened whilst the British commander, Lord Gort was actually in Hazebrouck! Guderian and General Thoma of the General Staff could actually see into Dunkirk from their forward position.

On 24th May Hitler issued his final halt order of the campaign; the Panzers were to halt at the line of the canal. . Dunkirk was to be left to the Luftwaffe. Guderian was left "Utterly speechless!" The decision was probably due to a number of factors; the shock inspired in the German high command by the British counter attack at Arras, the British willingness to fight to the last round rather than surrender at Boulogne and Calais, and Goering's (head of the Luftwaffe) influence over Hitler at HQ, Goering being desperate to claim some of the glory already achieved by the hard work of the Army.

For three days the Panzers sat on their side of the Canal whilst the British Expeditionary force and remaining French units withdrew to Dunkirk.

The British committed all RAF resources to defending troops on the beaches of Dunkirk; nearly 1,000 RAF planes were lost, but to a great extent this sacrifice rendered the Luftwaffe ineffective. By midnight on 2nd June over 338,000 allied troops (mainly British) had been evacuated to safety by the fleet of "little ships".

The next order for the Panzers was to withdraw to the south and mop up the last of the French forces, whilst the Infantry went in to occupy Dunkirk, after the British evacuation had finished. Thoma said of the "halt" order: "You can never talk to a fool. Hitler spoilt the chance of victory."

Sales Lesson:

Tactical decisions should always be heavily influenced by the people in the firing line, salespeople should beware HQ favourites and management flunkies who will try to take some of the glory for themselves without having to do the hard work. This is especially the case when there is an imbalance in leadership at the top, on the one hand autocratic and bullying born out of personal insecurity and a feeling of lack of control. There may be nothing the salesperson can do about this other than watch opportunities slip away.

Sales Example.

I will describe an actual sales campaign I was involved in, mapping the various stages of the sales campaign to a classic blitzkrieg campaign. As it turned out, the mapping turned out to be very accurate to the stages of a blitzkrieg campaign, although this wasn't intentional at the time of the sales campaign, it just seemed to be the obvious thing to do in order to win. And that would seem to be the point.

I was in a campaign to sell some software to a major bank. I had no competition except from an erstwhile partner company, who had their own inferior product, but massive account leverage because of the value of their incumbent software for which there was a big requirement for an upgrade at the customer site.

To overcome the competition's advantages we needed to push through the technicalities of the sale, and effectively overrun the command and control centre of the customer, i.e. get a senior management sponsor, before they could.

So from the perspective of a Blitzkrieg campaign we adhered to the basic principles:

Discover your enemy's dispositions and relative strengths.

We had good knowledge of our opposition's strengths and weaknesses, his offering in our product area was very weak, his sales force and technical personnel was low quality in the account, but his sales management was strong in opposition to us, but disliked by the customer, he was in a good position in his main product area for which the customer wanted a substantial upgrade, but through good account management the customer would (all other things being equal) prefer to purchase via us as a reseller.

We knew his product was weak through a close study of accounts where they had, unsuccessfully tried to deploy it.

We knew his sales and technical force was weak because we had taken time to study the individuals in their interactions with the customer, and had sought their opinions, which unanimously confirmed our observations, therefore although they had up to six separate individuals working the account to our two.

We knew that the sales management would fight us hard through gauging their reactions to our probes, and their avoidance of contact with us, even when legitimately approached about our intention to resell, the only contact they came forward with was to attempt to deny us the right to resell, which legally, because of our contract, they couldn't. We knew the customer disliked them, because the customer confirmed this to us.

Distract your enemy to draw away the bulk of his forces to an area outside of the decisive point (Schwerpunkt). This step may not always be carried out.
The real tactical advantage for me was that I had a contract that enabled me to resell the other company's products, and the customer's requirement was for their basic product that was not in competition with any of mine. The ability to take the fight to the competition's heart; my ability to resell the upgrade opportunity, denying them its full value should I win (my company's commission), was the "matador's cloak".

It was essential to keep the competition focused on the reseller deal to give us time to get the deal for our own product closed.

Concentrate your forces against his weak points (make this the decisive point or Schwerpunkt), moving fast enough to prevent your enemy realigning their forces.
The sword thrust would come by the purchase of our product; if the reselling deal came through us as well that would be a bonus.

We needed to concentrate our forces around building the need for our product, and as there was no budget for it, and it was not the type of product that readily lent itself to a demonstrable return on investment calculation. So the Schwerpunkt had to be a high level sponsor who wanted the solution badly enough, and who had enough power over budget and procurement to ensure that it went through. All our efforts, even those applied at a technical level, were aimed at convincing the senior manager of his need for the product.

Soften up enemy positions at the Schwerpunkt with an initial baombardment.
The initial bombardment was delivered through collateral showing the benefits of the product, and ensuring that he had access to it, albeit in the testing and pilot phases, so that once he got used to seeing it, he would be accustomed to it, making subsequently difficult to live without it.

If necessary use specialist forces to make the initial bridgehead and facilitate the advance of the armoured units.
The initial bridgehead was opened by technical staff installing a pilot of the product actually monitoring some live systems (which the senior manager was given access to). By setting up this strong deliverable as a bridgehead, actually providing benefit, even in this early pilot stage, the next stage became that much easier.

Use armoured forces to punch through enemy defences.
Once the bridgehead had been secured it was easy to use this as a springboard to sell the benefits at a high level within the customer's management, including the high level sponsor. The working bridgehead gave the narrow entry point to fully engage senior management within the account in the sales process.

Defend flanks and rear of armoured force's break out with slow moving units.
We used our technical support staff to keep the pilot systems up and running, embedding its use in the customer's day-to-day running and increasing their dependency. As long as the technical staff could keep the product up and running, and displaying benefit to the customer, the bridgehead was open and our main thrust to management couldn't be diverted or distracted. The actions of our technical people kept the flanks and rear of the sales thrust safe from competitive actions.

Use the armoured thrust to disorient defenders and break their morale, by cutting their lines of supply, communication, and reinforcement.
When it came to negotiating with the procurement department, they initially insisted on a formal ROI, however because we had identified the decisive point as being the desire of the senior management sponsor, when the procurement department questioned what the justification for the product was, the answer they got was "Senior Management want it!" This was outside of their usual procedures, but they had little option but to accept the situation, albeit with a cursory, and not exactly convincing justification document. Their dilemma was that we had cut through their normal procedural routes, and cut off their ability to present a united front.

Slower moving forces follow up on the armoured advance, protecting their flanks and rear.
We used the customer's technical people to propagate the use of the product to other departments to help open up new avenues for us to exploit, and to ensure the right things were

said about it to allow sales to advance throughout the account without fear of being let down by non-performance of the product.

Again the actions of the technical staff to ensure the perception of benefit from the product were essential to allow the advance to continue unimpeded by actions of competitors and hostile elements within the customer.

Enemy pockets of resistance (Kessels) overrun at leisure, by slow moving forces and armour as appropriate.
Still using the account's technical staff who had completely bought in to our solution, we then went on to mop up areas of resistance, we engaged various other departments to extend the use of the product, but having signed a group license, they had little choice but to go along with it.

Summary of Laws

So hear are the basics laid out as to how to mount your Campaign:

- Follow Fuller's **Four Principles** and apply his **Three Accentuating Factors** during the whole of your Campaign
- Use Tuker to identify the **Initial Pattern of the Campaign** you are entering, and if necessary change it from a **Siege** or **Linear Engagement** to a **Wide Area Engagement.**
- Use Liddell-Hart's Tactics to perform an **Indirect Approach** and produce a **Rolling Torrent** effect.
- Estimate the relative strengths of **Resources** and **E** within a specific engagement and apply the tactics of **Numbers**, **Concentration**, or **Equals** as appropriate.
- Emulate the **Initiative** and **Flexibility** of **Forrest**, the **Leadership**, **Determination**, and **Use of Ground** of **Henry V**, and the **Intelligence Gathering**, **Speed of Movement**, and **Concentration of Force** of Guderian.

The Principles

(To adhere to in your Campaign)

(Fuller)

Apply Fuller's boxing analogy to your Campaign, and to each stage of your campaign; **Think, Guard, Move, Hit**. These are the Four Principles; **Maintenance of Objective, Security of Action, Mobility of Action, Expenditure of Offensive Power**.

Maintain your Objective, make all your actions move you towards it, and measured the likely result of all actions against it.

Security of Action should be practiced at each step, do not be reckless, weigh possible gain against possible risk.

Mobility of Action is what will open opportunities to you, move within the target account, scout and probe, and look for opportunities to exploit.

Expenditure of Offensive Power at the right place and time will allow you to gain your ultimate objective.

Apply the Three Accentuating Factors to the Four Principles; **Economy of Force, Concentration of Force, Surprise.**

Economy of Force do not overextend your resources or use your reserves pointlessly, use only as much resource as needed, when it is needed.

Concentration of Force ensure that you "march divided" but fight united, when you need to engage make sure that all necessary resources are brought to bear to ensure victory.

Surprise will multiple your advantages in any manoeuvre, or encounter, surprising your opponent will give you a chance to wrong foot your competition, beat larger forces with smaller ones, and most importantly destroy your opponent's morale.

The Pattern

(Identify, Engage or change it as appropriate)

(Tuker)

Identify the type of Campaign you are engaged in. Is it a **Linear Engagement**, an **Area Engagement**, or a **Siege**?

Linear Engagement

A **Linear Engagement** will be fought on the customer's terms, if you have not dictated those terms, then the ultimate winner will be the customer, not you. If you have far greater resources than your competition you have a good chance of winning such a deal over them, but you will win it at a price, i.e. the customer will make price the biggest differentiator in the deal and drive your margins down. In general you should try to turn a Linear Campaign into an Area Campaign. To do this follow Tuker's advice; **"No army that is weaker in the mobile arm can hold a linear field defensive position which has an open flank or which can be penetrated"** so either find a flank and turn it, or cause a break-in and break-through to produce a gap in the line, and expose a flank.

Area Engagement

To win an **Area Engagement** the following must be the case:

- Flanks shall be tactically open or it shall be possible to create a flank by a break-in and break-through.

- The mobile arm shall predominate.

- It shall be possible to administer the mobile arm to the point at which it will decide the battle and gain decisive victory

Siege

If in a **Siege Engagement** you must decide if it is worth the time that it will likely take to bring it to a conclusion. If it is worth the time and effort then attempt to take the account by the following means, using the prioritised order below:

- Subvert a party in the account to gain you access without an engagement.
- Use a new technology that negates the defences.
- Attempt a fdull blown marketing and sales campaign to storm the account.
- Invest the account for an extended period, until their will to resist collapses.

Identify your resources, the **Mobile Arm**, **Arm of Defence**, **Siege Train**. The proportions and numbers of each will decide on the campaign you can best adopt.

The Indirect Approach and Rolling Torrent

(Liddell-Hart)

Do's

- Adjust your **ends** to your **means**.
- Keep your **Objective** always in mind.
- Choose the **Line of Least Expectation**.
- Exploit the **Line of Least Resistance**.
- Take a line of operation which offers an **alternative objective**.
- Ensure that all plans and dispositions are **flexible and adaptable** to circumstances.

Don'ts

- Throw your weight into a stroke whilst your **enemy is on guard**.
- Renew an attack along the **same line** (or in the **same form**) **after it has failed**.

The Indirect Approach consisted of a number of stages;

- Gather Intelligence; look for areas of weakness; joins and gaps.
- Probe enemy frontage to test intelligence, and distract enemy from true objective, approach along a line of least expectation.
- Use the line of least resistance to penetrate a weakness, throw the weight of the main forces against it, to widen and hold the gap.
- Pour fast moving troops through the gap and drive as deep as possible as quickly as possible to cause as much dislocation as possible, cut lines of communication.
- Overrun the enemy centre of gravity (Schwerpunkt) the centre of decision making. Separate the centre of thought from the centre of action; the head from the limbs.

The Expanding Torrent;

- Disruption: Push along lines of least resistance behind enemy front, extend area of damage and disruption, hit many centres of command, and communications.
- Protection: Cut off concentrations of enemy resistance, avoid direct engagements with strong positions.
- Destruction: Attack enemy concentrations showing signs of morale collapse.

The Tactics of Concentration

(Strategy of Concentration, Equals, or Numbers)

(Lanchester)

Stage 1 Decide on relative strength and Combat effectiveness

- Decide if you are numerically stronger than, equal to, or weaker than your opponent.
- Decide if your E is greater than, equal to, or less than your opponent.

Stage 2 Follow the relevant strategy

- If you are stronger than your opponent and have greater E, engage in a stochastic engagement as quickly as possible, do not take any risks.
- If you are stronger than your opponent, but lower in E, adopt the strategy of Numbers.
- If you are more or less numerically equal to your opponent and equal in E, adopt the strategy of equals.
- If you are weaker than your opponent, but higher in E adopt the strategy Concentration.
- If you are numerically weaker than your opponent, and have a lower E, then do not engage at this time.
- If you are uncertain of your relative numerical strength, and relative E factors, adopt the strategy of equals until a clearer picture is forthcoming.

The Strategy of Numbers

If you are stronger in resources but weaker in E than your opponent then adopt The Strategy of Numbers. This means preventing your opponent from operating the Strategy of Concentration.

- Study your competitor's weapons and tactics then copy them. This will reduce any actual or perceived advantage of "E" they may posses. If E=1 in the equation, then your more numerous resources will win all encounters, and even if your E is inferior to your opponent's you can still win decisively if Stochastic engagements are sought. This is called a Matching Strategy, and forms the Combat element of the Strategy of the Strong.
- Compete where your superior resources will stretch your opponent to breaking point, i.e. where their actual physical ability to respond to your initiatives is exceeded. This is called a Stretching Strategy, and provides the Positional and Temporal-Spatial aspects of the Strategy of the Strong.

The Strategy Concentration

If you are weaker in resources then your opponent than adopt The Strategy of Concentration.

- Compete on a narrow front, where their superior numbers are of no advantage. This is the Positional aspect of a Single Point Concentration.
- Fight serial, local battles, where you can outnumber your opponent in the immediate engagement. This is the Temporal-Spatial tactical element of a Single Point Concentration.
- Increase your combat effectiveness "E" to give you a significant advantage in local engagements. This is the Combat element of a Single Point Concentration.

Strategy of Equals

If you are equal in forces and E to your opponent than adopt The Strategy Equals.

The strategy of the Equal is to turn the current situation into one where you can outnumber your opponent at the critical time. You must bring about an engagement at the time and place of your choosing in order to separate your opponent's forces into smaller chunks so that they can be defeated in detail.

- Use very small detachments to distract larger portions of your opponents resources in non-citical areas, use the rest of your forces to attack his now smaller portion of resources in critical areas.
- Use superior speed to attack any separated units of your opponent's overall resources in detail, so that you can always manoeuvre larger numbers to attack his smaller numbers.

Winning Qualities

(Emulate in your Actions)

(Guderian, Henry V, Bedford Forrest)

Nathan Bedford Forrest

Initiative and Flexibility

- Show charisma and leadership and people will follow you.
- Have the confidence self belief, and desire to act outside of your comfort zone.
- Believe that your people are capable of doing anything and they will too.
- Place your art above your ego when acting as a subordinate, or in leadership.
- Take decisive and fast action to exploit an advantage.
- See no obstacles only opportunities for new ways of winning.
- Make your tactics, people and products fit the situation if the situation doesn't fit your tactics, people, and products.
- Walk away from hopeless engagements.

Henry V King of England

Leadership, Determination, Use of Ground

- Have a single simple objective within the reach of your resources.
- Good leadership out weighs poor conditions.
- If you meet unexpected circumstances carry on doing "The Right Things".
- You must only engage to win, not just for the sake of engagement.
- Choose your ground carefully. It is far better to fight with a weak army in favourable conditions, than with a strong army in unfavourable conditions.
- Once on the best ground, force your enemy to fight; do not allow the advantage to slip away, know your competition's psychology, use it to control their actions.
- Reduce your enemy's perception of the value in continued resistance. Force the risk reward ratio to a limit that makes continued engagement unprofitable.
- Carry out actions, that will undermine your enemy's morale. Sales are won when the competition looses the "will to fight".
- Once you are winning pursue it to the limit. Wring as much advantage out of settlement terms as possible whilst the opposition's morale is low.
- Do not confuse winning an account, with holding an account.

General Heinz Guderan

Intelligence, Speed of Movement, Concentration of Force.

- Discover your target's dispositions and relative strengths.
- Distract your target to draw away the bulk of their forces to an area outside of the decisive point (Schwerpunkt). This step may not always be carried out.
- Concentrate your forces against their weak points (make this the decisive point or Schwerpunkt), moving fast enough to prevent your enemy realigning their forces.
- Soften up enemy positions at the Schwerpunkt with an initial focused information bombardment.
- If necessary use specialist forces to make the initial bridgehead and facilitate the advance of the sales resources.
- Use sales resources to punch through enemy defences.
- Defend flanks and rear of sales resources break out with slow moving units.
- Use the sales thrust to disorient defenders and break their morale, by cutting their lines of command, communication, and reinforcement.
- Slower moving technical resources follow up on the sales advance, protecting their flanks and rear.
- Enemy pockets of resistance (Kessels) overrun at leisure, by technical and sales resources as appropriate.

Templates for Campaign Manual

Plan of Campaign for Account:

Time Period:

Define Objective
(Precise Black and White Goals)

↓

Outline Strategy
(Plan: What will you do in outline to reach Objective)

↓

Tactics
(Actions: Who will do what and when? Issue tailored sheet to each person in Sales Team)

Account Campaign Map

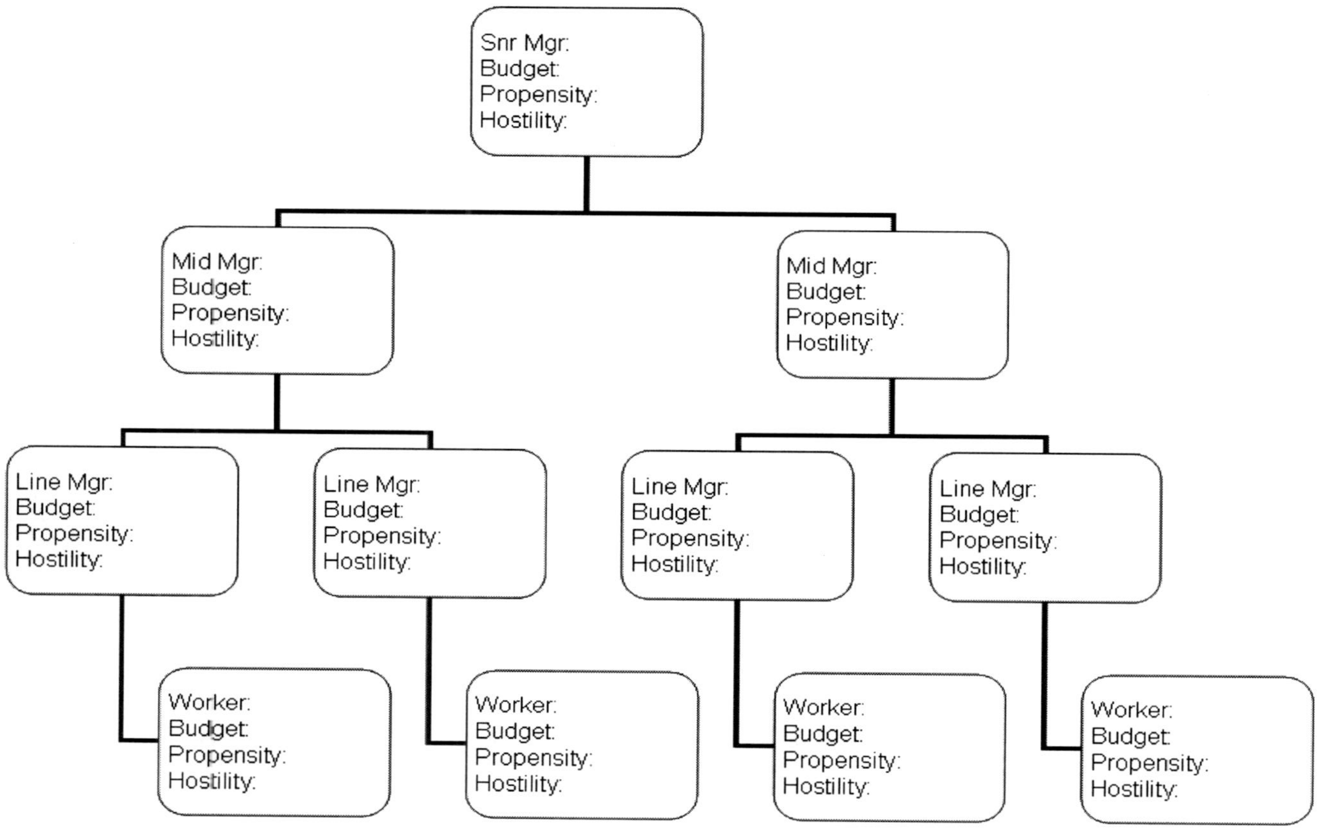

Engagement Pattern Identification:

	Propensity = -1	Propensity = 0	Propensity = +1
Hostility = -1	Siege	Siege	Linear
Hostility = 0	Siege	Linear	Linear
Hostility = +1	Siege	Area	Area

Lanchester Engagement Chart

	Your E is Greater	Your E is Equal	Your E is Smaller
Your Numbers are Greater	Immediate Stochastic Engagement	Tactics of Numbers	Tactics of Numbers
Your Numbers are Equal	Tactics of Concentration	Tactics of Equals	Avoid Engagement Use Tactics of Numbers if must Engage
Your Numbers are Smaller	Tactics of Concentration	Avoid Engagement Use Tactics of Numbers if must Engage	Avoid Engagement

Lightning Source UK Ltd.
Milton Keynes UK
172899UK00006B/132/P

9 781907 140013